W9-ARL-209

BELIEVE IN THE GOD
WHO BELIEVES IN YOU

by Robert H. Schuller

COME ALIVE NEW TESTAMENT CHURCH
P O Box 86
Medford, NJ 08055
(609) 654-8466

Thomas Nelson Publishers
Nashville

Other Books by Robert H. Schuller

God's Way to the Good Life
Your Future is Your Friend
Move Ahead with Possibility Thinking
Self-Love the Dynamic Force of Success
Power Ideas for a Happy Family
You Can Become the Person You Want To Be
The Greatest Possibility Thinker that Ever Lived
Your Church has Real Possibilities
Love or Loneliness Your Decide
Positive Prayers for Power-Filled Living
Keep On Believing
Peace of Mind Through Possibility Thinking
Reach Out for a New Life
Turning Your Stress into Strength
Daily Power Thoughts
It's Possible
Discover Your Possibilities
The Courage of Carol: Pearls From Tears
The Peak to Peek Principle
Living Positively One Day At a Time
Self-Esteem: The New Reformation
Tough Times Never Last, But Tough People Do
Tough Minded Faith for Tender Hearted People
The Power of Being Debt Free
The Be-Happy Attitudes
Be Happy You Are Loved
Success is Never Ending Failure is Never Final

**To my
Grandchildren,
my pride and joy,
I leave this legacy
of hope.**

Angie Schuller
Robert V. Schuller
Christina Schuller
Anthony Schuller
Jason Coleman
Christopher Coleman
Scott Coleman
Nicholas Coleman
Jennifer Dunn
Stephanie Dunn
Rebekah Milner
Ethan Josiah Milner

**Keep the faith! And pass it on!
God loves you and so do I!**

95015

Copyright © 1989 by Robert H. Schuller

All rights reserved. Written permission must
be secured from the publisher to use or
reproduce any part of this book, except for
brief quotations in critical reviews or articles.

Published in Nashville, Tennessee, by Thomas
Nelson, Inc., and distributed in Canada by
Lawson Falle, Ltd., Cambridge, Ontario.

Printed in the United States of America.

Schuller, Robert Harold.
    Believe in the God who believes in you / by Robert H. Schuller.
        p.   cm.
    ISBN 0-8407-5443-4
    1. Ten commandments.   2. Self-respect—Religious aspects—
    Christianity.   3. Success—Religious aspects—Christianity.
    I. Title.
    BV4655.S435   1989   89-38125
    241.5'2—dc20   CIP

Scripture quotations are from THE NEW
KING JAMES VERSION of the Bible.
Copyright © 1979, 1980, 1982, Thomas
Nelson, Inc., Publishers.

The Ten Commandments—God's Design for Divine Dignity

*Be
Hopeful!
For
Tomorrow
Has Never
Happened
Before*

R.H.S.

An Opening Word

Tell me, please:

Why does a book need an introduction anyway?

Why does a symphony need an overture?

Why does a building have a front portico?

Why does a star on stage need a warm-up act?

I've noticed some books have prefaces. Other books have forewords. Many books have introductions.

I'm confused. Who needs them?

The marketing folks? "Get a big name to write the introduction. It'll help sell the product."

The layout people? "The book's too thin? Fatten it up. Put in some stuffing. Yes! That's it! A foreword!"

The author? He finished the book but forgot something? Stick it up front and call it a preface.

The critic? She has to review this book and needs to get to the heart of the matter in a hurry.

The reader? He needs to be set up for what's coming. His mind is in a dozen (a hundred?) other places. You've got to draw his attention to what you're saying.

Preface. Foreword. Introduction.

I'm still perplexed. The rules are vague. The roles overlap. The job descriptions are not clear. The specifications are fuzzy. The definitive standards? There aren't any.

So for this book, at least, I'll do my thing. Call it sorting out my audience . . . screening the readers . . . separating my listeners into three categories.

So I'll do all three: Foreword, Preface, and Introduction.

The Foreword is directed to the agnostic or atheist or secular reader.

The Preface is directed to the religious reader.

The Introduction is directed to the Judeo-Christian reader.

So I trust I have written for you—whoever and wherever you are—so that you will indeed come to know and believe in the God who believes in you.

I
PREFACE

You're a skeptic, you say? Probably an atheist? No? An agnostic?

"What's the difference?" you ask. Why, an atheist has faith. He's a believer in *no God*. He has absolutely no proof for his belief, of course. When proof is possible, faith is impossible. Turn this around, and it's still true: Faith is only possible when proof is impossible.

An agnostic hasn't enough facts (or nerve) to make the leap. Yes! That's what faith is. Faith is deciding to:

- **Believe!** Before you can prove it.

- **Leap!** Before you can be sure you'll make it.

- **Answer!** Before you have all the facts.

- **Decide!** Before you have solved all the problems.

- **Commit!** Before you can be sure it's really the right move.

How will this book help? What's in these pages for the ones who have decided not to believe because they can't—or won't?

You're a secular humanist? You want to be a kind and decent person, but you don't want religion?

Then this preface is for you!

Welcome to a book that can help you where you need help most! For this book is about your self-respect.

Be honest—you cannot tolerate ridicule! Right?

I'm wrong, you say? You laugh it off, ignore the insult, and forget it? O.K. But wouldn't you be happier if instead of ridicule you got real respect? I hope so! If not, you have a problem with your self-image.

Believe In The God Who Believes In You

So that's what this book will do for you! How to get respect. How to avoid rude affronts in life. And how to respond to ridicule.

It doesn't matter? Come on! Be honest! Look at the alternative. Wouldn't you be thrilled—really!—if you were selected for a high honor?

Can you tell me your heart wouldn't suddenly start thumping if you got a telephone call from the president of the United States?

Honor. You love it. So do I. It's part of being human. It has motivated me—and you, too—to continue to do our best. And that's good!

Disgrace. This is hard to handle. It depends, of course, on who dishes it out. When, where, why—it's relative but always serious.

Mud spattered on the car.

Scratches on the new paint job.

A fender bender.

Any of these can be pretty unpleasant on a fresh, clean, sparkling new Chevy, Ford, or Cadillac!

Honor withheld, pride wounded, or embarrassments experienced are definitely not the sorts of things that make us whistle with joy.

A crack-up on the freeway! The car is totaled! You're lucky to be alive! You can't compare this event to spattered mud, scattered scratches, or a shattered window. Now we're talking about a disaster! In the realm of human relationships, we're talking about *shame*. Now, this is as tough as it gets.

How do you maintain your self-respect?

How can you salvage your self-esteem?

How can you preserve your human dignity?

How can you recover from shame?

Important questions!

How important?

Let me tell you.

I was asked to speak on a theology of self-esteem to two hundred psychiatrists gathered at the national convention of the American Psychiatric Association in Los Angeles. They heard what they expected to hear from me. I had already published my position.

"What is humanity's deepest need?"

The "will to pleasure"—that was Freud's answer.

The "will to power"—this was Adler's position.

The "will to meaning"—here is where Frankl stood.

So I led my respectful and sophisticated audience in a swift summary of the history of psychology. They understood this very well. Next, I proposed an alternative hypothesis:

The "will to self-esteem."

It was an analysis of the human will as created by God and seen by the writers of the Bible.

When I finished my remarks, one of the doctors came forward, excited, to affirm my position. "Guess what, Dr. Schuller?" he exclaimed. "The single most popular workshop at this convention is the one on SHAME!"

So you do not need to be religious at all to recognize the fact that we human beings have to learn how to handle rejection. That, after all, is what puts the weight in this heavy stone called shame.

Embarrassments? What is an embarrassment, anyway? A mild—or serious—touch of shame. We're talking about self-esteem now.

List your most unpleasant memories. Now analyze them. Chances are that *all*—not some, not many, not most, but *all* —of them relate to your self-esteem.

Embarrassments? Recall them.
- Solo performance—and you blew it?
- Tryouts—and you didn't make the cut?
- All dressed up—and you heard the rip?
- Secrets—exposed? Humiliated! The question now is how can I recoup my self-respect?

Guilt? Ever felt it? What makes this such a bad feeling?
- Of course! Your self-respect is shot.
- You blew your dignity.
- Worse, you may have ruptured a rich and rare relationship. Now what will this do to your self-esteem?

Anger? This is really bad—I mean a really bad feeling. What does this have to do with my self-esteem? Everything! Somehow I feel violated! Or victimized! Or threatened!

Perhaps someone you respect, love, and admire is treated unjustly. What do you do? Get mad? That's normal. But watch it. If you have a weak self-esteem, you'll make matters a lot worse. And if you have a positive self-esteem, you'll cool down, take control, and channel your anger.

But how? Where do I start?

Congratulations! You have just taken the first step to dignity and freedom. You are ready to listen; to begin.

So, agnostic, atheist, secular humanist, this book's for you! Look for the help you need. Chances are you'll find it.

"When I'm ready to launch a project," the late architect, Louis Kahn said, "and I think I have all of the answers, I can be sure of this: some of my answers are wrong."

Here's hoping this book will help you discover which of your answers need to be reviewed—and probably even rejected as wrong.

We can agree that moral reconstruction is desperately needed in an amoral and immoral world. Maybe—just maybe—the Ten Commandments need to be looked at again.

Congratulations! I can hear what you're thinking: "I'm willing to change my mind—*if* I'm wrong. I'm willing to become a Beautiful Believer if this will turn me into a Better Person."

Congratulations! You do have an open mind! Great! I'm proud of you. After all, people who never change their minds are either perfect or stubborn! Of course you're not perfect. And you're far too bright to choose to be stubborn.

Stay with me all the way through these pages. We're going to get along just fine.

II
FOREWORD

You are "religious"? Or at least "spiritual"? But you're of "another faith"?

What do you mean, *another* faith? Different from mine?

Are you sure you know what mine is? Maybe, just maybe, you and I can and do agree on some of the basics! If so, let's deal together on that level.

Wouldn't it be a beautiful world if all persons could be treated with respect?
- *Human Dignity.* I'm for it. So are you.
- *Human Integrity.* I haven't met a religion that doesn't advocate it. We all do.
- *Morality.* I know of no faith that touts immorality.
- *Suffering.* Pain, disease, death, concern us all—right?
- *Humanity.* We all want to be treated with courtesy and decency, don't we?
- *Arrogance.* Ugh. We all find it distasteful.
- *Egotism.* Revolting! We all agree.

Then all of us can be inspired—together—as we look at one of humanity's classic statements of morality.

The Ten Commandments.

They're too negative for you?

Wait a minute. That's what I once thought.

But my "answers" were wrong.

I've discovered that this ancient code is the modern road to real self-respect.

Please—let me share an exciting discovery.

These ten *commands* are *meant*
—not to take the freedom out of life
—but to build a positive faith in life that can free us from shame and spare us the oppression imposed by guilt and low self-esteem.

Yes, all of us want our freedom
  —and all of us really (I mean *really*) benefit from
    stronger faith.
So these ten *commands* are *meant*
  —not to inflict shame on humans
  —but to put liberating pride back into our lives!
Each of the ten rules is a *command meant* to:
  • *Protect* us from shame.
  • *Preserve* our self-respect.
  • *Point* us to a positive pride that will let us lift our
    heads, poised to praise and worship the Creator!

III

INTRODUCTION

And now an opening word to my Christian friends. We all are concerned about "ego problems."

They cut off communication. They block our listening skills. "My thoughts, my ideas are important."

We are so busy talking and expressing our point of view that we can't possibly hear what others are saying. Big egos have little ears!

EGO PROBLEMS!?

They're rampant! Wild! Weird! In the church, too!

"Could I get elected to the board?"

"Why wasn't *I* (that's not a little *i*—make it a full capital *I*) asked to sit on the platform with Billy Graham?"

They're all around us! Even on the freeway! "How dare you cut in front of me?"

You arrive at your parking lot. You've got a reserved spot—with your name painted in clear, highly visible lettering. Someone parked in your place?! Great!

The Office. How big is your desk? How high is the back of your chair? You have your own private bathroom? Wow! You don't?!

The Newspaper. You're mentioned. What a kick.

You're not?! What a letdown.

What? You didn't get top billing? Whose names were moved ahead of yours?

Rebuffed again!

The Convention. How did "they"
- get to travel first class?
- get assigned to a better room?

- get seated at the head table?
- get "named" *by name*—in the program and in the master of ceremony's comments?
- get recognition by the visiting artist?

THE EGO

We've all got our egos.

The ego is the core of being human.

If we could wipe it out, eradicate it, dissolve it, until it is no more, wouldn't that be wonderful?

Hardly! What you'd have left is something subhuman. The touch of the image of God within you would also be gone.

The *ego* comes wrapped in a package marked, "Fragile. Handle with care." What's that line? It's pretty good! "Handle with Prayer." Right!

So that's what this book is all about.

Totally stressed out?

Uptight? Fearful? Mad!? Guilty? Worried? Tense? or simply restless, dissatisfied, ill at ease, even a bit bored?

Something is missing in your life, and you don't know quite what it is, where you missed it, or how you can find it.

Do I ever have good news for you!

Chances are that if you could fathom the depth of your problem, you'd run into a taproot called "ego trouble."

This human condition has become a universal epidemic. What causes these ego problems anyway?

I am certain that the damaging and demonic problem of *the sinful ego goes back to Adam's tragic fall from glory to disgrace.*

His honor, which was also his halo, became his horn.

So the widespread interest in and hunger for self-esteem is not a secular fad that will go away. It rises from a classic, not a fashionable, human need.

The first sinless human was, after all, made in the image of God and was "crowned with glory and honor."

The pride of belonging to the royal family of God was Adam's created birthright.

And when he left Eden, he walked out having lost both his proper pride and his holy humility.

The Adam who walked out of the garden was not a humble man. He was a humiliated human. He was humble before he sinned and humiliated after he sinned. Ever since the "Fall of Man," every human being ever born has been torn apart with that hunger for lost glory and driven to recover his God-ordained pride.

So the human being found himself in trouble. Big trouble. Having lost his God-given pride he has to invent something to take its place.

Enter *ego*. Call it false pride. It is a manufactured substitute for that wonderful true pride of walking in the cool of the garden right beside the Father.

I recently found a line that I had scratched on the back of a Hope College psychology textbook. At that time I was a student under Dr. Lars Grandberg. The year was 1946. Here is the line written in my youthful penmanship: "The inferiority complex is the mother of the superiority complex."

Today I believe that more than ever.

The pride that is condemned in the Bible is the deviated, distorted, dangerous, and potentially demonic defense mechanism of a lost Adam trying in his own fumbling and failing way to put a crown of glory back on his head.

He simply feels naked and undressed without wearing that hat of holy honor.

What we must come to understand is—and I'll repeat it, I promise!—*The opposite of pride is not humility. The opposite of pride is shame.*

The good news I promised?

In Christ, Christians believe, we can once more become adopted children of God. We now discover that *positive pride and honest humility are not opposites, but are in fact front and back faces of one coin of unmatched spiritual value.*

In fact, this healthy spiritual sense of well-being is what every person in the whole world needs and seeks in his "ego tripping" and in pursuit of self-esteem.

"Christ in you, your hope of glory," is the safe, satisfying, sensible, and saving message of the gospel.

I am somebody—I belong to Christ.

Therefore I can do something and be somebody of profound value and worth in this world. Yes, "I can do all things through Christ who strengthens me."

When our pride is rooted in a redemptive relationship with Christ, our humility is total, healthy, and assured. I am somebody wonderful, but I can't take credit for it. I owe it all to Christ and His cross.

Yes, He bore the anguish of hell that I might not suffer that eternal torment. For what is the core of hell and death? In a word, shame. Total disgrace. Complete abandonment.

"I have known the worst torture," Nobel laureate and death camp survivor Elie Wiesel said in my hearing recently, "But the worst torture is when the torturer comes to you and tells you, 'No one believes you are alive anymore—they have all given up on you. You are abandoned'."

This was the real hell Christ experienced on the cross. "My God, my God! Why have *You* abandoned me?" It produced such shame that not a vestige of honor, dignity, glory—yes, self-esteem—was left in that sinless Savior. It happened in order that we need never be abandoned by God, but could be assured of eternal adoption into His family, belonging to Him forever and forever and forever. That's sanctified self-esteem!

Please—don't turn me off just because I mentioned "the cross!" Don't switch channels on me yet. The cross is not a negative, but a *positive* symbol. It's a giant minus turned into the biggest plus sign in the history of the human race!

"But Dr. Schuller, your messages all start out with a theology of comfort instead of the cross." I've heard this criticism more than once. My answer is always the same: "Well, that's where I was taught to begin."

As a young boy I was introduced to Christianity in a little book called the Heidelberg Catechism.

Its leadoff question is, "What is your only comfort in life and death?"

And the biblical answer is, "That I *belong* . . . to my faithful Savior Jesus Christ. . . ."

That faith has met my deepest need. Self-esteem through friendship with God in Jesus Christ. I now base my value as a person in my relationship as a human being restored to God through Christ.

I really feel important in Christ.

Yes, my ego needs are sweetly and safely fulfilled in my belonging to Christ.

How important am I, are *you*, anyway?

- *The cynic* would answer: You think you're so important? Just put your finger in a bucket of water. Pull it out and see how big a hole is left.
- *The chemist?* The materialist tells us the body can be reduced to chemicals that can be bought cheaply in a store.
- *The Christ?* "I am the Good Shepherd. You are one of my sheep. The Good Shepherd lays down His life for His sheep!" Jesus Christ! He would die—to save your soul and mine!

YOUR VALUE AS A PERSON—CHECK IT OUT!

How much is a sprinkler head worth? It all depends. Not much on a shelf in the hardware store. But attach it to a water line and it will bring life to plants, flowers, and fruit, feeding the human race.

Life and death—they're in the sprinkler head.

How much is a pen worth? It all depends. Whose hand holds it—and what that hand does with it.

What is a human being worth anyway?

It all depends. A disconnected human life is a waste. Connected to an uplifting faith in a loving spirit that flows from the living heart of Jesus Christ, this simple person becomes a powerhouse of life-giving hope!

I have practiced this positive faith for sixty years. I have proclaimed it in books and broadcasts worldwide to all cultures, creeds, and continents.

I have received well over twenty-five million letters in the past twenty years of ministry. Four words are repeated from every country and culture where I have been privileged to proclaim this gospel. The words are always the same: "You saved my life."

"You are saving people from emotional starvation; I am saving them from physical starvation," Mother Teresa said to me recently.

My passionate desire in this book is to share this proven, practical, positive, life-changing faith with you.

So let's go back—way, way back to the Book of Exodus in

the Old Testament. Back to the beginning. Back to the Ten Commandments. And we'll make this exciting, life-transforming discovery.

Yes, you'll discover that these ten *commands* are *meant* to lead you from
- oppression—to freedom!
- fear—to faith!
- insecurity—to security!
- sinfulness—to goodness!
- depression—to hope!
- unhappiness—to joy!
- egotism—to healthy pride!
- shame—to glory!

You'll discover the power and pride of being a child of God, the one true God who believes in you, loves you, and has given you good news that could just save your life!

Big egos have little ears

CHAPTER 1

BELIEVE IN THE GOD WHO BELIEVES IN YOU!

"THOU SHALT HAVE NO OTHER GODS BEFORE ME"

1

I can hear some sincere skeptic respond:
My! How exclusive can you get?
How intolerant is this God who laid down the opening words?

Hasn't He heard of religious pluralism, freedom of belief?
Is this really the voice of the God who says, "I love you"?

Well, remember that this commandment was written long before the modern era of intellectual enlightenment. Today, we have broader, more liberal understanding. How does it go, that inclusive statement? Oh, yes! "Different strokes for different folks."

Really, now! Isn't God being a bit of an elitist? Would it not be more magnanimous on His part to let us simply "pick and choose" among the vast variety of gods available in the free marketplace of ideas?

"Thou shalt have no other gods."
A bit standoffish, wouldn't you say?!
"Who does He think He is, anyway?"
"Does He have to be so narrow-minded?"
"Does He really think He can do more for me than—say . . .

> *. . . the god of war? Doesn't might make right?*
> *or*
> *. . . the goddess of love? Isn't sex still life's biggest thrill?*
> *or*
> *. . . the god of wisdom? Isn't intellectualism the ultimate fulfillment of life?"*

Isn't He a tad discriminatory?
Does He have to be so uncompromising?
He comes across with such a nonnegotiable attitude!
Couldn't He be just a little more tolerant of the competition?
Wait a minute—when did He write these lines? Maybe times have changed? Probably He didn't have so many gods to compete with then as he does in today's secular, modern world.

Of course, when He wrote this hair-splitting, rigid, inflexible

1

order there were no such things as Las Vegas or liposuction or Swiss bank accounts or cocaine. There were no call girls, computers, Concorde jets, nuclear power.

"Thou shalt have no other gods." But that was before Playboy or Penthouse, long— repeat, long—before the sexual revolution.

Or was it really? "The more things change," someone said, "the more they remain the same." Probably all the gods we recognize today were already alive, kicking, and calling for attention and affection way back when.

Nevertheless, why is God so dead set against sharing His role and His rule with all of the others that have so much to offer?

Does this God of the Ten Commandments really believe He can offer more fun, greater thrills, richer fulfillment than the other gods that this world is peddling from their carts?

The opposite of pride is not humility. The opposite of pride is shame.

Why doesn't He simply give us credit for a little intelligence? Couldn't He be decent about it and declare quite openly, "Pick and choose. It really doesn't make any difference to Me which god—if any—you choose"?

He is so unyielding. What's the word? Adamant! Arbitrary! Almost autocratic.

Why?

Maybe He knows something we don't know.

Maybe He just doesn't want to see us get hurt.

Maybe what He means to say is, "I love you. I want to help you. Please let Me!"

Maybe—just maybe—He knows that He is the only one who can deliver what we really need!

What could that be?

It just could be the answer to my biggest problem.

You guessed it—our—yes, yours and mine—ego problems! What could this exclusive God offer exclusively?

1

Is it possible?
- **Pride without arrogance?**
- **Self-esteem without narcissism?**
- **Self-respect without vanity?**
- **Dignity without conceit?**
- **Individualism without selfishness?**

That's it! Sweet, satisfying, self-effacing, sacred self-esteem!

Yes! That's it. That's what He—and He alone—can offer and deliver with total consumer satisfaction.

But why? Can't the other gods do as well?

Hardly—for one simple, obvious reason. The God of the Ten Commandments *is the only God who really believes in you.*

> But you say the entire subject of God is of no concern to you. It's O.K. for theologians and religious people. But you are far more interested in corporate mergers; personal investments; technological developments; business ventures; politics; medical advancements; world peace.
>
> Wait a minute! Maybe God shares your interest in these subjects too. If He's "for real," the two of you ought to get together. Think about it!
>
> Or maybe your wife shares your lack of interest in God—religion. She too is focused on career advancement, education, aerobics, fashions, children, house, furniture, weddings, birthdays, fingernails.

IF GOD BELIEVES IN US, WHY DON'T WE BELIEVE IN HIM?

I posed this question to Mother Teresa. "Distractions—too may distractions," she answered.

Of course.

It's not that we don't believe in God, we just have too many other things on our minds.

What's the old saying? "The wheel that squeaks the loudest gets the grease."

1

Distractions. No doubt that's our problem. Yours too? Believe me, I hear you!

I've got mail to sort out. Junk mail to discard is all mixed in with . . .

- *bills to be paid*
- *invitations to important events I wouldn't want to miss*
- *letters from friends*
- *these thank-you notes—do I have to answer?*
- *final notice to resubscribe to my favorite magazine (I wouldn't want to miss an issue.)*
- *political propaganda*
- *and now and then (rarely perhaps, but you never know when!) a letter with a check*
- *or a chance to win a million dollars*

Yes, there's the mail. I can't—I absolutely cannot ignore it. They'll turn my lights off.

And God doesn't send me checks. Or final notices. If He's in all of that stuff in the mailbox, I missed it! (You probably did!)

Then there's the telephone. I can't ignore a telephone that's ringing. Answering machines! I hate them. I love them. Whatever—the messages come and demand (I mean demand!) a response. If I ignored them, I'd soon be out of a job! Out of the house! Or on the "outs" with friends and family.

Part of my problem is that my telephone doesn't have any manners. It is totally uncivilized. It bursts right in on me when I've got my mouth full of food or when I'm in my bed or the bathtub. I can be eating, sleeping, praying. I may be watching TV or reading. My telephone is rude. It doesn't care and has absolutely no respect for my privacy!

For instance, I'm ready to go out; I'm late. I hear it ring. I can't ignore it. When I do I keep wondering with a mixture of guilt and anxiety who it was and what they wanted and if I should have answered it. Maybe I should get a telephone in my car?

> # The God of the Ten Commandments is the only God who really believes in you.

Believe In The God Who Believes In You!

1

Then there are distractions, my "to do" lists!
- *Replace the batteries*
- *Change the oil in the car*
- *Make appointment with the dentist, watch out for that plaque buildup*
- *Take the clothes to cleaners*
- *Go grocery shopping*

You think I'm busy? My friends' "to do" lists are worse than mine.

They've got a yard to keep up, weeds to fight! And no time to plant the flowers. Or cut them and enjoy them close to the eye and nose. They blossom and fade, never noticed by anyone.

They've got kids too. And pets. Kids + pets = busy. Add more items to their "to do" lists.
- *Take dog to vet*
- *Find dog sitter so we can take a weekend off*

Yep! They take weekends off—more notes on their "to do" lists.
- *Check on hotel and airline reservations*
- *Water the plants*
- *Give the darn goldfish away*

Some of my friends even have "second homes." You should see their "to do" lists.

Distractions? If I didn't have enough as it is, something always seems to come along that I didn't count on. It could be a simple thing like a hole in my sock, a broken fingernail, a stain on my suit (Why didn't I notice it before I was all dressed and ready to go out?).

It could be a humdinger of a surprise: the flu; or worse, a mysterious lump, an odd-looking mole. "Cancer!?" Doctor appointments must be made. "When will the tests be back, Doctor?" And what if the tests are positive? Surgery? Chemotherapy? How long? Yes, sickness. It can be so time consuming. Just staying alive and fit has a way of interfering with real living.

Then there are funerals. Even if I don't have to go or don't want to go or simply choose not to go, I still am bothered by the knowledge that someone I knew died.

Death can be a real distraction.

Especially if you have to plan the funeral. Even if it was all planned in advance, there are the announcements. Lawyers, accountants, changing names on bank accounts, subscriptions, insurance policies. Details can drag out for months. I can cry my

1

eyes out, but the business still has to be handled. Speaking of funerals, "funny thing how easy and harmless it was to cancel those terribly important appointments so I could go to the funeral."

Talk about distraction? You've heard about divorce? It's another death. It can add to the "to do" list. Even if there are no children and no ex-in-laws, you wouldn't believe it unless you've gone through it.

Distractions: I have the vague impression that I'm missing out on something. A concert, a game, a hobby. Maybe—at times I wonder—am I missing out on this whole thing called God?

I'm confused.

Maybe the atheist is right. Maybe not. I haven't time to think about it. I'm not even sure if I care—or dare—to really get into it. I'll put it on the back burner, call myself an agnostic. I'll defer, delay, postpone.

Perhaps your doubts are not based on distractions. You do care. You read. You do have a serious question? Let's have it.

Didn't I read that scientists are on the verge of proving that there is no God? What do they call it? A theory of everything (TOE)?

Yes! This theory of everything has really made the news. It is the work of Stephen W. Hawking, professor of mathematics at Cambridge University. "My proposal," he says, "is the statement that the universe is a closed system. We don't need to suppose there's something outside the universe which is not subject to its law. It is the claim that the laws of science are sufficient to explain the universe."

This theory of everything causes people to stop and question: "If laws of science can explain everything, then where does God fit in?"

Hawking's credentials are impeccable. When he speaks, people listen. They believe him.

For those of you who are impressed with Dr. Hawking's observations, I share the rest of the story: "Even if we had a TOE," Hawking admits, "we would still be left with one final question. *What*

Believe In The God Who Believes In You!

1

is it that breathes fire into the equations and makes a universe for them to describe?"

And does he have an answer? "If I knew that," says Hawking, "then I would know everything important."

So we're back to the possibility of God! . . .

Who puts fire not only in equations but in human hearts and souls!

What puts the romance in a rose?

If you did a biological analysis of a rose, you would study its various parts: thorns, petals, leaves, stem, and root system. You could carefully dissect the plant, part by part, and have a complete organic description and still not be able to answer the questions: What is love? What is romance?

If God believes in every person, why doesn't every person believe in God? Distractions? Yes, Doubts? Yes. But there are other reasons. I can hear someone say to me:

You may be interested, Dr. Schuller, in the God of the Ten Commandments, but frankly I'm more interested in politics. Who needs God when we have good government? The government has an obligation to take care of the people. Right? Who needs God if you've got Social Security? Unemployment insurance? Medicare? Welfare checks?

O.K. I'll admit government subsidies do precious little for my self-respect. The State can actually put a dent in my dignity to tell you the truth.

Money! That's the only God I need. I just might win the lottery someday. Maybe it won't do much for my pride, but it will open doors to lots of pleasures.

And if I have enough fun, I can escape from life's embarrassments. For sure, if I'm rich, I won't have so many distractions. "Wrong," you say? Explain that to me. The way I see it, I would hire people to take care of all my "to do" lists. On the other hand, I don't know if I'd like to have servants around. I like being able to have the house and yard all to myself. Not worry about running around from room to room in my shorts or closing the door every time I go to the bathroom. I wouldn't want to have someone else raid the refrigerator for me. I'd miss that.

1

"One of the pressures of affluence and wealth," someone once said, "is that the richer you are, the more options you have." When to travel. What to wear. Which house to live in. Which invitation to accept.

Wealthy people have even more decisions to make. Getting rich gives you the dubious luxury of choosing from among even more distractions.

"Let my lawyer and accountant worry about the bills, tax matters, investments. That's what I hire them for," a celebrity once told me. Suddenly sad lines crawled across her face like the tracks of little invisible worms, and she said, "You know, they really messed up my business. And I paid them to do it."

If God believes in you, why don't you believe in Him? I ask the question. I get still another answer from another mind stirring and stewing out there:

The God of the Ten Commandments!? I know people who really are into that. But frankly, I think they'd be better off if they learned to stand on their own two feet.

If there's a God, I'm it.

"I am my own God." Now that sounds enticing. Seductive. How does it go?

"You have unlimited potential."

"You have within you power—untapped, and unlimited."

"You are your own god. Believe it."

I like that. For sure it appeals to my ego.

What a kick. What a high.

On second thought, why, I wonder, would I want to be, or do I think I could, be my own god?

Don't remind me. It's true I had an alcoholic friend who was into that big ego trip. He kept on telling himself:

> # Money gives you the dubious luxury of choosing from among even more distractions.

- *"You don't need to go to an Alcoholics Anonymous meeting."*
- *"You're not an alcoholic."*
- *"You're not addicted; you can quit anytime."*
- *"You can handle this challenge all by yourself."*
- *"You don't need anybody."*
- *"Higher power? You don't need it."*

It's sad. He's still a lush.

I have to confess that this "I'm my own God" stuff comes across sort of flaky. Like gold-plated jewelry—the phony veneer wears thin, and the cheap reality is exposed. Bang. What a bang when the ego explodes.

The God of the Ten Commandments!? I don't know. I don't care. I'm really not into that. I don't need it.

Besides I have some serious doubts. You know Mother Teresa, Dr. Schuller? I admire her. I'd like to ask her this one question. "For sure you've seen it all. How can you believe in a good God when there's so much pain, evil, suffering, and tragedy in the world?"

What? You asked her that? What did she say?

"We humans, not God, create the pain and suffering. There is so much selfishness, Dr. Schuller . . . ." That's what Mother Teresa told me when I asked her that very question.

"You shall have no other gods!?"

You know, Dr. Schuller, maybe this is the root of my problem after all. Probably my ego has caused me to get my values all mixed up.

I'll admit sometimes I do get upset. Frustrated. Angry. I even want to cry—sometimes.

There's something else. I want to be treated with respect. I want to know that I am important. Yes, I do have ego needs. I cannot deny that. For sure, I don't like to be embarrassed.

If there's a tug of war inside me between indulging in forbidden pleasure and safeguarding myself from shame, I'll try to have it both ways. But, oh God (Hey! I said that word), I hope I don't get caught. If I really thought I'd be found out, I'm sure my fear of shame would win out over my appetite for fun.

Sin? I'm not really sure I know what that is. Shame? You bet. I understand that. Self-respect? Self-esteem? I want it. I need it.

- *Why am I this way?*
- *Big or little, healthy or sick, why does everybody seem to have an ego?*

The Opposite of Pride Is Not Humility!

The Opposite of Pride Is Shame!

1

- *Is it possible that this God of the Ten Commandments is for real?*
- *Does He really have the answer?*
- *O.K. I'll listen.*

How important is your self-esteem, anyway?

To understand the depth and breadth of this primeval emotion, first take a look at the English words that cast light on the subject:

- **Pride**
- **Honor**
- **Self-respect**
- **Dignity**
- **Glory**
- **Self-worth**

Can *you*—can anyone—live without these self-affirming perceptions?

Or look at it from the opposite side of the coin:

- **Humiliation**
- **Shame**
- **Embarrassment**
- **Disgrace**
- **Dishonor**

Can *you*—can anyone—live a healthy emotional life in such a desolate, demeaning climate?

But isn't pride one of the seven deadly sins? And humility one of the queenly virtues? Are we not winsomely attracted to the beautifully humble person and repulsed by the proud?

And if such is the case, then why do we tolerate and encourage pride in our family, our marriage, our educational accomplishments, our work? Isn't it true that we deplore the person who takes no pride in his labor?

Are we facing a shattering contradiction?

Or has our language confused the clarity of our understanding?

First, genuine healthy pride and authentic humility are not opposites—they are one and the same—only different sides of the same coin of human value.

We will be on the way to bright insight into human behavior when we see that what we all call repugnant pride and abhorrent self-interest and nauseating narcissism may

1

actually rise from the absence of that inner security that only healthy self-esteem bestows.

Any analysis of sin, selfishness, narcissism, pride, vanity, or egotism that fails to note this is, to say the least, a surface, shallow, and potentially misleading diagnosis of the real human predicament.

We will be helped immensely when we come to understand that (I promised to repeat it . . . it's so important!) . . .

The opposite of pride is not humility!

The opposite of pride is SHAME!

I

Where did this need for self-esteem come from anyway?

Why is every baby born with a force called ego?

What is the origin of the universal inclination to pride? Do the quantum physics folks have an answer to this? Where did this "fire of the Soul" come from?

Human beings are creatures designed to breathe the air of healthy, humble pride. In our heart of hearts, we sense a spiritual surge for greatness and glory. Of course! Why, the ego is the mark of the image of God within us. It's so obvious. It is not the product of an evolutionary process. It is the stamp of the Creator in our souls! Every human being that ever lived or lives has a hunger for self-respect. There isn't a single human being anywhere who does not face the possibility of ego problems.

That strange ego drive within you is the call of your ancestry. You are not an ape, not a glorified animal. You are the descendant of the first man called Adam, the first woman called Eve!

You are a human being created in the image of God to rule and have dominion! How does the Bible put it? And God created man just "a little lower than the angels" and

Believe In The God Who Believes In You!

"crowned him with glory and honor" (Heb. 2:7). So the ego drive in man is a blind desire to find his lost crown.

No wonder self-respect is so important. It is primal. It is instinctual. It is an incurable craving. It will never go away. Unfulfilled, left raw, this ego will erupt crudely, wildly, wickedly, even viciously. Destructive pride and demonic ego running rampant.

The end result of such untamed pride is shame.

Unless it is safely satisfied, that hunger for self-esteem will seek fulfillment in neurotic and even dangerous ego trips, all of which will ultimately prove self-defeating by adding up eventually to shame and humiliation.

> **Every human being that ever lived or lives has a hunger for self-respect.**

Desmond Morris, in his book, *The Naked Ape*, is awestruck by the question: "Why is Man—of all the primates—hairless?" If the pelts of all the primates were stretched out in a row, Morris reminds us, one pelt would stand out with startling uniqueness. It has no hair! Why? How did Homo sapiens get bald?

A far more important observation might be made if we placed all of the primates, alive and squirming, in a row of cages. We would note that one primate stands out from all the rest! One primate is driven by a hunger for *self-respect*. One primate has *dignity*. One primate has developed a *belief system*. One primate dreams, imagines, and professes a belief in God. Why are Homo sapiens the only species living on planet earth with these instincts and inclinations? How did this biological entity develop these distinctive spiritual qualities?

I have posed these questions to philosophers and psychiatrists that I meet. Frequently their reply was, "I don't know."

I accepted their answer as an honest, humble admission,

1

until I heard a lecture by Abraham Kaplan, formerly of the philosophy department of the University of Michigan. Dr. Kaplan was giving the Adolph Meyer lecture at the annual meeting of the American Psychiatric Association in Los Angeles. In his message he challenged the psychiatrists in attendance: "Oftentimes it seems to me that psychiatrists have a way of saying, 'I don't know,' when actually they are dodging their commitments.

"Cowardice is disguised as humility.

"You don't want to admit it, but the real truth is that the human being is this way because there is a God and we are reflections of God, just as surely as the moon is the reflection of the sun."

We have always been and will always be incurably religious. God has placed spirituality deep within our souls. We cannot fight it, run away from it, or ignore it. Consequently, we will find a belief system in every culture, in every society, no matter how primitive or how sophisticated.

Even atheistic states have unwittingly developed a belief system that is a mixture of scientism, secularism, and statism.

Even these other gods have not kept the God of the Ten Commandments from reaching into their human hearts.

This is the God you need, for God believes in you! Enough to want to put your lost crown of honor back where it belongs—on your head.

II

What happens to human beings who have never worn the crown of divine honor?

Somehow we will try to satisfy the heart's hunger for divine dignity.

Here's where the phony substitutes for God come in!

The human being will intuitively, instinctively, impulsively grope and grasp a force or a faith or a philosophy that will (1) relieve us of the pain of shame, (2) offer escape from the anguish of a low sense of self-worth, or (3) promise a compensation or fulfillment for low self-respect.

Believe In The God Who Believes In You!

1

False gods, like power or pleasure or false pride, make big promises. But they don't deliver what we need most: . . . humble pride . . . divine dignity . . . self-respect . . . self-confidence . . . mellow self-esteem.

These phony, fabricated faiths and philosophies that we choose as god substitutes really leave us grasping and gasping for
- **Self-Assurance**
- **Self-Belief**
- **Self-Confidence**
- **Self-Dignity**

People who
- do not have self-confidence will never dare to pursue creative adventures. Then they . . .
- lack the stimulation that comes from creative thinking! As a result they . . .
- miss out on the healthy excitement of constructive activity and may even submit to evil, sin, and immorality! What a potentially demonic ego trip!

That's why this command is meant to be number one.

> **It's not that we don't believe in God, we just have too many other things on our minds.**

Meanwhile, these false gods are always manipulating us by offering counterfeit emotions: egotism instead of self-esteem! And like all counterfeits, this cheap, false substitute, which we call vanity or arrogance, will lead the poor soul to an end that spells shame instead of glory.

Yes, every person will find and follow some ruling force to integrate his personality. It may be power, politics, pleasure, passion, or pathetic pride.

But where will these false gods lead us? To abiding self-

1

dignity? *No, just the opposite!* Isolation, alienation, rejection, and in the end—no respect, no honor, no healthy pride—only disgrace.

How sour on the emotional palate is the aftertaste of drinking the bitter elixir offered by the false gods.

No wonder God mercifully keeps on insisting, "You shall have no other gods!"

There is still no substitute for the original, the "Real Thing!" This God who calls Himself the heavenly Father just won't give up trying to rescue us.

Look at what this Creator—God—is doing today!

Even godless states—yes, even atheists—are switching to a belief in the God who believes in human beings.

My good friend Walter Anderson is the editor of *Parade* magazine. He's a believer today, after having been a proclaimed unbeliever. He came from the poor side of New York and as a child was abused by an angry father.

Considering Walter's negative home and childhood, it is no wonder that he wanted no part of churches or religion. He had no interest in a heavenly Father, especially since he had his fill of his earthly father. On his own he had managed fine by himself; he had no need for a belief system.

That all changed when he met God in, of all places, a Russian cathedral, while he visited the country as an American tourist. This is how he related the incident:

> About twenty-five miles south of Moscow is a little cathedral called the Church of the Trinity. It is a Russian Orthodox Church. I visited this little cathedral and was struck by the rope that ran right down the center of the church. On one side were people who viewed the cathedral as a museum. On the other side were people who were believers. I was with a monk named Longin.
>
> I heard this beautiful hymn—it was magnificent. I couldn't recognize it, but it touched me. Being a typical American I looked to see where the choir was. I couldn't find it. But I could hear this beautiful hymn. Finally I asked Longin, "Where's the choir?"
>
> Longin replied, "As the believers come in, they pick up the sound of the hymn, and as they leave, they

1

stop. So there is always, here in Russia, a continuing hymn."

I thought about these people who profess their belief and stand for what they believe—in a society which ridicules the notion of God, which discourages religion in nearly any form.

Still they stand; they continue to believe.

And I asked Longin, "How'd you come to be a priest, a monk? How did you even learn to do this?"

"When I was a child," he said, "we were taught the stories of the Bible as legends. All the students read them as legends and myths. Then there came a moment when I read the stories differently; I believed them; I heard them differently from the other children."

When Longin said that, it came to me that I now heard the stories differently, and I too believed.

III

*B*ut does it *really make a difference* if you choose to believe in the God who claims to believe in you? Will this belief system generate a healthy pride that can produce a positive pressure to rise to become a creative, constructive, humble human being?

Check the life of Dr. Ben Carson, a leading neurosurgeon. He was trained in the best schools in the country, yet he believes that only God can accomplish the ultimate healing that he witnesses at Johns Hopkins University Hospital.

Such was the case when Dr. Carson faced one of the greatest challenges of his life: to separate seven-month-old Siamese twins, joined at the skull. The surgical team practiced the procedures for months because they knew that even a minute could mean the difference between life and death.

After fourteen hours in the operating room, Dr. Carson said, "We did the best we could do. The rest is up to God."

In the publicity that followed, Dr. Carson repeatedly pointed to God's role in the successful operation.

1

Ben Carson knows that God can change people and situations, not only in the hospital but also in the streets. Born in the Detroit ghetto, Carson was accustomed to knives of a different kind. During a fight at age fourteen, he lunged with a knife at the stomach of another kid only to see the knife blade strike the belt buckle and break. It scared him! He realized that he needed to turn his life around. He couldn't do it alone. With God's help and the love and support of his mother, he came out of the streets and eventually went to Yale University.

Today he is one of the leading pediatric neurosurgeons in the country, and his successful operation on the Siamese twins brought him into the spotlight. "You don't have to be a brain surgeon to be important. God can manifest His glory through you if you'll stay humble throughout your success," Dr. Ben Carson, in characteristic modesty, says.

Today Dr. Carson is saving lives. He is rebuilding lives through hard work and his talent. But he is quick to point out that he wouldn't have achieved what he has if it hadn't been for people who believed in him—his mother and God.

There can be no doubt or debate something is sadly lacking in a society that replaces God with false gods—or tries to run on the energy generated by undisciplined and unregenerated egos.

Depression and despair follow when we're left to make it on our own.

In an unpublished lecture, Martin E. P. Seligman, nationally esteemed research psychologist from the University of Pennsylvania, asked the question, "Why is there so much depression today?" He studied and reports a dramatic tenfold rise in the depression rate in the last fifty years in America. In a study funded by the National Institute for Mental Health, he contrasts the low level of depression among Kaluli of New Guinea and the Old Order Amish of Lancaster County, Pennsylvania, with what he calls "California Self." By California Self (which could more accurately and fairly be called Modern International Secular Self), he means individualism disconnected from a support system in a society, family, or religion. This leads to helplessness which will lead to hopelessness.

By contrast, the Kaluli culture calls for "people to help

their own people." So asking for help is a right—and therefore produces no disgrace and is no affront to dignity.

The same spirit can be found among the Old Order Amish.

They caught this spirit, of course, from the words of Jesus: "Blessed are the meek, for they shall inherit the earth." This teaching encourages us to overcome our ego problems with this confession: "I need help! I can't do it alone!"

To ask for help and to accept help is not demeaning. In fact, without the self-affirming support of family and religion, failures increase; self-esteem is battered; depression spreads.

You simply need the emotional support of someone who will believe in you. Everybody needs this kind of support.

SO NOW THINK ABOUT THIS!

1. Is real self-esteem possible until and unless someone believes in you?

Answer: Perhaps—but it's doubtful. I can't imagine it.

2. What happens to people who never—ever—had anyone believe in them?

Answer: They do not learn to love themselves or anyone else.

Without a healthy self-love they are emotionally incapable of giving or receiving love.

They feel too unworthy of love to accept love and feel too empty of love to give any away.

Then, what? Listen to the evening news! Visit the prisons! Check the drug abuse epidemic! Studies of antisocial behavior keep coming up with this responsible and recurring diagnosis: low self-esteem!

3. What happens to people when they encounter people who don't believe in them—and express that lack of belief through indignities and insults?

Answer: They start wars! Little ones or big ones on the border; in the boardroom; in the bedroom; or on the playground, even on the freeway.

1

4. What happens to people who meet people who believe in them?

Answer: Miracles, as we shall see. Miracles!

5. A final, challenging question: Will you *dare* to *believe* in the God who believes in you?

I've met enough people that are so cynical and so lacking in self-worth that they actually distrust the persons who affirm them.

So they fail the test of this first commandment. They suspect that God is putting them on, or leading them on only to let them down someday. They should, of course, put God to the test.

You're already placing your trust in some god. Everyone does. Whether you realize it or not, you're placing trust in yourself, your country, science, ego, money, sex, things, personal power, pleasure, prestige.

Measure the sincerity of people's trust by the amount of freedom they offer.

IV

Does your god really believe in you?

Is there a way to test whether your god or whether any person really believes in you? After all there are a lot of flatterers and manipulators. Can we put your "god" or my "god" to a test?

Can you be really sure if someone really believes in you? The answer is yes. Ask these revealing questions.

1. *What trust do they put in you?*

Do they trust you with their money? The God of the Ten Commandments has turned the treasures of creation over to

1

the human race—to manage! And God trusted you with treasures called *intelligence* and *imagination* and *intuition.* Yes, the potential to be a creative person! That's trust! Add to that His gift of the capacity to love, the ability to exercise faith!

He has trusted you with a treasure called the instinctive inclination to believe.

2. *What freedom do they give you?*

You can measure the sincerity of people's trust by the amount of freedom they offer. Consider this: God gave Adam and Eve freedom.

He even gives us the freedom to choose to be believers or atheists! Yes, the possibility of doubt is proof of the possibility of faith. For there can be no faith without the freedom to doubt. "Yes" has no meaning without a "No." Talk about trust!

So didn't God take an awful risk here? Of course! But He faced a divine dilemma. He wanted you and every person to discover and develop a sense of divine dignity.

Dignity will never emerge without the freedom to make personal decisions. Self-esteem can only evolve through the process of making risky and responsible choices. So the next question will really expose the sincerity and integrity of a person who claims to believe in you.

3. *What responsibilities do they give you?*
• Little ones—or big ones?
• Easy ones—or "impossible" ones?
• Short-run responsibilities—or responsibilities that carry long-term—maybe even eternal—consequences?

4. *Are they honest with you?*
• Do they admonish you when you need it?
• Do they affirm you before they finish correcting you?
• Do they endorse you? Even if and when they know you could at times be an embarrassment to them? Do they still stand by you in spite of your failures?

Finally, do they respect you enough to let you make the big decisions? And live with the eternal consequences?

5. *Do they keep in touch?*
• Check on how you're coming along?

1

- Approach you at unexpected times and ways, through people, or through circumstances, to encourage, affirm, or admonish you?

6. *Do they build you up?*
Are they passing tough challenges on to you? Are they letting you face enough problems and pain to grow and mature as a person?

7. *Do they have time to listen? respond?*
Can you contact them anytime, anywhere, and be assured they have an open line for you?

8. *Do they share their "glory" with you?*
The real God does. God wants to spread His glory around. He expects us to keep on keeping on creating, for as we share in the process of creating, we share in the glory. There is no more glorious feeling than to create something beautiful.

9. *Will they make solid commitments to be your friends?*
Will they run the risks that serious relationships always entail? The true God does. The sacrifice that Christ made on the cross is proof of that!

10. *Do they still love you after they've seen you at your worst?*
Jesus Christ does!

Now, when anyone believes in you enough to satisfy these ten test questions, that's called LOVE! Apply this test of any "trusting relationship" to this God of the Ten Commandments.

1. He trusts you with treasures.
2. He gives you the freedom to become a unique person.
3. He shares responsibilities that will allow you to grow.
4. He is honest in relating to you.
5. He is available to be in communication with you.

1

6. He offers real encouragement.
7. He hears and listens and really cares.
8. He shares with you the credit, honor, and glory of being involved in creative activity.
9. He gets involved in your dreams and your disappointments.
10. He is able and willing to offer grace and forgiveness to anyone.

Add them all together, and you'll know the meaning of a statement so familiar that it may have lost its punch. It is the most powerful collection of three words ever put together: **GOD LOVES YOU!**

V

Now that's the reason you can't go wrong if you will only choose to believe in the God who believes in you!

His affirming trust in you offers the solid foundation for a healthy, humble Pride.

My father never used to say anything. He was the quietest man I knew. All through my childhood, my father and my mother had a good marriage. But they had their problems. My mother would get upset at my dad and say, "Why don't you say something? Why don't you talk?"

"What should I say?" he'd reply.

"Just something," my mother would always answer. Well, when my father died, I'll never forget how much my mother missed him. "But he never said anything," I said to her one day. "How can you miss him so much?"

"Oh," she said, "even when he was silent, I always knew he was there."

That's how it is with God.

Dignity will never emerge without the freedom to make personal decisions.

1

We may not be aware of God's presence, and if we are aware of it, we may not acknowledge it. Nevertheless, He is there— believing in you. He is like the air. You are so accustomed to breathing that you forget how dependent you are on the air until you are in danger of losing it. God is in your corner, encouraging you in silent, subtle ways.

Trust the God who's always there. Believe in the One who believes in you! He knows how unique and special you are. He understands you as you really are. And He alone can see your full potential. Discover what God already knows about you, that you are a beautiful human being.

God cares about you, and He has beautiful plans for your life. He doesn't leave you to flounder about. He has given ten positive principles, prescriptions for living to the fullest. Welcome them into your life today: ten *commands meant* to give to you what you need most.

GOD BELIEVES IN YOU
(Even if You Don't Believe in Him)

In Russia, I was with my atheist guide for over a week. She took me through the museum of atheism in Leningrad. A few days later she escorted me through another museum of atheism in Kiev. As we left the museum I prayed silently, "What can I say to her? If You're there, Lord, speak to her through me—please!"

My words came out without a forethought. I believe it was God speaking through me. I said, "I have good news for you."

"Well?" She looked at me; she waited.

"God loves you," I said, "even if you don't believe it. And God believes in you even if you don't believe in Him."

She was, I felt, startled. "And remember," I added as I boarded the train to Vienna, "it's not a debate, it's a decision. It's not an argument, it's a choice."

God believes in me? Even if I don't believe in Him? That's love! Then I must be something special! Then maybe I can start believing in myself too!

Now I'll begin to believe in the God who keeps reaching

1

out to me with invitations to believe or with unexpected, unsolicited, and unexplainable bursts of inspiration.

William Dooner was born to Irish parents in a Harlem ghetto. Despite his sober, praying mother, he was tough and drinking and selling hard cider at age nine. By age twelve he was an alcoholic. As a budding teenager he worked for the Mafia in the numbers racket. By twenty-one he had survived gunshots from chasing police officers and an ice pick attack from gangsters. At the age of twenty-three he woke up from a drunken stupor to find himself living on Chicago's skid row in a fifty-cent-a-night flophouse.

The dried blood on his shirt was three days old. Black pus was draining from the infection in his ear, which had been badly wounded in a street fight. He had experienced everything life had to offer, and it was a bad deal. For days, weeks, he'd been living on rubbing alcohol. Tonight he would end it all. He knew how he'd do it. He'd simply jump from his sixth-floor window of the flophouse. He'd be another statistic—a dead one. Minutes before midnight he went out for a last stroll. As he crossed the darkened, dangerous street, he saw a solitary figure standing at the lamppost. The stranger in a black suit turned, and his white turned-around collar reflected the dim light. The priest simply smiled. That's all. And a mood—a feeling—entered the young man's mind. He was instantly aware of a Divine Presence. He experienced the presence of God. A peace moved into his troubled, tortured soul, and he would never again be the same. There were no sermons, no condemnations. Only salvation! For the first time in his life, he knew someone believed in him!

Someone loved him. That Someone was God. Instantly,

> # Enthusiasm, self-confidence, faith in God, love, are all contagious, and you can help spread them.

1

permanently, the compulsion to drink left him, never to return. Suddenly, without words or warning, faith was born deep within him!

He would never drink again. He would clean himself up. He would discover what there was in him that God saw and believed in! Thirty-four years later he would stand in the pulpit of my church to receive the Christian Business Man of the Year Award from the prestigious Religious Heritage of America. By this time he had been married to his first wife for thirty years. Every dream he ever had came true! Children! Business success! He was a multi-millionaire. Three United States presidents had tapped him for high government service. Now he could give something back. He became a major donor to a $6 million, two-hundred-fifty-bed facility to house and help the homeless—in the same place where he had found God more than three decades before. The McDermott Center is named after and run by Father McDermott, the man in black standing at the lamppost thirty years before.

So don't be surprised if the God who believes in you meets your mind or changes your mood. "I never ever felt I was worthy of God. I had a horrible self-image—until God touched me," Dooner declares.

Now, that's why the next chapter is so terribly important!

CHAPTER 2

A SELF-IMAGE TRANSPLANT— GO FOR IT!

"THOU SHALT NOT MAKE ANY GRAVEN IMAGE"

2

"Eighty-three percent of all Christians in the world live above the poverty level," a lecturer reported recently to a gathering of 4,000 Christians in Manila. "The challenge to share our abundance with the poor is obvious and compelling," he added.

This startling statistic raised an exciting possibility in my mind. *Something in this positive Christian faith releases forces that tends to lift people from poverty to prosperity.* Especially when it is estimated that over 70 percent of Hindus live below the poverty level.

What astonishing conclusion can we safely draw?

When you begin to believe in a God who believes in you, what happens is exciting, remarkable, and positive!

On a purely human level, look at what happens to people when they meet people who really believe in them. They develop a positive self-image. Pride, self-confidence, and success often follows. Consider three case studies:
- The 1988 Los Angeles Dodgers
- Edna Buchanan
- Jaime Escalante

Tommy Lasorda, whose wife belongs to my church, was the manager of the Los Angeles Dodgers and the 1988 World Champions. I know him very well. Now, no one in the sports world will ever forget the 1988 World Series when the Dodgers won the world championship. Sports writers and newscasters all labeled the Dodgers as the underdogs. Their pitching team was analyzed, their hitting team was scrutinized, and when the predictions were handed out, the Dodgers were at the bottom of the pile. Now, that must have been devastating news to read every day, to hear every night. How do you get out on the pitcher's mound, how do you dare to step into the batter's box when everybody is telling you you are going to lose, lose, lose?

Yet, the Dodgers did it. They gave it their best and they won, won, *won!* I asked Tommy how they did it.

2

He said "Simply, it was a year of miracles. It wasn't just a baseball season. It wasn't just the playoffs, nor was it just the World Series. It was a sign and example of what you can do in life if you really believe in yourself. It is what you've been preaching year after year—about positive thinking, self-confidence.

"It was a group of players who began the season much the underdog. No one believed that we could win the Western Division title. And after 162 games, we prevailed, because we believed. And then we went up against the mighty Mets of New York, who had beaten us ten of eleven times. And no one, no one thought we belonged on the same field with them. But our players believed. And we beat them in a tough seven-game series.

"And then we went into the Fall Classic against the mighty Athletics of Oakland, who had won 104 games. It was the third best record in the last fifty years in the American League. They beat Boston four straight, and no one thought we even had a chance. And we beat them in five games because we believed and we wanted it.

"The difference between the possible and the impossible often lies in someone's determination and self-confidence. The most gratifying moment in the whole year was when we beat the Mets in the final game of the playoffs. Orel 'Bulldog' Hershiser went to his knees. It brought tears to my eyes because he didn't forget what was more important in his life than victory, and that was faith in God. That was beautiful!

"I knew every one of our players had faith in God. Because, in order to achieve success in any field of endeavor, we build on hopes, we build on dreams, and we build on faith. And the 1988 Dodgers had faith.

"As I told our wonderful president, when we were in Washington to be honored, 'It

> # The opposite of pride is not humility:
>
> # The opposite of pride is SHAME!

2

was a team that captured the hearts of America because it showed what you can attain in life if you want something bad enough.' And there's only one route to success . . . the avenue of hard work and faith in God."

I asked him," Tommy, when did you begin to believe that you could be the champions this year?"

"I believed that the day I went to spring training."

I couldn't help teasing him about it. I said, "Come on, Tommy. You're not talking to a reporter now. You're talking to a minister. Tell the truth. Did you really believe that the Dodgers would win the World Series on the opening day of spring training?"

"Oh, absolutely! I believed that the day that I went to spring training. If I didn't believe in my players, how could my players believe in themselves? Every year that I manage, I believe without a doubt in my mind that my team, our team, is gonna be on top. And if I didn't believe that, I shouldn't be the leader because enthusiasm, self-confidence, winning, faith in God, love are all contagious, and you can help spread them."

Edna Buchanan was a poor little girl who loved to read. Her pleasure in life was reading newspapers to her old grandmother. Edna loved the stories in the newspapers. Stories, stories, stories—she gobbled them up like candy. This tall, shy, awkward girl had little or no self-esteem. She was raised in abject poverty. She wore used clothing to school. She felt gawky and was sure that all the other children were laughing at her behind her back. But then life suddenly changed! Forever! Her self-esteem was trans-formed—from gangly to elegant! It happened in one split second when she was in the seventh grade. Her teacher made a passing comment as she handed back to Edna a paper she had written as part of her homework. Edna Buchanan became somebody when her writing teacher declared for the whole class to hear, "Edna, when you write your first book, I want you to dedicate it to me."

Edna was shocked. Somebody believed in her! Believed enough to predict that she would be a success! She would be somebody! She had talent! She had what it takes!

2

That moment propelled Edna to become a fledgling reporter for a small paper in Miami. After grueling years of working obituaries, Edna began covering homicides. Needless to say, there were plenty of murders to cover in Miami. Edna learned how to get to the scene of a crime before the police could rope off the area. ("I just drove fast! . . . The cops were too busy racing to the crime scene to stop speeders.") Arriving early meant she was able to interview witnesses and get their firsthand observations. Always Edna's concern was and is for the victim. She chooses to thrive in such a gruesome job because she helps people. "The authorities take action when a homicide is reported in the paper," she says. "Injustices can be corrected when the newspaper draws them to public attention," she adds.

Edna Buchanan is a street reporter. So it was with great pride that she received the coveted Pulitzer Prize for reporting. She recorded her stories in a book, *The Corpse Had a Familiar Face*. The book is dedicated to her writing teacher, to the one who believed in her—Edna Mae Tunis!

Jaime Escalante? We'll get to him later.

But first, consider the masses of people who never had a Tommy Lasorda or an Edna Mae Tunis who believed in them. Chances are they simply grow up with a pitiful, negative self-image.

"I'm no good."
"I'm a worthless failure."
"I'm a horrible sinner."

Sound familiar? It's the moaning of a negative self-image that will wipe out self-respect and self-esteem and will result in discouragement, depression, and despair. In reality this poor creature may be completely wrong, or this pathetic soul may be partially right. Either way—he needs a new self-image transplant! Without it his diseased, negative self-image can and surely will have disastrous impact on his emotional and mental health and may even move on to inflict serious sickness in the body itself.

Astonishing! Amazing! Incredible—what people are doing to boost their self-esteem to compensate for inferiority

A Self-Image Transplant—Go For It!

2

complexes. People today can walk into a local drugstore to purchase products that will hopefully give their faltering self-image a lift. There are drugs to help them lose weight, to grow hair, to remove wrinkles, and to clear up complexions. If the drugs don't work, they can see doctors who can lyposuction the fat off or hypnotize them into a slender shape. They can get a tummy tuck or a chin tuck. They can enlarge or reduce the size of their breasts. Now cosmetic surgery has its place. Physical self-improvement can be helpful, providing it doesn't develop a narcissistic personality. Maxwell Maltz, famed plastic surgeon, discovered and reported in his landmark book *Psycho Psyber-netics* that an improved self-image often followed cosmetic surgery. *However, most people today don't need a plastic surgeon as much as they need a self-image transplant.*

How can you be really sure when someone really believes in you?

Is there someone you admire that you would trade places with if you could? You wish you could have his hair or her eyes or his position at the company or her promotion? The truth of the matter is that it isn't their hair, eyes, promotion, or their position that you really want. It is their charm, their confidence and poise—in short, their self-image. You admire persons who are poised and confident, who really feel good about themselves. You want to feel good about yourself, too.

It's time to consider a self-image transplant, which means: Draw a mental image of a God who believes in you, and your self-image will be amazingly transformed.

The first commandment,"Thou shall have no other gods before Me" is the foundational step. This is a *command meant* to encourage us to believe in the One God who believes in us. The second commandment builds upon the first one. It is

DRAW A MENTAL
IMAGE OF A
GOD WHO BELIEVES
IN YOU, AND YOUR
SELF-IMAGE WILL
BE AMAZINGLY
TRANSFORMED.

2

"Thou shall not make for yourself any carved, i.e. false or phony, image."

Your self-image—what is it really? It is the way you see yourself. It may be quite a true picture of yourself, or it may be a distorted perception.

Volumes of studies have established beyond debate that one's self-image will, like a computer, print out what's pictured deep in the subconscious mind, whether that internalized programmed material is right or wrong. You will tend to become what you think you are. Think you're ignorant, and you'll avoid challenges to grow intellectually.

And controlled studies have shown that what you *think others think you are* will shape your own perceptions of yourself. So your self-image will be shaped by how you imagine others perceive you. Hence, "I am not what I think I am; I am not what you think I am. I am what I think you think I am!"

We shall see the importance of this later in this chapter when we ask the question, "Does the image I have of God affect my self-image?"

Our self-image is the inner program that charts our course, determines our choices, predetermines our reactions to what happens to us, even shapes our belief system, or generates our doubts. In fact, it is the control computer that, once programmed, takes over our lives!

The human mind was the first computer ever created and will remain forever the brightest and the best. When we are born our personal computer is "turned on" and the programming process begins. Erik Erikson, father of child psychiatry, has taught the world that the first thing a child must learn is trust. When I studied Erikson, I was forced to rethink my Theology Of The Person. I assumed, as did many theologians, that a child instinctively trusts the mother to whose breast he clings. Not so. The clinging is a demonstration of a lack of trust and inborn insecurity, a first faltering step on what will be a lifetime of learning (or programming) to achieve self-confidence. So Erikson has taught the nurses to stroke and speak tenderly to the newborn babies, to program them to trust!

2

This hoped-for emerging trust will be a fragile development. If the two-year-old computer is programmed with fear
teachings, his developing trust level will be impaired. If the
child is abused by his father, the computer will record this
negative experience. Later if that developing teenaged mind
is introduced to the concept of God as a heavenly Father, the
computer will light up the screen with a flash alarm,
warning, "Reject! Reject!" And atheism or agnosticism may
be programmed by the computer into the subconscious
mind, predetermining what may well be a lifetime
"Unbelief—Belief" System.

Good news, bad news—this incredible computer, the
subconscious, will keep on being programmed as long as
there is brain life.

If at the first-grade level the mind is programmed to
believe that God is a mean, unloving, super-spirit-power,
then we should not be suprised if the child that was reared
in this negative, legalistic religious atmosphere grows up to
react and reject the entire concept of God. Or he may reflect
an angry, religious lifestyle.

Even as the "computer" programming will largely
determine the religious belief system, so its programming
will determine the self-image. If the parent shouts in anger,
"You're stupid," the computer believes this. It does not
debate. It merely records the lie: *garbage in—garbage out*. The
mind is set to forecast predictions such as, "I am not smart
enough to get an A. I am not college material." The self-
image is evolving in the computer.

The computer never experiences a "power shutdown."

The teacher orders Johnny to go to the board and solve the
problem. Johnny's stomach churns. He breaks into a sweat.
"The subconscious is ahead of the conscious," psychiatrist
Scott Peck tells us. How true. The computerized negative
self-image is on the job, telling Johnny he's not too smart.
Now he's on the spot. He doesn't believe in himself as a
student. So he's thinking, "I'm going to fail in front of the
whole class." And of course he does, reinforcing the negative
self-image.

In the process the negative self-image has programmed
him for an experience which will leave him embarrassed,
humiliated. It's a downward cycle. The negative self-image

2

produces actions that feed and fuel it onward and downward. A failure cycle has caught hold unless a sensitive
teacher or an alert parent catches and corrects the damage
done. If not? Then a human life is on the way to developing
a negative self-image which will generate low self-esteem,
which will lead to failure, which will reinforce the negative
self-image, which will become a self-fulfilling expectation!

Our self-image tends to become a self-fulfilling prophecy.
So developing a positive self-image is of primary importance.
Without it, the hoped-for healthy self-respect is a lost cause.
Helplessness, perceived or real, leads to a sense of hope-
lessness in the mind of a person with a negative self-image.
That's a prescription for defeat, discouragement, depression,
and despair.

From time to time we see the havoc wreaked by persons
who ridiculously fantasize that they are gloriously gifted and
are sure the whole world is crazy not to recognize that they
are as talented as Pavarotti—even though they can hardly
sing on key.

Far more widely pervasive, however, is the negative self-
image infection in society that feeds and fuels an epidemic of
low self-esteem. Which explains why the bottom of every
professional ladder is crowded with genuinely talented and
often gifted persons. Why are they at the bottom? There may
be extenuating circumstances, but more often than not they
simply cannot believe in their heart of hearts that they are
really "that good!" Their thoughts keep them down!

- **Rejected?** They quickly give up: "I knew all along I didn't
  have it!"
- **Discouraged?** They abandon their dream too soon.
- **Disappointed with results?** They back away from new
  ventures.
- **Divorced?** "Never again will I try. There must be
  something terribly wrong with me."
- **Bankrupt?** "I guess I just don't have what it takes to be a
  success in business."

People who suffer with shame and wallow in negativity
will eventually search for a god who offers relief (an opiate),
retreat (an escape), or who generate a false and futile pride.
Tragically, such wrong choices will lead to false support

PMI—
POSITIVE
MENTAL
IMAGE

2

systems—false gods that will in the end generate a negative, not a positive, self-image.

Now you can see why it's imperative, essential, and all-important that you believe in a God who believes in you!

Now you can see how your self-image will be shaped instinctively when you listen to honest and perceptive persons who encourage you to believe in yourself.

Now you can understand how you must input a positive "image" of a positive God into your subconscious computer!

Now you can put the pieces together and analyze why persons who have an image of God as a negative, "I-don't-like-you" Person will end up not liking themselves either. "If God doesn't like me—and He doesn't make mistakes—I'm crazy if I like myself." So goes the distorted, sick reasoning.

We'll never know how many people have been infected with such a false image of God. This gives them a distorted view of themselves, feeding feelings of despair and defeat. And they are living with the fallout, all because they had engraved in their minds a horribly false image of what God is really like!

It's important to recognize that the image of God that's engraved in your subconscious will shape your self-image and in turn affect the state of your self-esteem.

• Does your problem with self-esteem stem from a negative self-image? Quite possibly.

• Is it quite possible that your inadequate self-image is the result of a false image of God? Very likely!

• Are the two "images" related? Yes, always!

• What are some of the false images of God that produce negative self-images?

• If the true image of a trusting God who believes in you is programmed into your computer, what will that do for your self-image? You'll experience a genuine "rebirth," that's what! Is it possible this could in fact, in human terms, amount to a self-image transplant? Definitely!

Consider how a transplanted heart brings new life to a body! Is it possible that a healthy, positive self-image transplanted in the place of a diseased and negative self-image will bring miraculous new life to a depressed personality? Most assuredly! Is this, in part, what happens

2

when a person becomes a born-again Christian? I'm sure of it!

Let's take a deeper look into these questions.

QUESTION ONE

1. *"Are the two images—our image of God and our image of ourselves—related?*
Does the God image you hold in your mind affect your self-image?"

Answer: Definitely! Emphatically! Beyond a doubt! And beyond calculation or analysis.

Illustration: Psychologists wisely counsel divorced parents never to put down or demean the ex-spouse in front of the children because of the danger that the child will develop a negative self-image and be infected with a lowering of self-esteem.

Explanation: In the child's mind, "If there is something so bad about my mother or my father, there must be something bad about me, for I am his (or her) child." This is only *one* way in which a negative image of the adult parent figure shapes a negative self-image in the child. This is one reason children of divorced families can develop a low self-esteem.

Another illustration: Children learn behavior from parents. An angry father programs an image in the son of what a father is supposed to be. To the growing son who sees his father as angry, there is programmed an image of himself as someday also being an angry father. The image we perceive of our parents, our role models, will no doubt affect the way we view God and profoundly, permanently (barring a born-again miracle) shape our self-images for good—or ill.

QUESTION TWO

2. *What are some of the false images of God that produce negative self-images?*

Answer: The Grim Reaper, The Punishing Patrolman, The Duplicitous Politician—these are only a few of the seriously flawed, false images of God engraved on human minds,

2

negatively programming us to believe less of ourselves than we should. Let's examine these and other false images.

THE GRIM REAPER

He was once a household name in the Christian churches of the United States, holding a high position in North American evangelism. Suddenly he shocked the world by renouncing his faith, giving up his religious profession, and is today a declared agnostic.

Not long ago I had a chance to ask him the haunting question, "Why?"

"I saw a process in evolution that shook my faith," he told me. He explained, "In nature, the strong survive. The weak die. I couldn't believe in a God who would let that happen."

I have reflected long on that judgement. John Stuart Mill, the great philosopher, once wisely observed, "You cannot accept any position until you have rejected the alternative."

So? Yes—the strong survive—the weak pass on. But to me this is a case to believe in God—not deny Him. Why? Because this is a positive process! *Consider the alternative.* What if the weak survived and the strong would die off? That would be a downward spiral! Impossible! The process of evolution is cause for hope in God! For in the historical process God is slowly and surely improving, upgrading, not downgrading His creation!

Does this mean He is a grim reaper, mercilessly exterminating the pitiful and weak creatures? Not at all. He rewards them with His own tender mercies and gentle graces in an ongoing creative process that is redemptive and constructive.

THE GRAND PATRIARCH

Another false view of God is that of the Grand Patriarch. This view perceives God like Santa Claus, a wonderful old grandfather—gentle, good, giving whatever we need or want. Yet the Bible does not present Him like this.

One of the funniest sights I ever saw happened a few Christmases ago. At a self-serve gas station, pumping gas into his car, was a full-bearded Santa Claus. Upon finishing his task, he proceeded to pay by credit card! When Santa Claus operates on credit, then we're really in trouble.

God is not a Santa Claus. He is more than a Grand Patriarch.

THE PUNISHING PATROLMAN

Someone once asked a young girl what she thought God was like. She answered, "God is Someone who watches to see if I am doing anything wrong."

In such minds God is pictured as a watchdog, armed with an assortment of weapons and means to keep the world humble and submissive. Lightning, famine, earthquakes—all are attributed to the "wrath of God."

We make a serious mistake, it seems to me, if we identify God with nature. He is free and above the laws of nature. Certainly God is not mean, vindictive, or brutal.

THE DUPLICITOUS POLITICIAN

There are others who view God as the Great Politician. He is imagined as One who manipulates nations, watches for His opportunity, and then mercilessly uses people, only to drop them when He has what He wants.

God is not a politician or a cheap opportunist. Some people confuse providence with politics, but God certainly is not responsible for the sins of the human race and the resulting wars and tragedies.

But what is true is that in His glorious providence He redeems miserable situations so that tragedies become triumphs, burdens become blessings, obstacles become opportunities, and problems become possibilities.

THE GLORIOUS PORTRAIT

The true image of God is indeed inspiring and glorious.

God, Christians believe, came down and walked around on this earth in a human body. And He was called Jesus! This Christ was not an ordinary itinerant preacher. This was God putting Himself in our shoes. It was the best way God could get through to the human race.

The true God is the God that Jesus Christ believed in. Jesus claimed to *be* God incarnate. He claimed to *be* a flesh and blood representation of who God is. It sounds incredible, but it makes sense when you realize how necessary it was for God to do this.

2

For years and years and years, humankind searched for God. Too often they lost Him. God was often misunderstood. He was feared; He was ignored. Humans turned their backs on Him and created impressions of what they thought God really was. Those impressions led them so far astray that God made the ultimate sacrifice: He came to earth as a baby. He was born to a common woman on a cold night in a dirty cave that was used as an animal stall.

This tiny baby was God in human form. His name was Jesus. As He grew, He began to fulfill His mission, which was to show the world what God is *really* like. So when we seriously look at Jesus and at His claims, we see a God who is loving, tender, caring, forgiving. He is the God who believes in the potential dignity of even the riffraff. Time and again, Jesus embraced the ones whom society had rejected. Time and again, He restored their dignity. Jesus taught them to believe in themselves.

Time and again, Jesus embraced the ones whom society had rejected. Time and again, He restored their dignity.

I see the *redemptive power of restored dignity* at work today in the lives of many dedicated men and women. God shows people that He believes in them through people like Jaime Escalante. You may have come to know about Jaime through the movie *Stand and Deliver*. This movie is based on the life of a middle-aged, balding, Hispanic schoolteacher. This unlikely hero took on gang-oriented, tattooed kids from East Los Angeles, kids that everyone else had branded as no-good and hopeless.

A Bolivian teacher, Jaime Escalante immigrated to America. He wasn't qualified to teach here, so he had to make great personal effort to qualify for teaching credentials in California. His first teaching assignment was a high school in East

Los Angeles. It was not what he bargained for. The kids in his classes were in no way, shape, or form ready to learn. In fact, the room was in a near riot; the kids completely controlled the classroom.

Jaime was disappointed. He loved to teach. He believed that teaching was sharing love and that education was a ticket to personal success. Nevertheless, he took on this rough group of kids who were destined to drop out of high school, headed for a life of crime and probably an early death. He started by teaching them manners and responsibility. He programmed them positively, "You're the best. You can do anything. You can go all the way to the top."

His goal was to help his students reach their highest possible personal potential. When the time to teach fractions came, he walked into the room with an apple and a knife. He began cutting apples into pieces. Meanwhile, he had precut pieces of apple in his briefcase. He started giving each of the kids a piece of apple. Then he asked them, "What do you have?"

"An apple."

"No." He continued to push for the answer he was seeking. "What do you have?"

"An apple."

"No, you have 20 percent of the apple." To another, "You have 50 percent of the apple." He turned to a girl, "What do you have?"

"I have three-quarters of an apple."

He applauded her and said, "You are a beautiful, intelligent kid."

That was just the beginning. Jaime's students went on to take calculus, advanced algebra, trigonometry. In most high schools, only 2 percent of high school graduates take the very difficult higher mathematics tests for entrance examinations, but 100 percent of Garfield High students take it.

I was so impressed with the movie and the man who gave of himself to these young people that I asked him if I could meet him and talk to him. He generously agreed to spend some time with me. I asked him, "Jaime, what's your secret? How do you motivate your students to such greatness?"

He said, "I look for the click. Sometimes it is easy to get, but other times I have to use five points:

- **"Desire**—They have to want it.

- **"Potential**—Potential is everywhere. The future belongs to those who can see it.

- **"Goals**—They have to set their goals and go for them. As you know, Dr. Schuller, the goals are there to direct the dreams.

- **"Dedication**—They have to put in the time. At least ten hours every week.

- **"Hard work**—"In my class room, I have under the clock a sign that says,

'**Determination + discipline + hard work = the way to success.**' I put that under the clock because my kids have the tendency to look at the clock during the class time."

Finally he added, "I believe in God. I believe that God wants us to be a success, and the only thing to do now is just follow what He said."

I can believe in the God that Jaime Escalante believes in. He is a God who believes in teenagers in the inner city. He is a God who believes in middle-aged teachers from Bolivia. He is a God who believes in young people like Ben Carson and Walter Anderson. He is a God who believes in me and in *you!*

QUESTION THREE

3. If the true image of a God who believes in you is programmed into your computer, what will that do for your self-image?

Now then, when Jesus is our mental image of God what happens to our own self-image? What will be the result? Healthy, humble, wholesome pride! Self-respect! Self-esteem! Sincere sacrificial service inspired by Christ will really make us feel great!

1. Yes, healthy honor—godly pride—is possible, IF we have engraved in our minds the true image of the true God,

not as a Grim Reaper, Wily Politician, or Grand Patriarch, but as the kind of person who was portrayed in the life and spirit of Jesus Christ, who said, "He that has seen Me has seen the Father."

2. Now, *I shall find real honor and glory when my life reflects this Christian image of God.* When this image of God is engraved in my life, even the wrinkles in my face will be affected.

"I don't like the looks of him." So Abe Lincoln said of one person considered for an appointment.

"But Mr. President, a man can't help what he looks like!"

"Oh yes, he can," the president answered.

Of course. I often meet older persons who have lived a long life of quiet and beautiful association with Christ. And they almost begin to look like Him. "Oh, but I've got wrinkles," the lovely old saint said to me.

"But they're twinkle wrinkles," I replied.

Our faces are sculptured, shaped—and silently but surely engraved by the thoughts we think and the feelings we harbor.

You can be proud of how you look when your face reflects the strength, the spirit, and the sweetness of Jesus.

The widespread, haunting, relentless fear of growing old drives people to a variety of market products. Why does our modern American culture glorify youth and disgrace age? Are we afraid we'll lose our beauty? Can we learn from the wisdom of perceptive artists who see the deep lines carved on the face of the well-traveled life as marks of honor?

Growing old gracefully in Christ assures us of true dignity all our lives.

Yes, a powerful and glorious self-respect is possible IF:

• **Our mental image of the true God who believes in us is sketched in our minds.**

• **We believe and receive Jesus Christ.** When we welcome warmly and sincerely His Spirit to come and live within us, then the image of God will be engraved on our spirits shaping our personalities. And yes! Our faces will reflect lasting, really attractive beauty.

2

• **We take time to learn who God really is so we can reflect His image.** We can sculpt the image of God in the face of our community.

Live out this living, loving Godimage and you can (Yes! One person! *You* can!) change your little world! Your family, your corner in the workplace, your club can and will be changed because you, the glorious engraver, are there, engraving, shaping artfully and beautifully an image of God through the Spirit of Jesus emanating from your heart to your social circle.

Then God's image will begin to be sculpted in society. You'll be proud—but completely humble at the same time. What joy! *You will be proud of the kind of person you are, but humble in the knowledge that Christ's Spirit living and loving within you is the source of your goodness.*

When your pride is rooted in your relationship to Jesus Christ, your humility will be assured.

Years ago when people from across America wanted to join my church, I found it necessary not to exclude but to include them. What form of commitment should I ask from them? What, if any, dogma or doctrinal standard for membership should I require them to sign?

I prayed. I sought guidance from the Spirit of God. And I was, I believe, led by the Lord to ask all who would join the Crystal Cathedral to sign not a *promise* nor a subscription to a *theological creed*, but rather to come into our family with this *prayer:*

> I offer my life to You, Jesus Christ, for You to live in
> me and through me.
> Here is my face—shine from it.
> Here are my ears—hear the cry of hurting persons
> through them.
> Here are my eyes—see the faces of those who need
> Your blessing and bless them with the healing
> look that radiates from You, my Lord, through
> my eyes.
> Here is my tongue—speak through it!
> Speak words of encouragement! Affirmation!
> Here, O Lord, are my hands—use them to touch,

stroke, hold, lift, and steady another human being.

Here, O Lord, are my feet—walk where You want me to go. And may those who follow me be following Jesus Christ!

Yes! You will come through an amazing self-image transplant! Yes! Being born again is beautiful. This is the life!
- Glory? Really!
- Honor? The highest!
- Self-esteem? For sure! "Christ in you, the hope of glory" (Col. 1:27).

Yes, now we know why billions of persons see God in their minds. By visualizing Jesus Christ. Picture, imagine Jesus, living in you. And that changes everything! Your thinking switches from the negative to the positive.

Discover the most positive pathway to positive pride through a personal faith in Jesus Christ. He won't let you down. He is the One person you can place your trust in.

You can count on Jesus Christ because He is the God who believes in you!

CHAPTER 3

DIGNITY— AFFIRMED! PROTECTED! REDEEMED!

"THOU SHALT NOT TAKE THE NAME OF THE LORD THY GOD IN VAIN"

3

*L*et's take time to see where we have come from.

I

"Thou shalt have no other gods before Me."
This is step one to a strong self-esteem.

I'm going to believe in the God who believes in me. The first word is a command meant to put me in touch with the One God who believes in me. I can now affirm: God loves me!

II

"Thou shalt not make for yourself any graven image."
This is step two to a sustaining self-esteem.

The second word is a *command meant* to give me a new life for my new journey. I have received the image of Christ in my life! I am somebody! Now I can affirm, "I'm going to believe in me! For Christ lives within me!" If Christ lives in me, I cannot, must not, will not put myself down. My life has become the place where Jesus Christ has come to live. That makes me a beautiful human being!

III

"Thou shalt not take the name of the LORD thy God in vain, for the LORD will not hold him guiltless who takes His name in vain."
This is step three to a divine dignity emerging within me.

This third word is a *command meant* to focus my attention on building a solid sustaining relationship with this God who believes in me! This affirming relationship will deliver and defend divine self-esteem in my life.

3

Now here is what God is prepared to do for you!

• *Declare* your dignity!
"You crowned him with glory and honor"
(Heb. 2:7).

• *Restore* your dignity when you lose it!
"Neither do I condemn you; go and sin no
more" (John 8:11).

• *Defend* your dignity!
"[His angels] shall bear you up, lest you dash your [foot]
against a stone" (Luke 4:11).

• *Drape* your departing spirit in divine dignity when you bid farewell to this world!

"Surely goodness and mercy shall follow me all the days of
my life;
And I will dwell in the house of the LORD
forever" (Ps. 23:6).

So these ten commands are meant to set us up to generate
genuine real self-respect. They are the divine design for
human dignity. How desperately urgently, passionately we
all need this holy pride.

DIGNITY

No wonder
• We are quick to hear good news that promises respectful
recognition.
• Awards for services rendered are genuinely welcomed.
• Honors handed over to us by our peers are really prized.
Our dignity is declared and delivered.
Somebody believes in me!
My faith in myself is charged up again.

Dignity—Affirmed! Protected! Redeemed!

3

I must be O.K. after all! Proudly I hang the award on the wall. I feel great. My self-image is renewed, revitalized, regenerated.

New, exciting visions, dreams, hopes stir in my positively charged imagination.

I'm a reborn possibility thinker again.

I've got what it takes to succeed after all.

I can do and achieve and become more than I ever thought I could.

I look at the honors, the recognition, the awards, the compliments, and my spirit soars.

But wait a minute.

Honors, without abiding positive relationships, can too soon lose their energy to affirm, preserve, and perpetuate a healthy self-esteem.

He is a famous actor. His name is virtually a household word. I have had the opportunity of ministering to him for over twenty-five years. I've laughed, cried, and prayed with him in his Hollywood home. The walls of his den are covered with honors, laurels, awards, and trophies. Still he is one of the saddest persons I've known. He is insecure. "Am I losing it?" he asks.

I listen. I sit there and say nothing. He has more to say, and I must be quiet and listen. I know what his problem is. Not alcoholism—that's only the ugly outward manifestation of the real problem. His real problem is a pathetically weak ego and inadequate self-esteem. Why? With all the brass, porcelain, bronze, and marble accolades that hang heavy on the wall, why?

He's lonely—that's why! He has been an abysmal failure in power-producing, positive relationships. Somewhere along the line—I suspect at the outset of his career—he became a victim of recognition addiction. It seemed to satisfy his need for self-esteem, but all it did was deliver vanity, a cheap substitute for the real thing. His life has been a race after recognition, which ruined all of his relationships.

Now he's old, lonely, suicidal. I'm praying for him.

HONORS WITHOUT SELF-AFFIRMING RELATIONSHIPS WILL NEVER DELIVER LASTING HONOR.

3

What you and I and every person need to put and preserve positive pride in our lives are personal relationships that

- AFFIRM our dignity,

- PROTECT our dignity,

- RESTORE our dignity, and

- SUSTAIN our dignity.

Now here's the reason for this third commandment, "Thou shalt not take the name of the LORD your God in vain, for the LORD will not hold him guiltless who takes His name in vain."

Quite bluntly, if you don't take God seriously you will never build a solid, sustaining relationship with Him, and you'll be responsible for your own loss of dignity and pride.

The truth is that relationships that regularly record fresh mental impressions of your value as a person are the only reliable reservoir of energy to sustain your self-respect.

Surely no award or recognition can compensate for the safe, satisfying, and sustaining source of strength that positive relationships supply to a human being's thirsty soul! Loving relationships are unequaled for safe, satisfying, and sustaining ego strength.

This fact is laid out frankly—up front—by God Himself! Here in the third commandment.

God cannot be held responsible for your emotional shortfall if you have not accepted His offer to seriously build a solid relationship with Him, taking advantage of all that He is prepared to offer.

Neglect Him—you're free to do so if you choose—and you and your dignity are on your own.

"Thou shalt not take the name of the LORD your God in vain, for the LORD will not hold him guiltless who takes His name in vain." "Taking the name of the Lord in vain" means "taking God's name lightly"—in other words, ignoring Him.

Thus, this is a *command meant* to take God seriously. I really hear God saying: *Take me seriously! Believe me! Trust me! Love me! Let's become best friends!*

3

I'll go to any and all lengths to bless you with the most wonderful pride and healthy humility. I promise you that.

I'll stop at nothing to restore glory to you and to your name. I'll even go to a cross.

I can and will even erase, eliminate, all shame, sin, and guilt, those terrible enemies of human dignity and noble pride. If you are too busy or too distracted to love Me in a beautiful relationship, then I cannot possibly be responsible for your loss of dignity, self-respect, and self-worth. You are free to treat our relationship frivolously and flippantly, but I, the Lord, cannot then be responsible for your ego problems and ego needs.

This third word is a *command meant* to lay the wise foundation for a positive relationship with God and with His positive people.

Nothing can be more important to a healthy, self-respecting, honored life than joining a community in which people affirm each other.

How do you begin to establish a healthy relationship? What is the starting point?

Loving relationships are unequaled for safe, satisfying, and sustaining ego strength.

Surround yourself with positive people, and the interpersonal relationships will mutually affirm and reaffirm each person's dignity! This is precisely what we find in the congregation of a healthy church.

The church stands alone in society as an institution dedicated to helping people establish positive relationships. I know of no other institution on planet earth that, at its best, does as much to affirm a person's dignity, restore a person's lost dignity, and protect a person's dignity from the barrage of destructive, negative insults in this world. The church has often been faulted for having too many hypocrites. In fact, the church is the only institution that spends billions of dollars to try to talk bad people into joining the ranks of converted souls. The church is not a museum for saints; it is a hospital for hypocrites and sinners.

Take the time and cultivate the patience to choose positive, forceful words that will uplift yourself and others.

In the congregational membership of the Crystal Cathedral you'll find lawyers, judges, and policemen mixed with convicted felons. Stars from the world of entertainment and professional sports along with captains of industry mingle and mix with common laborers.

What a phenomenon! What a class-free social circle. What a prescription for putting pride back into every person's life. What a creative community!

Yes, this third word is a *command meant* to build strong supportive relationships, the backbone of healthy self-esteem. Yes, this third commandment sets the direction that, if followed, will lead to a powerful positive relationship.

Now then, *how do you begin to establish a healthy relationship? What is the starting point?*

Begin by showing respect for the one with whom you wish to build a positive relationship. To start with, find out his name; make sure you can pronounce it correctly; and call the person by name with respect.

"Hey you!" isn't the best way to get a new relationship started.

Now learn the language of his culture and respect—don't rebuff—it. If the person has a well-earned title, note it and

3

use it respectfully: "Sir," "Dr.," "Officer," "Professor." Yes, effective relationships start with a respected and respectful naming of the name.

Now you can see the urgency, the desperate importance of this third commandment.

• You cannot expect to have a healthy, ongoing self-respect without positive relationships. Yes, success or failure in the process of becoming a genuinely self-respecting person will depend on how successful you are in your relationships.

• You cannot expect to have positive relationships unless you learn how to communicate with respect to those whose love is essential to your emotional strength.

• You cannot succeed in building positive relationships without "building up the name of the person."

So—If you hope to build rewarding, reaffirming, redemptive relationships, what's the very first thing you must do? Yes! Find out the person's name.

In the musical *Carnival*, a peasant girl leaves her little village of Mira high in the Italian mountains to join the circus. At first there is nothing but fun, excitement, people, performers, exotic animals, crowds of people. Then homesickness sets in. She finds that the pleasure stimulates her but leaves her lonely, with no affirming relationships.

One night when she's hungry for her little hometown, she walks forlorn and pathetic behind the tents where everyone is sleeping and sings a tribute to her home folks: "Now what

WHAT'S IN A NAME?

For twenty-eight years an escaped convict eluded capture. Then in April of 1989 he turned himself in. He'd succeeded in his escape by using a false name. When asked why he surrendered, Sylvan Carter said, "I wanted to see my own name on my tombstone." A person's name is important.

Dignity—Affirmed! Protected! Redeemed!

I like about Mira is—everybody knows my name. Now what do you think of that? What do you think of that!?! *Everybody* knows my name!"

And from the way her young soul sings it, you can be sure they name her name with respect and affection.

Perhaps the most embarrassing experience I ever had in many hundreds of weddings happened when I stood before the bride and groom and couldn't name their names. Unbelievable? Right! I was called in at the last minute to perform the ceremony. In fact, I had to rush from the airport and had only enough time to slip into my robe and race down the hallway into the altar area where the organist was already playing the wedding processional.

> # You cannot expect to have a healthy, ongoing self-respect without positive relationships.

There they stood, with a full church behind them, waiting for me to officiate. I was too embarrassed to ask their names. I felt that would certainly insult them.

Somehow I managed (never, never again!) the entire ceremony, and I'm certain (yes, positive) they never noticed that I never named their names.

"Do *YOU*?" I smiled, long, genuinely, warmly, drawing out the *you* as I fixed my eyes affectionately, respectfully, reverently on the groom. I repeated this formula for recovery through the ceremony. It was beautiful, but it haunts me to this day.

God. Jesus Christ. Speak His name softly. Let it flow reverently from your tongue. Send the holy words from your lips and life with profound reverence.

Honor the name of God, and you bring honor to yourself. A universal principle is at work here. It's called the law of proportionate return:

• "Cast your bread on the waters, and it shall return."

3

- The person who compliments good persons sincerely, compliments himself.
- "Whatever a person sows, that will he also reap."
- The person who pays his respects will be respected.
- "With what measure you give, it shall be given back to you."
- Communication is a boomerang.

By the time your life and your lips have honored the name of God, you will instantly sense His respect flowing toward you! That's the beginning of a powerful relationship.

This is the beginning of a new life for you. It is the introduction of a relationship that can change your life. You are no longer alone. You belong to Someone, Someone very special. This will be the most important relationship in your life.

Now you may say, *What a claim! How can you say this will be* the most important *relationship in my life? Aren't you being presumptuous, Schuller? Why is this relationship so important, anyway?*

Well, this relationship with God is no ordinary relationship. It is nothing less than that of a holy family relationship.

God becomes your Father. You now are adopted as His son or His daughter. His name becomes your name! He now becomes head of your family!

Provider. Teacher. Protector. Healer. Defender. Encourager. Restorer. Deliverer. Redeemer. Affirmer.

You have established a relationship with "The God Who Believes In You" that will prove to be a solid foundation for a safe, satisfying, and unfailing self-esteem. You are now a member of the human family of highest honor. You are the proud bearer of that name you spoke with such sincere reverence. Yes, you are a Christian. What an honor! Bear that title with divine distinction. Remember whose you are! Enjoy the pride of belonging! Relish the glory of membership in this elite community called the kingdom of God. Be conscious of yourself. Affirm it aloud!

- "I am a child of God!"
- "The God that Jesus called 'My Father' is *my* Father, too!"

Dignity—Affirmed! Protected! Redeemed!

3

• "I belong to a family, the family of the God who believes in His children!"

O.K., you say, I can buy that, but how can I be sure that this or any relationship is positive, not negative?

A very important question! For a positive relationship will build mutual self-esteem and self-worth while negative relationships tear down self-confidence, self-respect, and healthy pride. Be sure of this, God always builds people up; He never runs people down.

The power of a positive relationship lies in the encouragement it brings to a soul searching for self-respect: "You are somebody special!"

Every wise wife knows she must constantly be her husband's number one ego booster: "You're great, honey!" Every man needs that. (Remember, men, what's good for the husband is good for the wife, too.) Every marriage is strengthened by such positive affirmations.

> **Honor the name of God, and you bring honor to yourself.**

LET'S TEST THE HEALTH OF YOUR RELATIONSHIP WITH GOD.

Every relationship needs to be evaluated and reevaluated since we constantly grow and change. Here's a test to take from time to time to see if your relationship with God is working. Ask yourself these soul-searching questions. You'll observe that these questions will test the vitality of any relationship—human or divine.

1. *What am I doing with what He has given me? Freedom! Trust! Opportunities! Challenges!*

A priest was walking a dark and strange street when he saw a pitiful human being lying in the gutter. Suddenly his faith in God was shaken to the core, and in a dark moment of the soul he cried out, "Oh God, do you exist? Are you there? Do you care? And if so, why don't you do something about that pathetic soul?"

Into his mind came a message. Strong! Immediate! Authoritative! "I am. I see. I care. I am doing something about it. I just called him to your attention!"

2. Am I blaming Him for something that is not His fault?

The dam burst, and many lives were lost. Who engineered the dam? Who built the homes in the floodplain? Don't blame God!

The annual report is out: cancer and heart disease are leading killers. Who is responsible for the synthetic chemicals in the food supply? Who manufactured the tobacco, alcohol, and dangerous narcotics? Who established the tension-generated lifestyles?

Meanwhile . . .

3. Have I given Him adequate credit for all He has done and is doing?

Or have I projected a negative perspective onto a natural reality?

Illustration: Death.

God is responsible, you say. *How can I believe in a living God in a dying world?*

But God never designed us for death—He created us for life!

If we truly follow His path, we shall grow old with grace, charm, and dignity, then quietly and gently approach our new birth into eternity like "one who wraps the drapery of his couch about him and lies down to pleasant dreams."

Do we neglect to add up the gifts of grace God has given?

> **The fact that God silently allows the human race to take the credit for advancements doesn't mean He hasn't been ultimately responsible for them!**

Dignity—Affirmed! Protected! Redeemed!

3

Like education, medicine, technological advancements, institutions of mercy and compassion. Add it up! Do not take His name or His work in vain! The fact that God silently allows the human race to take the credit for advancements doesn't mean He hasn't been ultimately responsible for them!

4. *Have I been seeking His advice, and searching out His counsel?* Do I credit Him with "knowing something I don't know?" Do I really *want* His guidance? And if He makes it available in Scripture or science, will I listen? And follow?

5. *Do I feel gratitude? Do I take the time to tell Him, "Thank you"?* Do I recognize the treasures of life as gifts He has given freely to all persons? Do I have a grateful heart that God did not exclude me when He gave out the gifts— sunrise, sunset, birds, flowers, trees, parks, children being born?

6. *Have I taken His promises seriously? His invitations? His affirmations?* If I take the invitations lightly and fail to be proud to be on God's guest list, will I miss out on basking in the glory of His banquet of blessings?

7. *Do I trust Him to manage my life?*

> **Yes, God takes care of those who respect Him.**
> **"For He shall give His angels charge over you,**
> **To keep you in all your ways.**
> **. . . Lest you dash your foot against a stone"**
> **(Ps. 91:11–12).**

"I know [my sheep]. . . . and no one is able to snatch them out of My Father's hand" (John 10:27, 29).

Be sure of this, this powerful positive relationship represents God's total investment in your spiritual well-being.

Yes, this relationship with the Lord is the greatest gift you'll ever enjoy in your entire life! Know that! Value that!

Respect that! Treasure that! And *this relationship, more than anything else, will insure the stability of your self-esteem.*

Continue to honor this relationship, and you will continue to harvest the blessings of honoring—taking seriously—the name of your Father who wants to affirm, protect, and, if necessary, restore your dignity.

8. *Am I receiving, accepting, using, and enjoying the gifts God offers me?* God gives His children positive, priceless gifts to be used to affirm and strengthen a relationship that will affirm our human dignity. Gifts, both giving and receiving, reveal much about the health of any relationship. In negative relationships, gifts may tend to manipulate, control, or even insult a person. In positive relationships, gifts are measured and valued in proportion to their relationship enrichment value.

So we fulfill this third commandment when we in turn honor God by accepting His gifts. We insult a relationship if we casually ignore a carefully chosen gift.

"How did you like the birthday present I gave you?"

"Oh, I forgot to unwrap it." We know immediately that we have insulted the benefactor, and almost instinctively we add, "I'm sorry." And we further demean the gift—crudely, rudely—if we misuse it.

"What! You wore that good shirt working in the garden?" Now we are embarrassed.

> **God gives His children priceless gifts to be used to affirm and strengthen our human dignity.**

Accept God's gifts, and you honor Him. Honor God, and honor will flow back to you. When you accept a gift, you honor the name of the donor: "Look what God gave me!"

LANGUAGE IS GOD'S GIFT TO ENRICH OUR RELATIONSHIP

High on the list of God's rich and rare gifts to the human family is the gift of language. Positive words are symbols to

3

stimulate your self-esteem. Certainly the incredible power of language is a divine gift designed to deliver dignity. Rightly used, healthy language communicates respect, commands respect, and builds satisfying relationships that strengthen mutual self-esteem.

WORDS: SYMBOLS TO STIMULATE YOUR SELF-ESTEEM

Recently my wife and I were invited out to breakfast in a beautiful, elegant dining room. We were impressed with the restaurant, when we noticed a very distinguished gentleman who came and sat in the booth next to us. He was elegantly dressed. His choice of clothes, shirt, tie, hairstyle made him stand out as an impeccable gentleman. He was barely seated when he uttered a sentence that included about five words that I would never repeat. His language was crude and unnecessarily profane. The words that came out of his mouth contradicted his style of dress and manner.

*T*his third commandment has traditionally been interpreted to warn against the use of profanity. What does profanity really mean? To "profane" means to take something that was meant for good and turn it into an evil. The gift of language was to be used to communicate respect to the rest of the members of the human family to the end and for the purpose of creating mutually affirming and enriching relationships.

When language is used to insult, ridicule, embarrass, demean, belittle, or dishonor another member of the family, we put real stress on our precious relationships. In the end, God's name as head of the family and the name of every other member of the human family are disgraced. Precious relationships are not enriched, rather they are deprived of dignity and left impoverished.

3

Suddenly our image of the gentleman was no longer that of a gentleman. The crude style of his language was a crass contradiction of his style of dress. When he first made an entrance into the dining room, he attracted attention because of a nobility in his bearing, an elegance in his manner. Then he wiped out all of his gain in one sweeping, careless, crude sentence.

BECOME A CREATIVE COMMUNICATOR

Question: Does this mean we can never verbalize frustration? Or articulate objection to an injustice? Or vocally confront an evil or an error?

Answer: It is possible to communicate the harsh realities and still bring pride to the human race. But it takes work. We have to build up our vocabulary. You just can't keep repeating the same old trite, dirty, four-letter words that no longer even have any shock value and become a creative communicator. Become a craftsman of words.

Become a positive, creative communicator? How? Choose words as carefully as an interior decorator selects accessories; knowing one simple, inappropriate selection can wreck honor to the entire overall effect.

Protect your dignity and everyone else's in the process. Take the time and cultivate the patience to choose positive, forceful words that will uplift yourself and others within earshot. In the process you will honor God—and yourself. You will be proud when you

> **This third word is a *command meant* to lay the wise foundation for a positive relationship with God and with His positive people.**

3

sense how beautifully you are using His precious gift, the gift of language, especially when you see how it builds up your positive and powerful relationship with God and the rest of the human family.

There was a bus driver in Chicago who had a female passenger who expressed her irritation in a string of unrepeatable words. Everybody was ashamed. When the bus stopped and the profane passenger got ready to disembark, the bus driver said, "Madame, you left something behind."

She snapped, "Yeah? What did I leave behind?"

"A very bad impression," he replied.

WORDS: THEY WILL MAKE OR BREAK A RELATIONSHIP

At this point in our thinking, it is terribly important to understand the place and power of words, especially for building respectful and respect-generating relationships. Words are gifts of God. Wrongly used, they embarrass and dishonor us, the family of God, and the name of God. A chill sets in quickly.

Words rightly used protect, affirm, or restore human dignity. A wonderful warmth moves in beautifully.

So this all adds up to bringing honor to the name of the God who created the human species to be His friends and friends with each other.

Yes, high on God's gift list is the gift of language. The human being is the only creature that has languages that can be reduced to words. Remarkable! Astonishing! Why did God do it? Plan it? Engineer it? Why didn't He settle for the verbal cry of the animal or the song of the

> **The human being is the only creature that has languages that can be reduced to words.**

3

bird? Why of all living creatures does the human being have the honor of a gift of communication that takes the form of *words*, even *written words*?

Because God, the Creator, designed the human being in "His image," bearing His honored name. We are designed to become co-creators with God. Words hold powers of creativity.

God created the world. What tool did He use? He used creative energy: a word. He said, "Let there be light." And there was light. "Let the dry land separate from the waters." Whether you interpret these words literally or allegorically, the truth is: *Creative words generate energy; negative words drain out energy.*

Words are not just letters strung together. Words are the incarnation of emotions and the stimulators of emotion. A word can be a balm or a bomb. A positive word makes you feel good. A negative word leaves you feeling depressed and defeated. Words release energy. A single word can turn you on, or it can turn you off. A negative word can defuse your enthusiasm for a project. A positive word releases positive energy and becomes a creative force.

> # We are designed to become co-creators with God.

Have you ever been in a committee meeting when somebody offered a creative idea? Everyone is excited, and energy flows until someone arrogantly declares, "Look! what you are proposing is utterly impossible." Those *words* deplete enthusiasm, and when enthusiasm wanes, the energy drains out, and the creative force is dissipated.

I shall never forget visiting a friend whose husband had died. I said to her, "I'm so sorry that you lost your husband." Boy, did she straighten me out! She said, "Dr. Schuller, don't you ever use that word *lost*! That is a negative word." When you hear the word *lost*, the subconscious recalls a collection of negative memories:

- "I lost a coin."

3

- "I lost a job."
- "I lost this; I lost that."
- "Dr. Schuller, I have not *lost* my husband. I have agreed to let God take him home. He is not lost, for I know where he is!"

WORDS ARE SOMETHING SPECIAL

What kinds of words do you use? Do they create energy for positive relationships? Or are they a drain, a pain, a strain? Are they positive? Affirming? Do they build people up and, in the process, bring honor and glory to the name of God?

A member of my church teaches kindergarten. She believes in the importance of self-esteem and works diligently at teaching her students not only the alphabet and rudiments of beginning math, but also self-esteem. She tries to implant within all of her students the feeling that they are important and that they have value.

> **Creative words generate energy; negative words drain out energy.**

One day, one of her students dissolved into tears. She sat in the corner weeping. Mrs. Smith went to the little girl and sat down on the floor next to her and drew her into her arms. "Annie," she said, "what's the matter?"

"My mommy didn't hug me good-bye."

"Oh!" said the teacher. "It's hard to say good-bye without a hug."

"And Mommy is mad at me!"

"Oh! And we feel sad when we think someone is mad. Do you feel that your mommy doesn't love you right now?"

"Yes."

Little Annie cried unconsolably. The teacher wiped her tears and looked deep into her eyes. "I'm sorry you feel that

3

way. Maybe you can talk to Mommy about it this afternoon. I'm sure she would like a chance to tell you how much she loves you. Right now, I want you to know that I think you are a very special little girl. Did you know that you are special?"

"No, I didn't know that."

"Well, you can believe me. *You are very special.*" (Four very powerful words!)

Annie stopped crying. She looked into the teacher's eyes carefully, scanning them to see if she was telling the truth or not. Suddenly she got up, returned to her desk, and carried on with her work.

The next day Annie's mother talked privately with Mrs. Smith. "I just wanted to thank you for talking to Annie. She told me about your conversation. She said that you told her she was special. It really meant a lot to her."

Whoever you are—mother, father, student, teacher, employer—you have access to the power of positive words today:

• **Think of all the positive affirmations you can give yourself today.**

• **Think of all the positive affirmations you can give your spouse today.**

• **Think of all the positive affirmations you can give your coworkers today.**

• **Think of all the positive affirmations you can give your children today.**

And guess what you will have done? *You'll have affirmed God's name.* You will have vastly enriched someone's life. In the process you'll have enriched your own spirit! In the process, positive, rewarding relationships will have been enhanced. Yes, God's name—your name—is ennobled and honored. This, in short, is called *creative living!*

The remarkable fact is that dignity affirmed works like a boomerang. When you affirm someone else, you feel affirmed yourself. Suddenly you feel that you have done

3

A word can be a balm or a bomb.

something wonderful. And indeed you have. You have helped restore someone's respect, and that is a priceless gift. You will receive your reward immediately: Self-respect!

Yes, embrace the gift of language, for words are meant to be tools to *create*—what? Positive relationships that meet everyone's honest need for respect.

So the use of language, our choice of words, is *crucial* in the whole self-esteem process. "Sticks and stones may break my bones, but words can never harm me!" Wrong! Wrong! Wrong! Words can devastate a person, can lead to rejection, alienation, loneliness, bitterness, brokenness! Need I go on with the litany of human misery caused by the profanity of language? Words can be emotional bombs, swords, bullets. Or when used reverently, and sensitively, they can encourage, comfort, inspire, redeem, and yes—*create!*

Yes, create self-affirming relationships. You can't live without them. Not the least of creations is a society in which kindness, gentleness, courtesy, civility, and *respect* rule.

Yes, words have immense power to affect the way we feel about ourselves. *It may well be that the epidemic of low self-esteem in our society has been brought on or aggravated by the epidemic of profanity.* The horrific infection of demeaning words has proliferated in our society like a plague. We will—we are—paying the price in a spreading epidemic of a declining and depressing level of societal self-esteem. The widespread use of the censored four-letter words in homes, school yards, (yes even classrooms) and movies is having its telling, chilling effect in a cheaper, trashier, collectivized self-esteem—be sure of that!

What this commandment urges us to do is to discover the language and vocabulary that will elevate your sense of self-esteem, self-worth, and self-dignity and increase that beautiful civilized spirit of social respect. It is amazing what language can do to the collective self-esteem of a whole society. When the language in a culture is positive, it can raise the level of self-dignity. When it's negative, it can demean an entire community.

On the positive side—words can build a beautiful civilized, cultured, healthy society.

This was the Divine intent of language. So powerful and pivotal is language in the whole process of creating self-esteem in society that our attention is called to this, in the third command meant to help climb upward to respectability!

Oddly, tragically, devout believers in this commandment miss the point if they condemn such words as *darn*, *gosh*, as profanity. Real profanity is the use of language that strips people of their dignity, embarrasses them, and humiliates instead of affirms them; generating emotional blockage in the creative process.

"Stupid" * "Dumb" * "Idiot" * "Airhead" * "Dirt Ball" These are the modern words that abuse the holy gift of language by using something that was meant to create self-respect and turn it into a weapon that destroys human dignity.

Now you can see why Jesus never humiliated, embarrassed, or insulted a person by calling him or her a "sinner." Important: It is true that Jesus referred to a *group* of persons (plural) as "sinners"—but he never attacked a single, solitary, individual person (singular) as a sinner. This distinction is all-important! It's one thing for a teacher to throw out a blanket criticism to an entire class, but it's something else to single out one lonely student and force him to stand alone, unsupported in front of the class, to be embarrassed, humiliated, ridiculed.

That word *sinner* is, to put it bluntly, not a creative word. It does not create an environment where a positive, redemptive

> # When the language in a culture is positive, it can raise the level of self-dignity.

3

You change a person by using positive words that release positive mental pictures of what he can become!

relationship is likely to evolve. Rather, it communicates an insult!

You don't change a person by correctly calling him what, in fact, he may be: not if the truth embarrasses him. You will only reinforce his negative self-image, which will tend to express itself in negative behavior. Or the honest, insulting truth may anger him, and he will turn from your advice and be forced into a defensive posture.

You change a person by using positive words that release positive mental pictures of what he can become! This is using the power of language to be creative—or redemptive! So Jesus—Who was always in the business of affirming, protecting, redeeming, or restoring human dignity looked at imperfect (sinful) persons and said to them. "You are the light of the world! You are the salt of the earth!"

Now we see *how* the gift of language is the tool to create positive relationships! The creative use of words sustains the positive creative relationships between ourselves and other persons. As a result, *God becomes believable as we become loveable.* The healthy relationships stimulated and sustained through the appropriate gifts of creative language will go on to feed our mutual self-respect.

But there's more! Here's what makes this reverent and respectful relationship with the "God-Who-Believes-In-You" so vital to your emotional health: This relationship with God not only affirms your dignity, but restores your dignity when it suffers devastating blows.

3

POSITIVE RELATIONSHIPS RESTORE DIGNITY TO EMBARRASSED, HUMILIATED PERSONS.

God specializes in restoring lost pride. Society insults people. God honors people. Take your embarrassments to Him. He can restore your self-worth once more.

I'll never forget the day when Jim Coleman came to work for *The Hour of Power* as a full-time graphic arts designer. On his first day on the job, I received a call from his former employer, "Dr. Schuller, did you realize that the artist you just hired is an atheist?"

I replied simply, "I can't think of any better place for an atheist to work than in a church, can you?"

We all loved Jim's gentle spirit. But we were concerned by the despair deep in his eyes. Jim never bothered to hide the life he led. So we prayed that he would come to a personal relationship with Jesus. Months passed, years. One day we discovered Jim reading a Bible in his office. He told us that as he returned bleary-eyed from a weekend in Las Vegas, he had given his life to Jesus on the back of a bus.

The transformation was incredible. A spark that hadn't been there before glowed in his eyes. He became a faithful leader in the youth department and was outspoken about his newfound faith. All of his roommates realized that something was different about Jim when he put down his bottle of beer and suggested, to their shock and amazement, that they pray before they ate their dinner.

After a few years Jim started dating my oldest daughter, Sheila. They fell in love and married. Today they have four active boys. The plain and simple truth is that Jesus transformed this dear man's life. Jesus snatched him from the dark despair of pain and low self-regard and redeemed his dignity. He gave Jim a whole new life.

Today my son-in-law, Jim Coleman, says that nothing hurts him more than when he hears people use Christ's name as a swear word. Of all the profanity he has heard in his lifetime, this hurts the most. Why? Because he loves Jesus Christ. He knows how beautiful the name of Jesus is.

"Thou shalt not take the name of the Lord your God in vain, for the Lord will not hold him guiltless who takes His name in vain." Now look where this positive powerful command leads us. It leads us to our Lord's name. And His name is Jesus Christ.

RESPECT THE NAME
THAT SAVES FROM
GUILT AND SHAME.

Christ *protects* our dignity.
Christ *affirms* our dignity.
Christ *restores* our dignity.

Christ honored the name of God by restoring lost honor to lost souls.

Who is this Christ, whose name is used so glibly? He is the One who can forgive all sins,
wipe out all guilt,
heal the deep hurts!

He is the One who can redeem our dignity, restore our self-respect, rescue a lost self-esteem. Read the New Testament and see how sensitively Jesus deals with people and their shame.

JESUS: TAKE HIS NAME NOT IN VAIN,
AND YOU WILL BE HELD GUILTLESS!

Once, while gathering with His closest followers, a woman approached Jesus, loosened her hair to let it fall long, then took a perfume bottle, and poured the costly contents on His feet. Only a prostitute would let her hair flow loose and free in public. This then was her public confession and act of repentance. Judas, the treasurer of Christ's little band, a person who would become forever infamous as a traitor, publicly rebuked the woman for her awful waste of money. "You should have sold the perfume and given it to the poor rather than waste it by pouring it over Jesus' feet." How embarrassing to be rebuked in public, especially when you have done something that in your mind was good, kind, and generous! Enter Jesus, the Savior! Whereas Judas made her feel guilty, Christ moved in quickly to wipe out any guilt.

The response of Jesus was beautiful. Although Jesus was always concerned for the poor, he responded, "Not so, Judas! This woman has done this as an act of love for me. I will not be here long. But the poor will always be here."

Jesus swiftly moved in to redeem the woman's lost pride. He affirmed her good gesture in an attempt to salvage her shattered self-esteem. He gave her a gift more precious than the gift she had bestowed on Him. Her crown of glory as a person was restored by the positive accolade from the man who stood out and above everyone else—her Lord. *He held her guiltless.* Jesus erased the insult. He polished her pride. He replaced her shame

> **Christ honored the name of God by restoring lost honor to lost souls.**

with glory, her humiliation with honor. She, in this miraculous moment, was born again. Her dignity was affirmed, protected, restored. Such treatment of human beings really honors the name of the Father who created all human beings.

This *command* is *meant* to challenge us to do likewise.

Yes, we profane God's name when we miss the opportunities to build pride in the human family that carries the name of God's children. So we honor God's name when we protect someone's dignity, affirm someone's dignity, restore someone's lost dignity. We honor the name of God when we honor His children, whatever they may do.

3

RESPECT THE NAME THAT TAKES GUILT OUT OF FAILURE

Human dignity—it is hard to hold your head high when you've suffered an embarrassing failure. No wonder people are afraid to set high goals. Enter Jesus Christ!

Consider how Jesus dealt with the professional fishermen who were His closest followers, His disciples. One morning as the dawn rose over the hills, Jesus appeared on the shore and recognized His closest friends in a boat not far from land. A brief interchange followed. "We did poorly. We toiled all night and caught nothing." (Failure often carries guilt in its bag: "We must have done something wrong.")

How did Jesus reply? With jibes or cheap remarks? Such a response would have been, to say the least, inappropriate for men who had worked hard, tried their best, and now were fatigued with nothing in their hands to show for their efforts.

"We have toiled all night and caught nothing." The hurt of coming home empty-handed is painful. Jesus never takes delight in seeing people flunk out, fall on their faces, or eat the bitter dust of failure and lose their self-esteem. Jesus calls out with this inextinguishable note of hope, "Throw out your net on the other side." *In other words, when you think you've exhausted all possibilities, remember this: You haven't.*

The amazing part of this story is that the fishermen didn't retort cynically, "Forget it! We fished this whole area for hours." Rather, they obliged without argument, casting their net on the other side of the boat only to have it immediately catch hold of a school that was so thick and heavy they could hardly haul in the catch.

JESUS: THE TRULY GUILTY CAN BE HELD GUILTLESS UNDER THE BANNER OF HIS NAME

So this is how this third commandment shapes up. "Thou shalt take (receive) the name of the Lord respectfully, and the Lord will hold guiltless all who receive His name reverently."

The truly guilty can be held guiltless under the banner of the name of Jesus.

3

In Jesus' time, some of the most despised persons in the Jewish society were those Jews who had sold out to the Romans. One such person was the tax collector. This Jewish person solicited burdensome and unjust taxes from his own people and turned the exploited money, the extorted funds, over to the Roman governor.

Zacchaeus was such a tax collector. When Jesus was passing through the city of Jericho, rumor preceded Him that He would be passing through town. By this time Jesus had gained a reputation. Crowds of people gathered wherever He went. Zacchaeus, short of stature, and moreover despised, preferred to distance himself from the unfriendly crowd by climbing into the branch of a tree. There, in the safety of his own space, protected from the unfriendly crowd, he commanded a good view of Jesus.

As Jesus approached, He suddenly looked up and saw this unpopular character sitting in the tree above Him. Christ was always seeking to lift people from shame to glory. He declared for all to hear, "Zacchaeus, come down! For I'm going to your house today!"

The Bible does not say who was more surprised and shocked, Zacchaeus or the people. After all, to visit someone's home was to pay that person a high honor. It was one thing to meet a celebrity in public. It was another to be singled out of the crowd and be embraced as a friend.

When you think you've exhausted all possibilities, remember this: You haven't.

I've often pictured Zacchaeus running home, shouting to his wife, "We're having company! Jesus is coming to *our* house!"

How beautiful. Jesus must still remain head and shoulders above all human beings as a healer of the mind and the heart. How profoundly He understood every person's need for restored pride, healthy glory, healing honor, redeeming self-respect!

Dignity—Affirmed! Protected! Redeemed!

3

This is where the third word leads us, to the possibility of living guiltless, guilt-free lives! "Thou shalt take the name of the Lord your God reverently, for the Lord will hold guiltless all who take His name seriously and sincerely."

JESUS: GLORY SEEKERS MAY BE HELD GUILTLESS, TOO, BY THE AUTHORITY OF HIS NAME

Jesus was not about to condemn glory seeking itself when two of His finest friends were caught in a debate over who would be seated closest to Him in heaven. Jesus understood so well and sympathetically the root cause of our need for glory. He would not condemn it; He would fulfill it. Hostesses have faced the same glory-seeking problem through the centuries. Who shall be seated at the head table? Who will be seated at the right hand of the honored guest of the night? Who should sit at the captain's table? In this understandable human dilemma, Jesus moved in and offered them the key to real glory. "He that is least shall be the greatest," was His consistent teaching. The path of humility is the path to glory.

Understand the social setting.

It was a time for a religious ceremonial feast. In keeping with the custom, the feet were to be washed. A bowl of water and a towel were passed. Then, before the shocked apostles, a scene unfolded that left them stunned. Jesus—the leader, the commander, the captain, the most honored one in the group—took the bowl and began to wash the feet of His disciples. The point was instantly clear. If you want to have glory, be prepared to do the common tasks of life.

Self-effacing and sacrificial service is the safe and satisfying source of sincere self-esteem. To this day, I remember that scene and am inclined to salute the janitor, compliment the caretaker, applaud the maid, and give honorable recognition to the simple person who works calmly, quietly, conscientiously at a task that lacks social status.

It is interesting how different societies have created their

3

levels of social status in public service. Historically, the warrior ranked high. In nations and tribal groups whose survival depended upon the bite of the sword, the warrior was honored because he protected the colony and community. Along with the warrior there was the priest, the mystic person who called upon powers unknown and unseen, weaving magic or marvelous spells to connect with divine forces for help and healing. The priest was held in high honor. Towering above all were the rulers: kings, governors, tribal chiefs, elected officials. Below royalty but on a high level were the property owners, the plutocrats, who controlled

The path of humility is the path to glory.

food output. Then there were the artists who through tedious years of painful discipline cultivated and finely honed their crafts, creating jewelry, utensils, ornamentations, and implements of service or safety.

Finally there were the peasants, the pawns on the chessboard of society. They could boast no clever craft, could display no unique talents or skills, were never favored to be in places of honor, or fortunate to be property owners, priests, or warriors. They were just simple folk. They worked the land. They did the menial tasks. They were viewed as cheap and expendable.

ENTER JESUS CHRIST

He was attracted to these, the unheralded, dishonored, socially and emotionally disenfranchised persons.

Criminals? In some cases, yes.

Disreputable prostitutes? Yes, indeed.

Farmers and fishermen? Most assuredly.

Why was Jesus attracted to them? Why did He not seek out the prestigious, the powerful, the nobility of His day as

3

His friends and confidants and first followers? I submit He *first sought out those who needed Him most, the persons who had no awareness whatever of their intrinsic value. The holy light of human dignity was virtually extinguished in* their darkened souls. Hardly a spark of self-respect remained within them.

Dignity restored! That's real redemption.

The Savior came to them because the Father God in Heaven had sent Him to the world to tell every human being that he or she was glorious, beautiful, wonderful, and could be saved from guilt to glory, from haughty shame to humble pride.

Yes, Christ's life is the ultimate fulfillment of this third commandment. He affirmed the dignity of God's children and restored dignity to the members of God's human family when they disgraced themselves and the name of God by sinful behavior. Relationship established! Dignity restored! That's real redemption.

Is any embarrassment more shameful or devastating than to be caught publicly in an act of sexual immorality? There would be embarrassment enough in suddenly having uninvited intruders breaking into your private place when you are in an act of love with your legitimate mate. But shameful to the point of devastation of every shred of self-respect would be the horrific emotional tragedy if you were caught in an act of sexual immorality, exposed to the uninvited eyes of those whose respect for you was all-important.

It was exactly such a scene that Jesus came upon one day. He saw a trembling woman covering her nakedness with a piece of cloth that she had grabbed quickly. Hovering around her, preparing to stone her to death, were the religious leaders. "This woman was caught in an act of adultery! The law says that this sin deserves to be punished with death—by stoning!"

So the haughty, arrogant leaders explained and defended their position to this interloper named Jesus. Without saying a word, this quiet man stepped in between the woman and those who were about to kill her. Kneeling, He wrote in the sand then spoke what would remain one of the classic sentences in recorded literature, "Let him who is without sin cast the first stone."

Then, staring at the men who were so quick to condemn, He passed silent judgment on their own faulty and imperfect lives. They could not pass the test. They simply dropped their stones and drifted away. Then turning to the sorrowfully shamed creature, He gave her the greatest gift a person can give another person: nonjudgmental love. "Where are your accusers? Neither do I condemn you. Go, and sin no more."

> **To be forgiven is to look into the face of redeeming respect until its glory falls upon you and you are saved from shame to healthy pride once more.**

To be forgiven is to look into the face of redeeming respect until its glory falls upon you and you are saved from shame to healthy pride once more.

I doubt if there is any embarrassment or shameful experience that you have encountered that has not been dealt with by the Lord of my life—Jesus Christ.

You've had your love, your gift, rejected and spurned? They sent the gift back without opening it? Does this remind you of Judas' reaction to the woman whose perfume was poured over the feet of Jesus. You've been embarrassed by public failure? You were supposed to be great, and now you have turned in a performance that is amateurish to say the least. Does this not remind you of the fishermen who toiled all night and caught nothing?

The press has reported on your improper behavior?

Dignity—Affirmed! Protected! Redeemed!

3

Whatever your shame is, let Jesus redeem your dignity for you.

Perhaps correctly, perhaps incorrectly. So you have been caught and revealed to be a sinful person. Could it be worse than the woman caught in adultery?

Whatever your shame is, let Jesus redeem your dignity for you. Let Him restore your self-respect. He's the God who believes in you. You'll start to believe in yourself too. And when you do, you will recover your lost glory, and God's name will be honored as your Savior. That's bringing respect to the name of God and—yes—you'll respect yourself in the process. To honor God is to honor myself. For we all belong to the same family name.

So that's what living out this third command is meant to do: put us in the center of a powerful, positive, redeeming relationship.

"Lord, I respect You! Lord, I honor Your name!" Say it gently. Whisper it sincerely.

Listen! You will hear a still, small voice within you whisper back, "Likewise, My child!"

CHAPTER 4

RETREAT, REGROUP— AND REGAIN YOUR PEACE OF MIND!

"REMEMBER THE SABBATH DAY TO KEEP IT HOLY"

4

*T*he place?
Alton, Iowa. A farmhouse in the country.
The year?
1933.
The day?
A Sunday morning in spring.

A seven-year-old boy named Robert Schuller wakes up. The sun rises to a clear day. No mist or haze dims the bright rays of morning light. The dawning is so sharp and crisp it makes his eyes blink and the grass seem yellow in the golden sunlight.

Birds sing.

Crickets that have been partying all night are still making music.

He can hear the corn growing? Of course not!

But he can smell the mixture of natural fragrances that rise from budding leaves and blooming flowers.

What is strange about the morning anyway? Oh, it is the quietness. Something is missing. Of course! No grinding sounds of heavy machinery slicing through fields and grinding huge chunks of overturned earth. Seems like all the machines are asleep, or they died last night. That's why he can hear the birds singing! Plus the gentle rustle of wind in the trees. He can even hear the leaves laugh in the gentle wind.

From miles and miles away drifts the distant sound of a single muffled car on a lonely country road.

Somebody is going to church early.

Now it is quiet again. Then he hears it.

The sound of a bell.

A church bell.

From the country church three miles away.

It's Sunday.

These are the sounds and the silences of Sunday.

4

"Time to get dressed, Robert." And it's my chance to get all dressed up with a shirt and tie and a Sunday suit and my single pair of black, shiny shoes. They are shiny all right. Mom polishes them every Saturday afternoon.

Ours was the only car on the road. Others were already arriving at the little white church. Every farmer wore a shirt and tie and a suit, for we were going into the presence of God in His house. Reverence for Him dictated that we should make ourselves presentable. Not that He saw us differently from when we were dressed in denims. And not that He respected us more because our hands were washed and not covered with grease or dirt. But it was our way of doing something special that would make us feel more respectable as we prepared to pay our respects to the Lord as we came calling at His house on this, His day.

The farmers' voices were always made strong through years of calling commands to their horses from behind the plow. They could really sing lustily and loudly. Their whole families sang. The farmer with his wife and children filled the whole pew. Every pew included a man, a woman, and some children.

I never did see a pew filled with heads all the same height.

There were always low places in the horizon in every pew to mark the presence of short folks and little children.

"O God, our help in ages past, Our hope for years to come."

They sang peace into their souls. They sang power into their lives.

Pardon, peace, and power all came into the gathering minds of the people of God as they reverently worshiped their Lord in this house on the Lord's day.

This was Sunday.

This was the quiet day of the week. This was the still day. The slow-down-and-listen-to-God-speak-to-you day.

The place?
    Jerusalem.
The year?
    1961.
The time?
    Friday evening. Sundown. The Sabbath has begun.

Retreat! Regroup! And Regain—Your Peace Of Mind!

4

Lights in shops are turning off.
Locks click under turning keys.
"Have a blessed Sabbath."
"Shalom."
Merchants and clerks move their way through crowded
streets toward home, change their dress, and go off to the
house of the Lord. In an hour the darkness will creep in
quietly. The mechanical sounds of the street will be replaced
by foot traffic as the feet of the devout shuffle reverently to
the synagogues.

The Sabbath has begun. Prayers soon will be offered. And
quiet blessings are bestowed on the people of faith. Now
they will return to the stillness of the home: a gentle bed and
a soft pillow.

They fall asleep with warm blankets of holy thoughts
having just been drawn over the exposed surfaces of their
minds.

This is good. The blessings lightly spread on their spirits
only an hour or two ago are left alone to sink slowly into the
soul. Slowly, through the sleeping hours, the spirit of the
Lord can seep deeply into the lower levels of the human soul
as soft and gentle rains fall quietly through the night. The
raindrops soak slowly and deeply to reach thirsty mouths
and deep roots. There is no sun at midnight and no wind in
the calm before the dawning to dry up the raindrops before
they can penetrate to the lower levels. Like raindrops left
free to seep slowly to the levels where they can do their best
good, the blessed thoughts of the worship hour in the
synagogue are free to find their probing way to the hidden
hallways of the mind where powerful, silent, unseen forces
gather and wait for daylight. Now they will advance into the
awakened mind, bringing pleasant moods, healthy thoughts,
and creative ideas. What a blessing to the human heart is the
gift of the Sabbath.

The place?
  Orange County, California.
The year?
  1989.
The day?
  Sunday.

4

A harassed young woman is rushing to get to work. She is a clerk in the big store in the mall. And there is a sale starting today. The mall is going to be crowded. How could the traffic be so heavy!? What's going on anyway? It's Sunday morning and the traffic is bumper to bumper already. Where are all these people going? Of course! They are headed for the mall. No, that car is pulling a boat. They must be headed for the ocean. Noisy thing, I'll bet.

And that pickup, with two motorcycles tied down on it is headed for the desert. I can hear the roar of the engines already. It's going to be a noisy, dirty, fun day for them.

"Watch it, stupid!"

"You just don't switch lanes like that!"

The radio is blaring now: "There is a sig-alert for freeway travelers on Interstate 5 southbound. Heavy traffic is slowing to a near standstill. There is an accident with injury near the Washington offramp."

(There ought to be a law against freeway accidents, at least on Sundays!)

> # Even positive relationships are easily subject to fracture.

"Motorists are advised to take alternate routes."

Suddenly there is a screech of brakes. The driver cringes. She'll never get used to the sound. If only she could maneuver into the outside lanes. The rearview mirror? Boy, is the traffic coming up fast behind her! She tightens up. Got the seatbelt on? There is a break in the traffic coming up. Quick, quick! Take your chance. Cut in! She made it.

Why did the fellow behind her give her such a dirty look?

It's Sunday. Just like every other day. Monday. Tuesday. Wednesday. Thursday. Friday. Saturday. You really can't tell much difference.

That's an odd-looking family in that car. All dressed up! Surely not for the mall. Or the beach. Or the desert. Or the mountains.

Could it be that they're going to church? Who goes to church anyway?

Retreat! Regroup! And Regain—Your Peace Of Mind!

4

I don't hear any church bells. They may be ringing somewhere, but all I can hear is heavy traffic. The air smells terrible. It's smoggy again. Where are the birds anyway? And why do most of the drivers look so tense, just a thin slice away from anger?

There ought to be a law against heavy traffic on Sunday mornings.

"Turn that noisy radio off!" She's talking to herself. *"There ought to be a law making one day a week a day of quietness and peace."*

. . . (Maybe there is!)

So now we see why this commandment is what it is and where it is: (1) Remember the Sabbath Day to keep it holy." Of course!

Relationships are fragile. Even positive relationships are easily subject to fracture. Handle them with care. Keep in tender touch. . . .

Relationships are perishable. Without steady and strong nourishment, they can wither and die.

The relationship between you and your God is vulnerable too. Communication lines between the two of you need to be kept open, clear, and clean and to be used regularly and respectfully. Constant attention without distraction or obstruction is the natural requirement to sustain the life in love.

That flush of early enthusiasm for the new relationship can wear off too soon. Under life's stress and new setbacks, that initial burst of pride can lose its luster.

The booster forces that feed your dignity lose their energy too quickly. Your one essential relationship needs an unfailing power source to keep it pumping your self-esteem up through good and bad times.

Set aside regular times to draw close to the God who believes in you.

4

Self-respect, positive self-regard, wholesome self-esteem, healthy humble pride have short lifespans as did the manna from heaven that was given to the Israelites on the move from Egypt to the Promised Land. It was sweet; it was nutritious; it was delicious. They couldn't get enough of it. So they tried to horde it, stash it away, and save it for a rainy day. But it soon spoiled.

The prescriptives? Set aside regular times to draw close to the God who believes in you.

But there are so many distractions to the person with eyes and ears, plus a variety of body organs, each with their separate demands. The competition for my time, attention, and devotion is fierce. The stress generated in me is enough to put static into the communication lines with the Eternal Silent One.

Tensions interrupt and cut off the clear signals.

"Remember the Sabbath day to keep it holy."

How is this *command meant* to help me sustain my one essential relationship? Simple. Not easy, but simple. Set aside one day in seven to:

Relax!
To quiet your mind and hear the inner voice,
Retreat!
To get a fresh perspective, on your life with its problems and possibilities,
Regroup!
Your spiritual resources, marshall their potentially creative power and focus on your God-inspired dreams again.
Regain!
Your peace of mind. Let your spirit flow again in harmony with the eternal Spirit!

Your relationship will be strengthened. You'll be emotionally healthy again. Your self-esteem will blossom.

Now check these health tips out carefully.

Retreat! Regroup! And Regain—Your Peace Of Mind!

4

I

RELAX

Tension seems to be our constant companion in this stress-torn world.

The inner calm that is our birthright is continuously assailed by
- Noise,
- Pollution,
- Inflation,
- Illness,
- Personal problems and a
- Myriad of other discouraging, disappointing, and positively depressing experiences.

Result? The tension produced in our minds and spirits often results in mental and physical illness and the inability to achieve our life goals effectively.

Even worse, more basic damage is done to relationships, for tension blocks and obstructs clean, clear, and kind communication.

Q. Is it possible to eliminate tension from our lives and replace it with peace of mind?
A. Stress can be reduced to a safe and manageable level if we follow the instructions clearly written by our Creator.

It is not coincidental that the rise of tension as an emotional epidemic parallels continuing reports of breakdowns in personal communication. One reason communication breaks down is that inner tension blocks the mind from hearing what others are really saying. It also blocks the mind from hearing what God is saying.

Once when I was a young man, I had a strange, beautiful, transcendent experience with God in the mountains. But then I came back to civilization, to the "real world." Suddenly the good feeling was gone, and therefore I suspected its integrity. *I was manipulated by the idyllic setting,* I falsely reasoned. I crudely concluded that the world of traffic and crowds was "reality," that the peaceful world of the silent hills was "unreality."

The truth is that our Creator has, like a brilliant cosmic architect, designed an incredible organism called *human*

4

being. In His basic planning, God conceived of engineering this creature with a built-in tranquilizing system, so that every person, when relaxed, would be sensitive and receptive to receiving daily spiritual communication from the Creator.

I learned this from the architect Richard Neutra and his friend, the founder of sociobiology, René Dubois. They talked about "bio-realism." I never learned it in seminary. But it's imbedded in psychology and biblical theology. The doctrine of bio-realism holds that the human being is created with a built-in tranquilizing system;

• **eyes to see the trees, the hills and colors of the flowers.**

• **ears to hear the singing of the birds and listen to the rustle of the leaves and the whisper of the wind.**

• **nose to smell the fragrance of the flowers and the new-mown grass.**

• **skin to feel the caress of the sun and the silent, stress-relieving strokes of the cool breezes.**

The biological reality is that God created these senses to be channels of tranquility entering your system.

God created us with eyes to see clouds sliding silently through the soundless sea of space, green trees bending gently in soft breezes; water shimmering in the moonlight. Sensing and seeing this scene of serenity, the man and woman would enjoy deep calm and quiet inner peace.

They would be in tune with eternity to hear that still, small, inner voice of God, who designed the birds to fly, fish to swim, and persons to walk in gardens. Sounds too! The God who designed our ears to hear tranquil sounds: the rustle of the wind; the song of the bird; the trickle of a friendly brook.

In harmony with our natural habitat we now experience healing, harmony-induced peace. Deeper relaxation; heightened sensitivity to the sounds of the Spirit of God follows.

But a terrible thing happened. Today we have left the garden behind. The ears and the eyes, designed to be channels of tranquility, have become loud corridors where a mad assortment of tensions rage and race in wild conflict.

The biological organism is in trouble. The static of many

4

tensions jams the spiritual wavelengths. The human being is in an ecologically, psychologically, and spiritually polluted environment when he leaves his natural Garden of Eden and is thrown into a foreign jungle of cars, buses, concrete, and asphalt.

Dr. René Dubos said it in words to this effect: "What I fear is man's ability to adjust." By that he meant that human beings inherit an evolutionary capacity to adjust downward in order to survive in an alien, hostile, destructive environment.

"In the struggle to survive, an organism will adapt to the tragic point of becoming abnormal, even evolving into a deviate." Apply this to human beings and we will lose touch with the Spirit of the Creator and become bright, brilliant, intelligent, but unnatural and abnormal unbelievers in the God who created us to be in communication with Himself. Why fear that? Because we will one day no longer know or care that we are destroying ourselves spiritually and emotionally in the adjustment process. Spiritual apathy and ignorance will erode our enlightened awareness. For the human mind has an almost infinite capacity to rationalize its negative, compromising adjustments. Enter unbelief, doubt, secularism.

How *you* are going to feel today is a decision *you* make.

I have heard the questions. I have heard the objections. "Where is God?" "I have never felt any of those religious feelings that people talk about, so they must just be a figment of their imagination or brought on by the stirrings of music or a charismatic preacher."

It is no wonder, then, that people are skeptical, doubtful, cynical, slow to believe in a God who believes in them. It has become increasingly difficult to hear His message of belief. It's been a strain to hear the affirmations, assurances that He is there and that He cares about us and what we are about.

4

Q: Whom do you believe? The person who says he's felt God's presence or the person who says there is no God?
A: If a bird that has spent all its life in a cage declares, "I do not believe in the sky! I do not believe in soaring. It's impossible," I would not believe that bird.

If a fish that has been living all of its wet life in a fish bowl denies belief in the lakes, streams, and seas, I would not believe that fish. If a person who has spent his life in an environment of cars, streets, curbs, concrete, and asphalt, breathing exhaust, pushed, shoved, elbowed, and dehumanized by his own species and depersonalized by a computerized, technological, materialistic world—if such a person says, "I do not believe in God," I would not trust his doubts.

A bird was designed to fly; a fish to swim; and persons to enjoy God in a garden. Gardens soothe to tranquility. And tranquility makes spiritual communication possible.

When I went to Richard Neutra and asked him how we could create a church where people would be more free to communicate with God, Richard said, "We can't demolish our cities and bulldoze all the asphalt. However, we *can* shield the eyes and the ears from those tension-producing stimuli."

So, Richard and I designed a church where you can hear the birds sing; you can look out and see the clouds drifting in the sky. We created a garden retreat from the tension-producing sounds and sights of the world.

Now, many of us live in cities. We don't live in a house where we can be protected from the sights and the sounds of the bustling city. What do we do? Go to church on Sunday. That's a place where we can go and feel God's presence. Within the sanctuary of stained-glass walls, we are shielded from unsightly parking lots and power poles. In these beautiful retreat places called churches, the sounds and sights that would fill us with negative emotional tensions can be drained out like dirty oil from a car.

"Be still, and know that I am God."

"The LORD is my shepherd,
I shall not want. He makes me to lie down
   in green pastures . . .
He restores my soul."

Retreat! Regroup! And Regain—Your Peace Of Mind!

4

Every morning before my children left for school, my family and I would repeat the lines of Ella Wheeler Wilcox:

> I'm going to be happy today,
> Though the skies are cloudy and gray.
> No matter what comes my way,
> I'm going to be happy today!

As our children were growing up we taught them this cybernetic reality: the brain is like a radio dial. All of the ideas that bombard you are like sound waves. You can switch the dial and pick up stress-relieving music or you can pick up propaganda and tune in to some tension-producing messages.

If my children got depressed, cynical, crabby, we would simply say to them, "Come on, turn the dial."

Make the choice that is *positive. Choose to feel good today.*

What does this have to do with the Ten Commandments? Everything! *The Ten Commandments are the ten most fundamental principles that God gave to you, to me, to the human race, to help us feel good.* Ultimately, you know, feeling good is really living. Not feeling good is death. And a lot of people—young people, middle-aged people, old people—are dead just because they don't feel good about themselves.

This wholesale deprivation of positive emotional power is so pathetically unnecessary for God has given us principles of emotional health and spiritual fitness that, if we live by them, will make us really feel good. But if you or I, in our freedom and rebellion, resent them and ignore them, then we will pay the price in a life that is deprived of positive emotional energy and wellness.

The Bible says, "The wages of sin is death, but the gift of God is eternal life." What does that mean? It means that the death of joy, the death of hope, the death of faith, the death of enthusiasm—yes, emotional death—does not come from God. It comes from ourselves as a result of an unnatural spiritual lifestyle. When spiritual communication is blocked by stress, emotional malnourishment is inevitable. God does not offer death. God offers life. The gift of God is life, eternal life.

4

How does He give life to us? He gives this to us with positive principles found in these Ten Commandments.

We've looked at, analyzed, and discovered the power of the first three of these potent, basic, classic, emotional vitamins. We are now on the fourth, "Remember the Sabbath day to keep it holy. Six days you shall labor and do all your work, but the seventh day is the Sabbath of the LORD, your God."

This commandment protects our emotional well-being by protecting us from burnout.

God knows His children need to relax.

If we ignore the warning in this principle, if we don't set aside one day a week for positive emotional treatment and a spiritual therapy session with God, we will suffer emotional problems.

Now, if we are honest with ourselves, we will have to admit that we have neglected this principle. The statistics show that most of us treat Sunday just like any other day. Most of us don't have a Sabbath day. Most people don't rest one day in seven. Most people keep working, working, working until they are suffering from fatigue, tension, lack of enthusiasm, even depression.

Here are the comments that I hear too frequently. I call them the terrible Ts. Each one clogs the otherwise open channel of communication.

• "I'm so TIRED!" ("I NEED A DAY OF REST!")

Fatigue is rampant among Americans. We are operating on overdrive. We need to learn how to relax without feeling guilty. Tired people are poor communicators. Fatigue produces short tempers. A tired body and a fatigued mind make even God's approach difficult to detect.

"I've lost my faith in God, Reverend Schuller."

I couldn't believe it. Not John. "Been working hard, John?"

"Yep!"

• "I'm so TENSE!" ("I NEED TO GET AWAY FROM THE DAILY GRIND!")

When you're tired, you're apt to be uptight. Your fuse is shorter than normal, and you're bound to be tense. Result?

Retreat! Regroup! And Regain—Your Peace Of Mind!

4

"I don't want to talk right now." "Leave me alone." "Give me my space." People can't say they feel good when they're walking around wound up as tight as a bomb waiting to go off at the slightest provocation. Believe me, we see the effects of tense, uptight people on the freeways here in California. Everyone is in such a hurry to get somewhere. With gridlocks and airport congestion, there's just no way to get anywhere in a hurry anymore. It takes time. We all have to learn to be patient. We have to learn to relax when we're stuck in heavy traffic.

• "I've been so TEMPTED to quit!" ("I NEED HELP TO KEEP GOING!")

When you're uptight, tense, and overworked, then there's little emotional strength left for resistance. The idea of quitting, of walking away from it all, becomes tempting.

• "I've been so TROUBLED lately!" ("I NEED TO FIND A QUIET PLACE WHERE I CAN THINK!")

Problems manage to mount; worries reproduce themselves. It happens to all of us. *Where is God? The stress is clogging the channel. I can't seem to get through to Him. What can I do?*

Phillips Brooks experienced one of the most devastating experiencs a human being can endure. He was a public school teacher, but he failed miserably and was so wracked with self-doubt that he almost allowed his famished self-esteem to annihilate his spirit. He suffered what was called a nervous breakdown. Humiliated, he left home and traveled the world. On Christmas Eve he found himself in the Holy Land, out in the shepherds' hills that overlook the little town of Bethlehem where Jesus was born two thousand years ago. Here in that starlight of the silent, peaceful night, he penned these words:

> O Little town of Bethlehem,
> How still we see Thee lie!
> Above thy deep and dreamless sleep
> The silent stars go by.
> Yet in thy dark streets shineth
> The everlasting light;
> The hopes and fears of all the years
> Are met in Thee tonight.

4

Here he found his faith again. Fresh faith! Real faith in God and in himself! Now he had something to say. He had a message. He had a reason to live. God was real after all! Life had value again. He was important! For he had discovered that it was really true that there was a person called Jesus, who lived and was born in this town.

He went back home to become one of the greatest ministers and communicators for faith that the world has ever known.

"Why do you believe there is a God?" he was asked. "Because I believe in Jesus," he answered, "and Jesus believed in God. I trust and rest on his wise conclusion! I don't think He was wrong on this point. I trust the faith of Jesus more than I trust the doubts of anyone else when it comes to the subject of God." Well thought out and wisely spoken! His self-respect was rescued from total destruction by the decision to embrace faith. Result? A fantastic life of service to humanity.

• "I feel TORN!" ("I NEED TO GET IT TOGETHER AGAIN!")

Are you torn between the bad and the good? The good and the better? The better and the best? Choices are hard to make when you're on the verge of burnout. Leadership becomes weak when it has neglected time for quiet reflection.

Tired? Every seven days I need to go to church to stop and meditate, reflect, and be refreshed.

Tempted? Every seven days I've got to come to church and be reminded what the boundaries are. We all need boundaries. Take away the banks, and the river is free. But it will soon become a swamp.

Troubled? Every seven days I need to come back to my church to be comforted.

Torn? Once a week, I need to be restored and built up and reminded of the best choices.

The movie *Chariots of Fire* received an Oscar as best film in 1981. At first glance, it seemed improbable that a movie

4

based on this story would have achieved such popularity and such critical acclaim, for the movie is simply the story of Eric Liddell, a man who would not run on Sunday.

Eric was his country's hope for a medal in the 1924 Olympics. He was a senior at Edinburgh University when he joined the Olympic team. He was known for his fierce religious convictions. The son of a Scottish Congregationalist missionary, Liddell inherited his father's devotion to the church, to Jesus Christ, and he was unwavering to the commitment he had made to put that relationship first and foremost in his life, above every other event and potential honor—including an Olympic medal.

When the games and races were scheduled, Eric's race was set for a Sunday. Eric would not, could not run on a Sunday. He was firmly, resolutely committed to keeping Sunday a day of rest.

But then the opportunity arose for him to run the 400-meter race. This was not his race. This was not his best running event. He had not intended to run it. But it was either run in this event or not run at all. Eric chose to run.

Eric was victorious. Through sheer courage, discipline, and character, he won a gold medal in the 400-meter run!

After the Olympics he returned to China where he taught science and athletics. He married a missionary's daughter and carried on his strong evangelistic work with the Chinese. His wife and family left China when the Japanese invaded. Eric was arrested by the Japanese and died in 1942. He was mourned as a Scottish hero by his countrymen. He is remembered still today, but not for winning a race. How many other Olympians have won races only to be forgotten? Eric is remembered for his commitment to Jesus Christ! Can anything be more victorious than that? Can anything bring greater honor to a life than those costly decisions of self-denial made on the altar of "Preserving Precious Relationships"?

RETREAT

Sometimes wisdom advises us to retreat. Sometimes this is a necessary strategy for winning the big prize. If you always advance without taking time to rest, evaluate, and plan, then

4

you'd better expect a resounding defeat. The same is true for emotional health. There are times in life when it is vital to plan to retreat.

We all need to retreat sometimes from the accumulations of the multiplied tensions. We need to have:

- Our spiritual oil drained and changed,
- Our emotional batteries recharged,
- Our attitudes realigned.

II

NOW, RENEW!

Your strong self-confidence can be quickly withered on the vine, and your positive pride can turn to strong misgivings under the assaults and blows of unexpected attacks. A positive mental attitude is like a beautifully washed window. Now you can reflect; you are transparent; you can see *out* clearly, and others can see *into* your soul. It's a healthy situation.

But even as an unexpected rainstorm spots the windows, as the dust and grime of the air can cloud the windshield with a thin film of sediment, so your sparkling, crystal-clear confidence can be soiled under a subtle film of accumulated negative thoughts and expressions that will distort the clarity of your spiritual perception. Life, after all, is a constant flux and change. Persons who were a major source of your emotional support are now gone. Your job position never remains static. New faces appear. New forces emerge. There is constant change.

A toddler needs to learn how to function confidently outside the home when he first begins preschool. He is away from his nursery and family, which up until now have been his sole source of affirmation. Then when he graduates to go on to kindergarten and first grade, he will need to have his self-esteem bolstered as his self-awareness and self-value begin to bud in the environment of new classes, new rapport with new teachers, and new friends. Junior-high kids, of course, find this a crying need. This is why the absence of self-esteem may force youngsters to surrender to peer pressures and engage in illicit drug activity or promiscuous

4

A positive mental attitude is like a beautifully washed window. Now you can reflect; you are transparent; you can see *out* clearly, and others can see *into* your soul.

sexual practices. But those in their twenties and thirties also desperately need renewed self-esteem, for they are moving out into the job market, establishing families. "Will this marriage succeed? I'm scared!" "Will I fail as a mother? Do I have what it takes to be a parent in today's world?"

The strong, quiet, confidence that claims "I've got what it takes," that "I can do it with God's help," is needed at every age. Just when you think you have made it, you enter a new passage of life and embark on a new stage of fresh relationships. So you've reached the top of the ladder? For the first time in your life you are number one, only to discover that you need a self-esteem boost. You need to feel that you deserve to be number one. You need to believe that you can fill the spot.

Self-esteem is never, ever a permanent condition! Peace of mind is not an acquired possession! Life is in a constant state of change. New deals are dealt. Blows are felt. Stress is a natural result of change. Every transition brings tension with it. The bigger the change, the tighter the tension. The broader the transition, the deeper the stress.

It's no wonder that we need to take the time to retreat, readjust our mental attitudes, and restore our self-esteem.

4

III
REGROUP

Now discover the power of the one-in-seven principle. I live by this principle. The one-in-seven principle is critically important. I have a friend. Every Monday morning he takes his car, leaves it at the garage, and says, "Check it out." They know what he means. He wants them to check the front wheels, among other things, to make sure the tires are aligned. He gets triple the mileage that I get out of my tires. I wait until the treads are worn off and they say, "Hey, your wheels are out of alignment, and you need new tires." My friend gets them checked every seven days. It's what you call preventative maintenance.

My wife and I discovered this years ago. We decided the most important thing in our life was our marriage. We decided that once in every seven days we needed to be alone. So we established our Monday night date night. Absolutely no excuse is good enough for us to cancel our date night.

A few years ago I received a call from *Good Morning, America*. David Hartman wanted me to participate in a televised discussion on religious television. I wanted very much to say yes. I have always respected David Hartman. But agreeing to the engagement would mean leaving Los Angeles on Monday, and I had a date with my wife on Monday night. I agreed that I would be willing to get up early on Tuesday morning and go into the ABC office in Los Angeles if they wanted to do it by satellite. But, I explained, I could not give up my date with my wife. As it turned out, they responded to my suggestion and even offered us a beautiful hotel accommodation in Los Angeles. So my wife and I had our dinner date on Monday night, and ABC's *Good Morning, America* picked up the check!

My wife and I have five children. We have always kept Sunday as a day of rest, to retreat, and regroup as a family. I remember when Sheila, our oldest daughter, was about four years old. Her neighborhood playmate came to the house one Sunday to ask if Sheila could come out and play. I wasn't prepared for that. I said, "No, not today. She can play

4

tomorrow and the next day and every day the rest of the week, but not on Sunday." I wanted one day completely different so that she could regroup with the family. We held to this family rule while all of our five children were growing up. Today they all comment positively about this discipline.

Sunday can also be a day to regroup your thinking. Henry Ford hired an efficiency expert once to go through his plant. He said, "Try to find nonproductive people, tell me who they are, and I will either retrain, remotivate, or replace them." The man returned and reported that he definitely found such a person: "Every time I walk by his office, he is sitting with his feet propped up on his desk. When I go in, he stands and shakes hands, and we exchange a few words, and when I leave he props his feet up on his desk again. The man never does a thing."

When Henry Ford learned the name of the man he said, "I can't fire him. I pay him to do nothing but think."

We all need one day in seven when we can do nothing but *think!*

Whether you live by this one-in-seven principle or not is your choice. My job is to tell you it's an option open to you. God wants you to feel good, to have peace of mind, but you have to take care of yourself. That's the positive purpose behind the Ten Commandments. When you buy a product, the manufacturer gives you an owner's and operator's manual. I have to confess something here. I am not a perfect person, and if there's anything that turns me off, it's the owner's and operator's manuals. I never do read them. "When all else fails, read the instructions," God advises.

God created the human being with an inspirational gas tank, and it only holds a seven-day supply. It needs to be refilled, refueled, and recharged. That's why God gave a great gift to the Jewish people—the Sabbath. We Gentiles have inherited it, but over the years we have ignored and thrown away one of God's most important instructions on how to get the most out of what He created.

I've made three trips to the Soviet Union, two trips to the People's Republic of China, and remarkably many Communists observe the Sabbath. They know the one-in-seven principle. They know that people are far more productive in five- or six-day stretches than seven-day

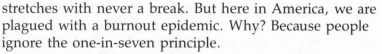

stretches with never a break. But here in America, we are plagued with a burnout epidemic. Why? Because people ignore the one-in-seven principle.

Are you tired? You need one day in seven when you can really rest for twenty-four hours. Are you tense? Once in every seven days you must come to a place like a church, a synagogue, a temple, where the tensions can be dissolved and where you can have an effective spiritual renewal. Tempted? You need to come back once in seven days (especially in our culture) to discover where the boundaries are. Troubled? You need healing and comfort from grief, disappointment, and rejection. Torn? Then go to a positive church that will inspire you to choose the best.

My friend, you may have what it takes to live successfully, but there is no way any person can be successful in his most important relationships for any length of time if he ignores the invitation of this commandment. Great values await the person who makes a resolution to attend church every week. I need this. So do you. Make a commitment now to observe this commandment: "Remember the Sabbath day, to keep it holy." By so doing, you will tune in to life and will learn how you can feel good today and every day.

You'll be amazed how your channels of communication with God and with your own soul and heart are cleared, opened.

IV

REGAIN YOUR PEACE OF MIND

William Wolcott, the great English artist, came to New York City in 1924 to record his impressions of that skyscraper city. After a week of feeling the lifeblood of the city, he found himself one morning in the architectural office of a colleague for whom he'd worked years before in England. Now, suddenly, the urge and the surge to sketch came over him. He quickly said to his colleague, "Please, I need some paper." And seeing some paper on a desk, he said, "May I have that?"

The architectural colleague said, "That's not sketching paper, Mr. Wolcott. That's just ordinary wrapping paper."

4

Wolcott, not wanting to lose the inspiration, reached out and said, "Nothing is ordinary if you know how to use it." And he took the wrapping paper and made two sketches. One sold for one thousand dollars and the other for five hundred dollars. The principle: Nothing is ordinary if you know how to use it. Sunday is not an ordinary day if you know how to use it!

I love the fact that the early Christians were inspired by the Holy Spirit to change their day of rest from Saturday to Sunday so that their day of rest would be not just a negative retreat but a positive renewal. The Muslims set Friday aside. The Jewish people set Saturday aside. Most Christians set the first day of the week aside to commemorate the Resurrection of Jesus Christ.

Yes, the Resurrection of Christ happened on this day, *and we want to be resurrected.* We want to be renewed. Don't miss this God-ordained prescription for your peace of mind. Business may be rotten, but only you can vote to throw in the towel. You may be frustrated in achieving your heart's desire, and a lot of people and pressures and problems may be keeping you from the success you want. But only you can say, "I quit." And if you have enough strength to hang on for six days, Sunday will come again. If you have found a positive church, you will receive another shot of rejoicing and renewal. Power to fulfill your dreams will be God's gift to you!

Traditionally, Sunday has been a day of creative quietness for faith, for fun, for family, for church, and for community. But something has happened. In the past fifty years we have seen a growing, deepening sense of depression in the widespread epidemic of emotional ailments like anxiety and stress, with its effect on the human organism. This emotional epidemic of negative mental and spiritual problems in our country has risen sharply in proportion to our forsaking that one day in seven as a useful day of healing.

The truth is you desperately, urgently need one day in seven to rest the heart, the soul, the mind, and the body. The Bible says, "In quietness and confidence shall be your strength." I work hard six days a week, but I take Mondays off. My Sabbath, as you might expect, is not Sunday, and it is not the Jewish Saturday or the Muslim Friday. My Sabbath is

TURN EVERY SUNDAY INTO A PERSONAL RESURRECTION DAY!

4

Monday. I do not go into the office on that day because I believe that if I can't get my work done in six days, then I am overloaded. I either need to reprioritize, reschedule, or reorganize my work. I would rather live longer and do more than try to accomplish a lot in a few years and die too young.

So choose, then, to use your Sabbath as a day of rest and renewal.

All my life as a pastor, I've heard the objection, "I don't have the time!" Well, I hear what you're saying. Time is a valuable commodity. It's impossible to put a price tag on it, but time is money. There's no doubt about it. Consider S. Truett Cathy, a prominent, successful businessman from Atlanta, Georgia.

In 1946, right after World War II, Truett opened the restaurant, "The Dwarf House," that gave birth to the Chick-Fil-A chain. He and his brother, Ben, had just been released from military service. They pooled their resources, accumulated four thousand dollars, combined that with a six-thousand four-hundred-dollar loan, bought some property, bought equipment, and started their business. Their business today is worth several million dollars. They have hundreds of outlets across the country.

This successful, *busy* man is an active member of the Lord's Day Alliance, which is an organization that attempts to remind people to set one day aside to revitalize their faith and their family. In other words, *preserve, empower,* and *enrich* the most important relationships in your life. In fact, if you wanted to eat at one of Truett's restaurants, you'd better not try to eat there on a Sunday because it will be closed.

CLOSED ON SUNDAY—do you ever see those signs any more? Believe me, they're few and far between in Southern California and many other places in America. I was frankly surprised to hear that this successful entrepreneur could operate a chain successfully even if its restaurants are closed every Sunday! I called Truett and asked him, "Why is Sunday so special for you?"

He replied, "Sunday is a very special day for me today. I'll tell you why. I was brought up in a boarding house, and I and my brothers and sisters had to wash all the dirty dishes every Sunday afternoon. I can't think of anything more distasteful than dirty dishes on a Sunday afternoon. More than that, I believe in setting Sunday aside because it gives people an opportunity to be with their families and to worship, if they choose. We've seen the family disintegrate. If we close our restaurants on Sundays, maybe families will eat together at home."

I persisted, "Are you telling me that all four hundred of your stores are closed on Sunday?"

"Yes. And most of our units are operating in shopping malls. We're in one shopping mall which has 350 tenants. We are the only tenant that closes on Sunday. We included a clause in the lease that we will be open on Sunday at our option, not theirs."

This man is successful. He is busy. But Sundays are important to him. The truth is: *Relationships are all important to him!* He not only has put this principle to work in his business; he also practices it in his personal life. On Sundays you will find this great entrepreneur teaching Sunday School to a class of thirteen-year-old boys at the First Baptist Church in Jonesboro, Georgia.

> **The Sabbath should be a time when hope is reborn, dreams are rekindled, self-worth restored.**

One day in seven you need a positive injection of positive emotion. You have to have an experience in which you laugh or cry or feel love or get a lift.

Sabbath should be a time when hope is reborn, dreams are rekindled, and self-worth restored. When you are renewed, when your dreams are reborn, when your ideals are rekindled, then you will regain your dignity, your self-esteem, your peace of mind.

"Sunday is my only day to play golf," someone once said defensively to me.

"Like Sunday is my only day to clear my lines of

4

communication with my God," I offered. "And this relationship is the most important thing in my life!"

That is just one step ahead of building a strong family. So now, let's go to work on that in the next chapter.

WHEN I'M GOOD,
I'M GOOD!
WHEN I'M NOT,
I'M HUMAN.

P.S. LOVE ME ANYWAY.

CHAPTER 5

TAP INTO THE POWER OF YOUR ROOTS

"HONOR THY FATHER AND MOTHER"

5

We're halfway in this book which is designed to be a God-inspired, ten-step path to self-respect and self-esteem and powerful self-dignity. Time for a quick review, a short quiz. Check your progress so far.

1. *I'm a believer (at least I'm trying).* Let me hear you say it. You dare to believe in the One who believes in you? Great!
2. *I did it! I went for a self-image transplant.* Fantastic!
3. *I'm working at building pride through a positive relationship!* Wonderful!
4. *I'm keeping the lines of communication open!* I'll pay the price to enrich my priceless, positive relationships. Terrific!

Ready for the fifth lesson? Here it is.

5. Tap into the power of your roots.
   "Honor your father and your mother . . ."

For me, this commandment is a delight!

But for many persons—a growing number, I'm afraid—this fifth word is hell!

Just because you've gotten into positive religion doesn't mean you will magically wipe out, erase, obliterate memories of a family that may have been neurotic or even destructive to your budding self-image and self-esteem.

If this sounds like your family, let's try to work through this tangle of tormenting memories together.

Wait a minute! Hold it right there, Schuller. You don't know my dad or my mother.

I doubt if you would respect them if you knew them.

Child abuse. You've heard of it? I'm the victim.

Could that be why I wince and really have to struggle with this concept of God as my heavenly Father? One father was bad enough! It's enough to cause me to be repulsed by this God-idea. God is love. I like that. I'm not sure I even know what "love" is. But it sounds so nice.

5

Is there any hope for me?

There must be something really bad about me for my mom and dad to have treated me the way they did.

Honor your father and mother? You can have this one, Dr. Schuller. May I pass, please?

As a pastor, I've had to hear that sad story too often.

Right now, I'm thinking of Judy (not her real name).

Judy suffers from a horrendously low self-esteem. She has been in counseling for only a short time. She could never look in a mirror and declare, "I'm pretty!" By the cultural standards of the modern world she'd be labeled fat, and physically unattractive. Is the extra weight the cause or the effect of her low self-esteem? Right now, it doesn't matter because the taproot of her pathetically low self-esteem is obviously rooted in a terribly troubled family background. She and her mother have a sad, mutually insulting relationship.

Q: What is her hope?

A: First, counseling and therapy may help bring this estranged mother and daughter together. Then much of the damage that has been done may be controlled if not completely eliminated.

Second, extended family may be helpful. Here the church steps in. In the Crystal Cathedral, we have dozens of specialty small groups that have become a healthy synthetic family. Members know each other, affirm each other, encourage each other, and *maintain* each other's emotional health through their recurring and periodic dips into depression.

One such small group in my church is made up only of incest victims. Perhaps no other group of persons have had their self-worth, their human value, their dignity assaulted and violated more disastrously than victims of incest. All suffer from a condition I call "emotional amputation."

You may never be able to draw any dignity from the memory of your father and mother. You may never be able to honor your parents because of the horrific humiliation they inflicted on your still-youthful and emerging identity. Face up to it the way my daughter faces up to the fact that her

Tap Into The Power Of Your Roots

5

amputated leg will never grow back. You will most likely have to live with some of the scars all of your life.

So come to terms with reality. Accept and admit that your father was despicable in his behavior. We think of what Jesus said: "Whoever violates one of these little ones, it would be better for him that a millstone were hung around his head and he were drowned in the deepest sea." So Judy lives with the hell of a little girl's memories. But she belongs to a like group of damaged souls, and she is surviving! Her dignity is constantly being affirmed, defended, reinforced, and strengthened by her caring Christian sisters in a small group in our church.

One of the twentieth-century's greatest psychiatrists, Dr. Karl Menninger, a friend of mine, once asked me, "Why do we in our day hate children so much?"

There are many answers and probably more mysteries to that question. But what is noticeable is the rise in child abuse.

Is there a cure for the damaged faith potential inflicted on children from troubled families? *Will they ever be able to believe that there is a God who believes in them?*

Most definitely yes. However, for many persons the natural taproot of faith—is severed or poisoned by
- Physical,
- Sexual,
- Emotional,
- Verbal, or
- Spiritual abuse!

The result may be "spiritual retardation." Is this cause for despair? Not so! But reality must be faced!

Let me try to help you.

Here are nine tips on how to build self-esteem by tapping into the power of your roots.

1

ABANDON THE "IF ONLYS"

When I reached the bedside of my teenage daughter who had just had her leg amputated, I said, "Carol, you must be

5

on guard against one thing—and that's self-pity."

"Don't worry, Dad," she shot back. "I've got enough problems without adding that one!"

A psychiatrist had several sessions with a client who suffered from depression. He listened quietly for several sessions, taking copious notes. Then one day he spoke to his troubled patient: "I've noticed that two words keep coming up again and again in your conversations with me. They are 'if only':

- *If only my father . . .*
- *If only my mother . . .*
- *If only our family . . .*

"My advice to you is forget the 'If onlys.' Put them behind you. For that is where they are. They are in your past unless you allow yourself to bring them from the past into the present and into your future."

The next time you're tempted to think, "If only," think:

- *At least . . .*
- *Nevertheless . . .*
- *However . . .*

Now try substituting

- *Next time . . .*

Your father and mother are hardly worthy of your honor? Well, try thinking, "Next time I enlarge my family, I'll help to make it an honorable family!"

> **Replace useless self-pity with an inspiring dream of what you can do to become the kind of parent that your child will be proud of.**

Replace useless self-pity with an inspiring dream of what you can do to become the kind of parent that your child will be proud of.

Coming to terms with your parents is often a tough assignment, but it cannot be neglected.

Many parents have failed to produce self-reliant, inwardly assured, self-respecting children because they have believed the so-called experts. Psychologist John Rosemond believes

5

that a child's self-esteem is more important than happiness. He wrote the following article in his column, "Parent Power":

The biggest mistake made by this generation of parents was that of believing the experts knew what they were talking about. And the biggest blunder made by the experts was that of promoting the entirely ludicrous idea that happiness and self-esteem go hand in hand.

That's right, ludicrous, as in absurd, ridiculous, patently false. Self-esteem and happiness are not one and the same. Keeping a child happy is as simple as giving the child everything he or she wants. That may prove expensive, but it's not difficult. Keeping a child happy takes less effort, less stamina, and certainly less courage than helping a child grow up.

I guarantee that I can keep a child happy for 18 years. In the process, however, I will have no choice but to completely destroy the child's self-esteem. Self-esteem, you see, is composed of equal parts initiative, resourcefulness, imagination, autonomy, and determination. Self-esteem is an attitude of "I can do it myself."

Such an attitude develops not as a result of parents constantly doing things for you, busying themselves in pursuit for your happiness, but as a result of parents who expect you to do for yourself, take responsibility for yourself, and pursue your own happiness.

Self-sufficiency is the yardstick of self-esteem. But the road to self-sufficiency is paved with frustration, tribulation, trial and error, disappointment, falling flat on one's face, and other equally "unhappy" experiences.

Believing the experts (they write books, don't they?), the majority of today's parents have dedicated themselves to the cause of keeping their children happy. In the process, they give their children too much attention and too many things. They expect little of them around the home, do their homework for them whenever the going gets the least bit rough.

5

When the time comes for these children to leave home and begin fending for themselves, many of them will not be prepared for self-sufficiency. It's interesting to note that between 1976 and 1985, the number of 22-year-olds still living at home nearly doubled.

The experts deceived themselves and passed the deception along to us. The cause to which parents should dedicate themselves is that of helping their children out of their lives (and into successful lives of their own).

When the time comes, the child with self-esteem wants to leave. He's not only impatient to take on the challenge, he's also convinced he can make a better life for himself than his parents were willing to make for him. He's prepared to take responsibility for his own happiness because his parents wouldn't accept much of that responsibility for him.*

2

DOUBT YOUR DOUBTS

"Doubt your doubts" is the next word of counsel abused children must be given.

If you don't believe in yourself, please don't trust the negative thoughts you may have about yourself or about God.

Your father and mother may have left you emotionally deprived. Therefore you are famished at a point in your memory system where you should be nourished. The result could most naturally be a lack of faith in God, in yourself, and in others.

Don't trust the negative thoughts about yourself or about God.

It is impossible to know how many atheists, secularists, and agnostics are what they are because of where they came from— homes and families where the

*Honolulu Advertiser, Feb. 15, 1989

5

mutual sharing of love and respect was completely lacking. Complex systems of distorted reasonings rise from their dwarfed or deprived self-esteem. They erect elaborate and often brilliant rationalizations to prove to themselves that there is no God. "Doubt your doubts" is a fundamental step to coming to terms with a tragic childhood.

3
FACE YOUR FEARS.
DON'T RUN FROM THEM.

This advice, I realize, can be horrendously painful. Many victims of incest try to blot it out and refuse therapy when they could release and heal these horrible memories. But if you face them, you can erase their damaging effects on your self-image.

You are afraid even to probe into the mysteries of your past. That's common with adults who were abandoned as children and raised apart from their blood relatives. You have already been hurt. So now face your fears. You just might run into some happy surprises.

You may find that if you cannot honor your father or mother, you might be able to honor your grandmother or your grandfather. Your parents may have been rebels against great family values and traditions. You can restore the tree to its heritage of great fruitbearing. You can—and you will, you *must*—find someone in your past who had noble values. Surely, you're not the first.

It happened in my church a couple of years ago. Every Sunday I say to my congregation, "Turn around, shake hands with somebody behind you; tell them who you are and where you're from."

On one Sunday a young airline stewardess was sitting in the cathedral. She turned around and shook hands with an older lady behind her. She said, "Hello. God loves you, so do I. My name is Lisa."

The older woman said, "Oh, I have a granddaughter named Lisa. Are you a member here?"

"Oh, no, I live back East," Lisa replied. "I'm an airline

5

stewardess, and I'm on my way to Hong Kong on a free pass to shop."

"I have a granddaughter named Lisa," the elderly lady said, "and I've heard that she's an airline stewardess."

"Oh?" Lisa was intrigued. "Who does she fly with?"

"I really don't know. You see, I have never seen her. They took her away right after she was born."

"Really?" said Lisa. "How sad." She added, almost as an afterthought, "What was her mother's name?"

"Eleanor."

Lisa was stunned. "I have a mother by that name! And I know I have a grandmother living in California. But I've never met her. I don't even know if she's still alive. Oh, it can't be! You couldn't be—my grandmother, could you?"

"It can't be! You can't be my granddaughter!" the grandmother declared.

As it turned out, they were indeed grandmother and granddaughter. It was beautiful.

"Grandmother!" Lisa cried. "You are my grandmother!"

You can be sure they know and believe there's a God above who loves them and believes in them. The odds of these two persons being in the same service at the same church, on the same Sunday, and sitting in front and in back of each other, in the three-thousand-seat Crystal Cathedral defy comprehension.

A young man once came into my office for counseling. All his life he had been rejected by his father. His alcoholic father left his wife and son for "greener pastures," paying the price of many broken marriages. This philandering father went on to make it to the top of a national corporate ladder. However, the father's total rejection of his son severely pained this young man, who carries anger within him today. Indeed, this anger is justified and not altogether unhealthy. But he has learned to handle it. For although his mother is also a problem to this young man his grandmother is an inspiring and positive person. She has been his father and mother rolled up in one. Unquestionably her love was enough to give the boy what he needed—a sense of family pride anyway.

Don't be afraid to check out the family tree. You may find

5

a problem or skeleton in the closet, but you'll undoubtedly find some honorable and inspiring souls too.

4

KEEP THE DOOR OPEN TO PARTIAL
IF NOT COMPLETE RECOVERY

This is the third piece of helpful counsel to the innocent wounded children of the world. A prostitute in Tokyo abandoned her unwanted child on a doorstep. He was adopted by a Christian who made God's love so real that this child grew up reacting positively and became one of the great evangelists and social reformers in twentieth-century Japan—Toyohiko Kagawa. Call this complete recovery.

Lee Ezell was born and raised in an alcoholic home in Philadelphia. At the early age of seventeen she accepted Christ into her heart at a Billy Graham crusade. She had just graduated from high school. She was excited about life. She had a job in San Francisco as a typist. She had worked there just a short time when a salesman, who came through the office twice a year, raped her one horrible night.

As a virgin teenager, Lee was unprepared for that violent intrusion into her life. She didn't report that rape. The majority of rape victims do not. Twenty years ago there were no hotlines, no crisis centers. She thought that it would all go away if she was quiet about it. That might have happened if she hadn't found out a few weeks later that she was pregnant.

Lee herself had been told by her own mother when she was a child that she was unwanted. Here was an unwanted child carrying another unwanted child. However, as a new Christian she kept in close touch with Jesus Christ through this difficult passage of her life. As a result, abortion, in her mind, was not an option.

Lee signed up at the Los Angeles County Adoptions to give her child away at birth. She felt that it was the best that she could do for her baby. She told me later, "Dr. Schuller, I found comfort in the story of Moses. I related to his mother who took that little baby, put him in a basket, and placed him in the reeds along the river's edge. I hoped and prayed that God would find someone like Pharaoh's daughter to claim and love my baby."

Her child was born, a baby girl. Lee never saw her or held her. She didn't realize at the time that this little unwanted baby would be the only child she'd ever deliver.

Understandably, Lee became very distrustful of men. So it wasn't until she was twenty-eight that she fell in love and married. With her new husband came with two children, whom she adopted legally as her own. How ironic! Lee, the young mother who gave away a child for adoption, was now herself an adoptive parent.

Then one day the phone rang. It was Julie, the little daughter she had given away twenty years earlier, her missing piece, her unwanted daughter.

"Lee, my name is Julie. I'm your daughter! I want to know you, Mom. I'm married to a wonderful man, and I'm the mother of a little baby. You're a grandmother!"

And so they arranged to meet, and they were beautifully reconciled.

When Lee introduced me to her lovely daughter, Julie, I was overwhelmed by the uncanny resemblance. I was so impressed by this remarkable young woman. She told me about her search for her mother. She told me how her adoptive parents graciously gave her all of her adoptive papers to help her in her search. Julie's burning desire was to know if her mother knew Jesus as her personal Lord and Savior as she did. This was, in fact, the driving impetus behind her search for her mother.

She wrote to everybody and every place that she could think of—the hospital, lawyers that handled cases, social workers. Then, lost in some twenty-year-old hospital records, Julie deciphered a phone number, and on a whim she called it. It was the phone number of the couple that Lee had stayed with while she was waiting for her child to be born. Imagine! Twenty years later, the same couple still lived in the same home, with the same address and phone number. None of that important information had changed in all that time!

Had Julie called the telephone number only two months later, she'd have reached a disconnected number, for eight

5

weeks after Julie contacted them, they moved out of that home.

Julie didn't know who or what her birth mother was. Frankly, she expected the worst. But when she met her mother, she was delighted to find that Lee Ezell was a successful wife, mother, and lecturer. Their love for each other was immediate and they are today very, very close.

Lee said to me, "I found my missing piece, and I believe others can, too. They can find God's peace for their missing pieces. Life can be whole again if we allow God to fill up the empty hole with His divine mortar through Jesus Christ."

5

TURN YOUR SCARS INTO STARS

Now if—and when—full and complete recovery is not feasible, then it's time to turn your scars into stars. In fact, this is the last best hope for some abused children today. The story of David Rothenberg is told in a book and was made into a TV movie. His father poured gasoline over him, lit a match, and left him burning in a motel room ten miles from the Crystal Cathedral. He was only a mere child. He did survive physically and is surviving emotionally. How?

By becoming a believer in Jesus Christ. The Lord moved in to rescue him and save him from disaster. I think of the psalmist, who said, "When my father and mother forsake me, then the Lord will take me to His heart." That is what happened to David. Fortunately his mother rushed to his rescue, and skilled surgeons, along with countless numbers of unknown people have spared nothing to help him. He can indeed give honor to his mother and hence receive honor in return. A very courageous young man, David has exercised what I call possibility thinking:

- I cannot change what has happened to me, but I can control to a great degree how I will react to what happens to me.
- I shall become a compassionate, sympathetic, caring, sensitive person to help others who are hurting as I have been.

5

And so David Rothenberg received from our ministry the Scars into Stars Award.

6

NOW! DETERMINE TO UPGRADE YOUR FAMILY NAME

Still another piece of wise advice to the children whose parents abused them, neglected them, or innocently deprived them of developing a healthy self-respect is this: Determine to do a better job of parenting than your mother and father. Learn from their mistakes. Correct the errors in instruction you picked up from them.

Did their behavior disgrace your family tree? Then redeem the honor of your family name by becoming the kind of a person that will restore dignity and respect to your family name.

Many years ago an English convict was sentenced to a prison exile, half a world away. He brought dishonor and shame to the family name. But out of that progenitor came a son destined to become one of the greatest Methodist ministers in Australia. That convict's son and grandson and great grandson followed in a dynasty of Methodist ministers doing wonderful Christian work which has had its impact on all of Australia.

One of those sons, Alan Walker, conceived of and launched in Sydney, Australia, the world's first twenty-four-hour live telephone counseling ministries. I learned from him and was inspired to "do likewise" in America. So in 1968 we followed his example and started NEW HOPE, America's first and longest running (to this very day!) crisis intervention, suicide prevention telephone counseling programs!

Thousands of persons have been rescued from the brink of suicide these many years through our telephone ministry at the Crystal Cathedral in Garden Grove, California. Over four hundred volunteers man the telephones every minute, round the clock, to pick up the telephone that rings when a desperate soul, somewhere in America or the world, dials

5

the area code 714 and the letters N-E-W H-O-P-E. Yes, the Walker name was turned from shame to fame.

Yes, look at your family and know there is always the positive possibility of making improvements in your generation and the next. It is no disgrace to disagree and depart from your family's traditions if you can bring a brighter faith and a healthier love and a more honorable religious tradition into the bloodstream of your family. We honor the ongoing family name when we make corrections that upgrade it.

One way to upgrade and, in the process, really bring honor to your family name is by bringing positive religious practices into your home. Pray before family meals. Pray by holding hands around the table. Turn a night a week into a spiritual sharing time. For our family this was Saturday evenings. It set the stage for the entire family attending church the next day. The customs of Bible reading and prayer life must be revived to reverse the erosion of secularism.

When I had Mother Teresa as my guest on television and told her the program would be seen in her homeland, Yugoslavia, she replied, "I'm so happy!"

"Do you have a special blessing or a special prayer to all the people who are watching you and listening to you now?" I asked.

"Yes," she answered. "I would like them to bring prayer back again into their families, because love begins at home. And it begins by praying together. The family that prays together always stays together, and they stay together united in love for one another, and they never allow anything to break that unity and peace.

"It is very, very important," she continued, "that the families teach their children to pray and pray with them." She added with passion, "And we have enough reason to trust God because when we look at the cross, we understand how much Jesus loved us. It is wonderful to be able to come to Jesus! That's why God made Him—to be our bread of life, to give us life! And with His life comes new life! New energy! New peace! New joy! New everything! And I think," she added, "that's what brings glory to God, also, and it brings peace. I've seen families suffer so much, and when they've been brought to Jesus, it changes their whole lives."

Believe In The God Who Believes In You

5

7

The Pride of Belonging—Tap into It and Enjoy It!

You can be sure there were brave people in your lineage. They kept the lifeline going. You are proof of that. Did not they, a century or more ago, face uncertain seas and leave a familiar homeland, to emigrate to a foreign land? Did they face unpredictable illness? Loneliness? Did they rebound after defeat? Did they come back after loss? Search and find the positives. They are there.

Be proud that you belong to survivors. Was your great-great-grandfather a slave? He was a survivor. Be proud that you belong to such a tough and strong lineage. Whatever your race, ethnic lineage, be proud of it. It's very important!

Be proud that you are alive and belong to the living human race. Your very existence is a miracle. I can prove this to you. My father's father was almost killed a year before my father was conceived. How close I came to never being born. The same is true for every person alive on earth today.

Each person could find a parent—or grandparent or great grandparent—who survived persecution, survived the epidemic, survived the war, survived the plague, or survived the passage across dangerous seas and across violent borders. They survived for a purpose, God's purpose. *To bring you into existence.* That's exciting! *There is a divine destiny to your life.* Discover it. Be proud that God has honored you with life and a future filled with possibilities.

If your ancestors were a part of the Christian faith, then you can honor your parents by keeping this family faith alive. Stand guard against the pervasive dangers inherent in our pluralistic society, the tendency to water down your spiritual inheritance. Tolerance is important, but tolerance must not lead to intimidation to abandon the family faith.

Now, if your family was secular, nonreligious, all under the guise of being tolerant and broadminded, then here's where you can make an improvement in your family tree. You can discover, then share with your children, a positive faith in a God who gives dignity to any and every life that trusts Him.

Yes, the heartbeat of faith is in the family. I once recall a

5

young man who wanted to be a believer in God but couldn't find it in his heart to sincerely make this commitment.

"Where can I really feel the presence of God?" he asked sincerely. "I began to sense the possibility of an eternal creative God when my baby was born two months ago," he added.

"Tonight," I advised him, "when your precious baby is lying sweetly and soundly asleep in her crib, try kneeling at her bed. Try to connect with the Spirit of God at her slumbering side. For God lives in that precious life. Be sure of that."

"I've found Him!" he confessed later. "I'm ready to commit my life to the heavenly Father." He's a beautiful Christian today.

Yes, your self-esteem will be profoundly, perhaps even pervasively, shaped by your self-image. And your self-image will be shaped for better or for worse by your family history. You cannot ignore your roots. To achieve emotional well-being, deal with history, don't ignore it.

Your concept of God and your consciousness of God will unquestionably be influenced by the father-mother-family relationship. For myself, *I could never be an atheist if I wanted to be.* My childhood memories are of a father who was tender, honest, caring, sacrificial, and totally devoted to my best interests. The earliest imprints in my childhood subconscious mind are recordings of a tough but tender father, a firm but friendly father, who really loved me. Often he showed soft tears of love for me. And when that kind of a father taught me about the God who is my heavenly Father—well—my evolving faith was certainly and surely positioned for healthy development.

Four children were playing in an empty lot in New York City. "What religion are you?" one boy asked.

"I'm a Jew," one replied.

"I'm a Lutheran," another answered.

"I'm a Catholic," the third boy announced.

The fourth boy was quiet. All eyes looked at him. "Well, what are you?" the three buddies chimed in unison.

"I'm nothing."

Find your place of honor in your family's faith. If they did not embrace a religion, then you can start this noble tradition.

8

NOW, FOCUS ON HONORING YOUR FAMILY!

Yes, draw close to your family. Do welcome family invitations to parties and celebrations. By all means invest heavily in time, telephone calls, cards and dinners with parents, brothers and sisters. Again and again the honor you show to the family will come back to you. Again and again a father, mother, brother, sister, or child will help you recover your pride when you have suffered embarrassment, insult, and loss of self-respect.

Honor—what a great word. Honor your family. Draw respect from your roots. Pluck the fruit of self-esteem from the family tree.

Honor—what a challenging word. Build your family relationships and make them strong. They will rescue your wounded spirit again and again. No other relationships, save your relationship with Christ, will pay such rich dividends to your spirit.

I recall how impressed I was one day when I was with Dr. Norman Vincent Peale in his private study in New York City. It was many years ago when his book *The Power of Positive Thinking* was on the best-seller list. We were in a deep and earnest conversation when his secretary interrupted us, saying, "Excuse me, Dr. Peale, but your daughter Elizabeth is on the line."

Without a moment's hesitation, he picked up the phone. It was obvious that Elizabeth was very important to Dr. Peale. "Lizzie, how are you?" His face showed deep concern. The telephone conversation lasted for nearly fifteen minutes. All of his attention was focused on his teenage daughter on the other end of the line. He listened for a long time. Finally he spoke. "Now, Elizabeth, don't you worry. So you didn't win the election. That's no disgrace to the Peales. I know you conducted a clean, Christian campaign. Now you have a good opportunity to show everyone you know how to be a good loser. Your mother and I are proud of you, Lizzie. You're beautiful. You're the greatest. Oh, yes, and never forget—you're a Peale!"

When we honor our family, of course, we bring honor to ourselves. For we are all in the same lineage. I build self-respect when I honor my father and mother. For I rediscover who I am. And I can't love a stranger, can I?

Self-identity and self-respect are siblings:
- "I am the husband of . . ."
- "I am the wife of . . ."
- "I am the son of . . ."
- "I am the daughter of . . ."
- "I am the brother of . . ."
- "I am the sister of . . ."

Yes, we discover our identity in family relationships. And as we honor and encourage each other, the level of dignity rises. The pride of belonging expands and grows.

I am the father of five beautiful children. All are happily married. All have brought pride to our family name. I attribute that to the fact that they themselves have a healthy family pride. I attribute that to our positive faith. We started teaching our first child and each of the others in turn what a family is.

"The world is made up of nations," I taught them, "and each country has its own laws, its own cultural and behavioral and social patterns. America is the country where we belong. But America is made up of fifty states. Each state has its own laws, and many states have their own peculiar traditions and cultural reflections. We live in a state called California. California has a cultural climate different from the cultural climates of the other states. It also has some cultural values that are similar.

"California is made up of counties and towns and cities. Each town and city has its own laws. Some cities and towns have qualities and characteristics and cultural patterns quite different from other cities and towns within the same state of

California. Now, within each city and town there is a collection of families. And every family has its own laws.

"The world is made up of nations. Nations are made up of states and providences are made up of cities and towns. Cities and towns are made up of families. Now families may live on the same block, in the same city. But they may have completely different family rules and regulations. They may eat different kinds of food. They may speak different languages. They may hold to different religions.

"In the United States of America, all governments in the states and cities exercise some form of democracy. But in our family," I declared to my children, "democracy is not the form of government that will control order in this little society called the Schuller household. In our family, we have a government called a Christian monarchy. I, the father, am the king. Your mother is the queen. My son is a prince. And every daughter is a princess. You see we have some distinctive beliefs and values in our family. Learn them. Enjoy them. Treasure them and pass them on!"

Each family is unique, free to be different, a fact that must not be lost in a society that is an amalgamation of cultures, values, and belief systems. The perils of pluralism threaten every family's unique identity. The little family unit is being intimidated by the society that surrounds it.

The family coat of arms was once very important. It called to mind through a dramatic collage of symbols the history and values of this social unit. Our respect for diversity must not be allowed to subtly eliminate or neutralize the positive distinctions from our family value systems.

Self-respect, self-esteem, positive self-regard, and healthy pride is built into each human being in our growing family. It is no wonder that our family gatherings continue to be positive times of sharing. These events sustain and feed our pride as a family group. In building the dignity of one another, we become encouragers at a deep level, not a shallow level. And having been encouraged, we are truly happy. Our self-respect has been renewed.

What if you have no family? Then find a "family" and become a part of it. That's what the church offers. It was

5

Christmas morning, 1968. I had conducted Christmas Eve services the night before. The church had been filled with candles, twinkling lights, and glorious Christmas music. The next morning, my children awakened early in anticipation of the presents piled under the tree.

After the gifts were opened, I decided to return to the church. My mind and pockets were filled with little notes that people had given me at the Christmas Eve services only hours before. I wanted to organize them before I forgot some promise that I had made. Sheila, my teenage daughter, the oldest of the family, agreed to ride with me so that I wouldn't have to drive to my church office alone.

The church was abandoned. There was only one lonely car parked in a corner of the parking lot. As Sheila and I approached the Tower where my office is located we noticed a petite young girl, huddled against the doors, almost asleep on her feet with her head hugging a pillow.

"Hello," I said, tapping her on the shoulder.

She opened her eyes. "Can I help you?" I asked.

Her eyes filled with tears. Her narrow shoulders trembled. "I spent the night in my car," she answered.

It was pathetic to think that this poor young girl slept alone in her car on Christmas Eve. "Where are you sleeping tonight?" I asked her.

"I don't know."

So Sheila invited her to come and share a room at our house. She accepted and remained as our house guest for quite a bit of time. During that time she was exposed to our faith. Then we began to encourage her, "You can go back to school, you can go to college, become anything you want to be! Just let God take control of your life. He believes in you. So do we."

Well, she joined my church and discovered the pride of belonging to a community of caring persons that brought honor into her life. Her shattered self-esteem was repaired. She went back to college. She is today a very, very successful C.P.A.

Jesus said, "I've come to seek and to save that which was lost." Do you know what a lost soul is? A lost soul is a person who really doesn't know where he belongs. That's being lost. The umbilical cord of self-esteem is severed. An emptiness haunts the hollow cavities of the heart. And where there's a vacuum, boredom, frustration, anger, or depression will move in. This vacuum, you can be sure, will be filled with something—drugs, alcohol, sexual promiscuity. Something negative! Unless it is first filled with positive love, hope, and faith.

9

BONDING WITHOUT BONDAGE—
GO FOR IT!

Now, whatever your family background is, build your own family into a social unit where positive thinking, positive talking, positive laughing, positive praying, and positive disagreeing take place. What cannot be tolerated is insulting, demeaning, negative put-downs. In my thirty-eight years of marriage, *not once* did any member of my family *intentionally* ridicule, humiliate, or fail to show respect to each other.

Intense disagreements, yes! Positive, respectful disagreement can actually build pride into the family. A family in which verbal attacks are insultingly hurled between members is certain to spread an infectious sickness in this little community, a serious epidemic of poisoned self-esteem.

Families in which sharp and serious differences of opinion exist only to be "swept under the rug" with false smiles will only violate the dignity of the individual members. Children raised in such an environment will tend to be easily intimidated, pitifully nonaggressive, and quickly manipulated. Strong self-esteem development may be retarded.

The fact is that debates can be very constructive in the development of family pride if the disagreements are aired with respect.

Even heated debates can enhance our self-esteem and self-worth if the communication is respectful, open, and honest.

Can you hear yourself say this? "I'm proud of the fact that I spoke up. And I'm proud of the fact that I did it with such dignity—in such a sensitive way—in such a quiet manner— in such a private place."

Tap Into The Power Of Your Roots

The fact that you're not compatible at times doesn't mean you have to be combatible.

Failure to speak up, politely disagree, respectfully debate may do great damage to one's self-respect. "I'm ashamed of the fact that I just sat there and didn't say anything!"

The point is that pride is possible only when *respect* is operating in the relationships.

Families: Bonded? Broken? Or Blended? Whatever happens, maintain respect at all times. How do you tap into the power of your roots *when the bough breaks*?

Divorce.

Where does the child belong?

With Mom? With Dad? With Grandma? Grandpa?

A famous American psychologist, who has counseled couples going through divorce, once told me that when children are involved, both the husband and the wife are strongly told never to make negative statements about the ex-spouse in the presence of the children.

She repeated to me the story of a husband who came to see her after his first wife chose to walk away from the marriage. There were two children from that marriage. It was the most painful experience the family ever went through. Added to the immense emotional pain was the unhappiness that the divorce did not bring pride to the family, but instead brought embarrassment and shame.

The two beautiful children continued to visit their grandparents often. Intuitively, the grandparents knew that they must never make a statement that could be construed as negative about the children's mother. This was terribly important. For as we noted earlier, a child's evolving sense of self-esteem cannot be separated from his self-image and that is, like it or not, connected to his impressions of his parents.

As the doctor said, "If they had told their grandchildren, 'Your mother has done some bad things,' They would probably think that they have a bad mother. And on a subconscious or perhaps a conscious level, their minds would say, 'If I have a bad mother and I am her child, that makes me bad, too.' Thank heaven these grandparents wisely watched their words!"

5

When real trouble hits the family, then the family pulls together. All families can expect trouble, even tragedy, and when that happens, each one comes to the rescue! That's bonding without bondage! That's what "honor your father and your mother" adds up to.

I was in Korea with my wife when the telephone call came: "Your daughter Carol was on a motorcycle. They're amputating her leg. She has lost seventeen pints of blood. They have saved her life—but. . . ." The words trailed off. I was faint.

"Call her brother and sisters," I said. "Her brother Bob is in London; her older sister, Jeanne, is in college in Chicago. Her oldest sister, Sheila, is at home in California. Try to reach them."

It was twenty-four hours before my wife and I could be at her bedside. But already gathered there in Sioux City, Iowa, were her two older sisters. My wife and I were never more honored than when we found they had rushed to comfort their sister in great pain.

Bonding—beautiful! It sets a positive, pride-producing cycle in motion.

The mother of the late Len Bias knows all about that. Trouble struck her family in a big way when her son Len suddenly died of a drug overdose only days after he'd been picked to play high-priced professional basketball.

Can you imagine the possible self-recriminating thoughts a mother could feel if her child is accused of being involved with narcotics? Or, if her son who is supposed to be one of the greatest superstars ready to earn millions of dollars suddenly lies dead from cocaine? "So many of our problems exist because children feel they are not loved," she says. "You have to hug and love these babies like they are infants! And believe me, they eat it up. They need it every day. The worst form of abuse is letting a child go to school every day feeling that they are not loved. Your kids are walking around smiling in your face, but they are hurting. I tell parents to turn off the TV, turn off the radio, go into their room, and find out what they are all about."

Tap Into The Power Of Your Roots

5

After the tragedy of her son's death, she decided literally to turn her scars into stars. She threw herself upon her faith in God to seek strength and guidance. This wonderful mother quit her bank job and has no doubt at all that God is directing her to turn this tragedy into a triumph for others. To high schools and colleges across the country she brings her messages of hope, love, and joy. It is always the same: "Life is what you make of it. You have a commitment and you can't give up. *You are somebody! You must love yourself!* It's not going to be a cakewalk, but you can't give up. You can make it. Life does not serve you beautiful pieces of cake all the time. But that's life. So *know who you are.* Someone says, 'Hey, you think you're too good.' You say, 'You're right, I am too good!' and walk off. Everyone who laughs and grins in your face is not your friend.

"When things get tough, the family pulls together", she declares adding, "This is the real world, and it gets tougher. *Tough is having to bury your baby on national TV. If you don't know who you are, you'll be swept away.* To our knowledge, Len never used drugs. His closest friends said he never used drugs. Apparently he unknowingly drank something that was spiked with a drug. When I got the call that he had some problem and was sent to the hospital, I figured I would get there and look in his eyes and say, 'Son, how are you feeling? What happened?' When I got there he was already dead.

"Treat your students," she tells teachers, "with love as if you will never see them again."

To the children she says, "There is nothing wrong with going to your parents and hugging them. You know, your mom and dad need a hug, too."

Yes, the mother of Len Bias is *proud* of the way all three of her children handled their grief and loss in the face of the painful, but inevitable taunts. Harsh words were thrown at them. Their dead brother was called a dope addict. They were accused of being drug users as well. Meanwhile the brother, Jay, continued to play ball in the same gym where Len had made his mark.

One day he found a note taped to his locker. It said, "What did Len Bias and plants have in common? They both die three days after being picked."

5

Jay could have reacted in horror and said, "The world is terrible! I don't want to have anything to do with it."

But instead, he went on to the state championships, scoring forty-nine points in thirty rebounds in two games.

Where does the Bias family find this inexplicable strength to live through and beyond such a horrific tragedy? Their strength comes from a deep religious faith. Many people think that Mrs. Bias is home counting the millions. She says, "Mrs. Bias is counting nothing. My son is gone. I only care about God, my family, and the rest of the poor kids who are out there in trouble.

"Though it is my belief that God took one man to save millions," she says, "Len Bias has done more in death than he could have done in life. *You have no control over when you are born or when you die. What you have control over is the dash in between. That's your life.*"

Do you see how everything we have been trying to teach in this book works in the true story just told? A cruel world delivers taunts, insults, and threats to self-respect and self-esteem.

Where is the hope for dignity in life's disasters?

How can we live above humiliating insults hurled by an uncaring world?

God's prescription is a

> **God's prescription is a positive family that is the emotional fortress where every person's honor is treasured.**

positive family that is the emotional fortress where every person's honor is treasured. There we will learn to honor ourselves as members of a proud family and go on to build an ongoing self-respect. We turn our hurts into halos and use our grief to bring relief to others. "Honor your father and your mother"—this is where it starts, in a family blended

*Taken from the *Honolulu Advertiser,* Wednesday, May 20, 1987 [C 5].

and bonded together to share and spare each member's honor. Bonding without bondage!

The family can be your best fortress against stress. In such an emotionally healthy environment, you might even live to be one hundred. This command is meant to hold out that possibility. "Honor thy father and mother *that thy days may be long . . .*"

Go for it!

CHAPTER 6

LIVE! LOVE! AND LIFT— YOURSELF— AND OTHERS!

"THOU SHALT NOT KILL"

6

*S*ome men die in shrapnel,
  Some men die in flames,
Most men perish inch by inch,
Playing at little games.
  Yes, we all die.
  By disaster or disease.
  By guns or germs.
  By crashes or cancer.
  Some die by growing old.
  Too many others die by pathetically losing the will to live.
  Only a very, very few will be murdered.
  Few, if any, readers of this line need to be told it is a sin to
  • press the trigger
  • plunge the knife
  • explode the terrorist grenade
  • draw blood
  • or practice birth control by casual abortions.
  Surely this is a *command meant* to shield us from shame
and, more positively, lead us to a life crowned with glory
and honor. "He has made us just a little lower than the
angels and has crowned us with glory and honor."
  This word is a *command meant* to motivate us to discover
the glory, the honor, the pride of loving and lifting people
from despair to hope. Then discover the joy of the
overflowing heart and overflowing eye.

  How does the sixth commandment get broken? How do
we violate the deeper pride-producing principle hidden here?
  Yes, the drunken driver kills. So does the raving maniac,
the wild-eyed extremist, the reckless patriot marching under
the banner of bigotry and dogmatic ideology.
  But how about the rest of us who simply let people die?

  G. Studdert Kennedy has lines that are most moving:
  When Jesus came to Golgotha,
  They nailed Him to a tree.

6

They drove great nails through hands and feet
And made a Calvary.

They crowned Him with a crown of thorns;
Red were His wounds and deep,
For those were crude and cruel days,
And human flesh was cheap.

When Jesus came to Birmingham
We simply passed Him by.
We never hurt a hair of Him,
We simply let Him die. . . .

How then are we to fulfill this commandment? Simply by
never murdering, killing, terminating, or aborting life?
   Hardly.
   We can't get by that easily.
   Let me explain.
   My father was an Iowa farmer. When all of the fields were
cleared of weeds and the broken black earth was raked clean,
it looked as if a massive dark blanket had been rolled out.
No weeds. Clean. Clear. A perfect field? Not quite. A symbol
of a sinless, holy life? Not so. It is not a "good field" until it
produces fruit or wheat, food or fuel to sustain life.

   So the fulfillment of this command will lead us to
excitement and enthusiasm. Respect life! Reverence life!
Restore life! Revive life! Release life! That's the power-packed,
pride-releasing possibility this command offers to us all!
Now, how do we get started on this perfect path to positive,
proper pride?
   God, the Creator, wants us to be His creative partners in
the excitement of generating life where there is no life!
   God's in the life, not death, business! He wants, He needs
our full and enthusiastic participation.
   How can this work out? In real life? Here's how.

6

1. Reverence life! Catch the beautiful spirit!

This is the first step to unlocking the treasure this command is meant to deliver.

Plants, insects, "all creatures, great and small" are interdependent—balancing each other in an ecological phenomenon!

"You shall not murder" is a beautiful sentence. It reminds you and me that God looks upon all of life on this planet as something with infinite potential. Over twenty years ago, I coined this line: "Any fool can count the seeds in an apple, but only God can count all of the apples in one seed." *God values the life potential in each life and in each seed.* That's why I say, "Give me one fertile seed and I will give you a garden, an orchard, an industry, or a family." If you can't plant a garden, be one. Your heart can be the soil; Christ's love, the flower; His spirit, the fragrance.

> **God values the potential in each life and in each seed.**

I will always remember Asa Skinner. He was a member of my first church in Chicago, Illinois. He was a fine executive who was always active. He underwent brain surgery for a tumor, and I wondered how he'd be able to tolerate the long recovery period at home. I called on him shortly after he was dismissed from the hospital. His wife met me at the door. "How is Asa doing?"

"Oh, very good," she replied.

"How are his spirits?"

She answered, "They're fantastic. Follow me, you'll see why."

I found him in his tiny backyard, sitting in a chair with his bathrobe on and his head bandaged in white. As I approached him, I noticed that he was looking at the ground with binoculars. When he saw me, he said, "Oh, Bob, look

6

at them!" He was watching the ants building a home and transporting material. "I've been noticing the wasps. Look at the nest they built." Then he pointed to a tree in the far distance. "See, in that tree a robin is building a nest.

"The ants, the wasps, the robin. This world is throbbing with life, and all of life is so beautiful. It's a pity that a single insect has to die." He spoke with real enthusiasm.

The real issue is; Is all life equally sacred or is some life more sacred than others? In Christianity and in Judaism, we have great reverence for all life, but human life is the highest form that we revere. Hence in Judaic-Christian culture, we say the question frequently is not whether or not it's right to kill. The real question is, What life form should be given the privilege and the priority to live? I could not agree with Hindus in India who allowed human beings to die of starvation while they allowed the rats to live on grain that had been imported and held at the docks. In their religion, no animal, not even a rat, may be killed, even though it consumes the limited food necessary for the survival of human beings.

I have never, thank God, had to kill a human being. And only once in my life did I kill an animal. I remember it well. My mother would not allow guns in our Iowa farmhouse. However, the neighborhood boys had a gun, and one day they invited me to go hunting. I saw a rabbit, and I took a shot at it. I watched as it hit the ground, first kicking and then dying. I ran over and picked up the soft, warm, dead body. We did not need it for food. It was pure sport. It made me ill. I've never been able to go hunting since then.

What if a rapist came into my home with a knife to attack me and to kill my wife and daughters and the only way for me to stop him would be to kill him? I would have to make an impulsive, instinctive, intuitive, immediate judgment. The question is not, Is it right or wrong for one person to die at the hands of another? The right question is, Whom should I allow the privilege to continue to live? The rapist? Or my wife?

6

2. Respect life—your life! Reward yourself—with a high value on your own life.

"You shall not murder." It means *don't destroy your own life or anyone else's.*

Don't undervalue your own self. Many people do. That's why we say the bottom line of all healthy theology comes back to a theology of self-esteem.

When we lose our self-esteem, we lose the ability to be possibility thinkers. When we cannot cope, we lose hope. When we lose hope, the will to die takes over, and we'll want to die.

Even if we don't attempt suicide, we may self-destruct through a degenerate lifestyle. We all know that the alcoholic is really trying to destroy himself because he can't cope. The people who seek relief with chemical addictions are really choosing a lifestyle that's self-destructive. They kill themselves by killing their awareness of the world around them.

"Thou shalt not kill" has a powerful, positive, provocative meaning.

• **Don't undervalue yourself.**

• **Upgrade the potential worth of your own life.**

• **Give yourself credit for being intelligent, creative, inventive.**

• **Exercise your freedom to dream dreams, set goals, and make commitments.**

Yes, you have the potential to handle difficulties you may face in relationships, marriage, business, school, or even in your own health. Even if the doctor says it's terminal, that does not necessarily mean you will die. It won't kill you until you give up. It doesn't give you the right to quit fighting to live!

6

Value yourself and your life highly. This isn't as self-centered as it may seem. For when you value yourself, you will, in turn, value others. We project our own values onto other persons. A person who treats himself shabbily will treat others shabbily too.

All of life is to be valued most highly. In Christian morality, can war ever be justified unless it is an absolute last resort to keep good, innocent people from being shot down and destroyed? I think not! That's why we call our military forces "Peace Forces." The positive interpretation of this commandment is to preserve life at every level.

Many times as a pastor I have had to deal with women who came to me for counseling after they had chosen abortion as a solution to a problem. There are strong arguments on both sides of this issue, but no one will disagree that abortion is almost always a negative, unpleasant, and regrettable option. We must ask, is this the most positive solution to the problem?

Value yourself and your life highly. For when you value yourself, you will, in turn, value others.

"You shall not murder." Somehow we have to learn that there is always a positive solution and a negative solution to every problem. And somehow we have to learn how always to choose the positive above the negative.

3. Revive life—deal with anger positively.

Yes, immense anger is loose in the world today, and Jesus interpreted this sixth command with the teaching, "Whoever is angry without a cause commits murder in his heart."

Anger—what is it really, this strong surge of a sometimes

6

silent, sometimes shouting emotion that generates such an incredible force in mood, mind, manner, mouth, and muscle?

Anger—what is this passion that powerfully transforms weak nations, quiet persons into marching, shouting, screaming waves of meat, hair, bones, and blood?

Understand the roots of anger, yours and everybody's. Any analysis of this strong emotion that fails to probe and observe the source and the force behind all anger will be too shallow.

No one really becomes angry unless somehow, some way, sometime at some level, conscious or subconscious, human dignity is violated. Righteous wrath caused Christ to drive the money changers out of the temple. Why? He saw religious authorities using their pious power and position to demean sincere but sinful souls who were seeking rescue from their shame. In that day, the Hebrews sought salvation through the sacrifice of an innocent animal—a lamb or a bird. The priests of the temple arranged for merchants to sell these animals to the contrite worshipers. In this way the hypocritical priests were able to manipulate guilty souls by manufacturing a sense of guilt and then monopolizing a market that offered relief from their shame. Could *anything* be more offensive to a person's dignity than that?

Anger is human dignity violated.

Few persons have contributed more to an understanding of the roots and fruits of anger than psychiatrist Dr. Gerald Jampolsky. He saw—and sees—anger as an expression of fear. He came upon this revelation when, as a young psychiatric intern, he was called to an emergency in a ward of the mental hospital. "There's a raving, naked maniac in there," the nurses reported.

Through the small, thick glass window the inexperienced doctor could see the madman wielding a weapon, a part of the wooden molding ripped off a door frame, nails

6

protruding like teeth. "You have to go in there, Doctor," the orderly ordered.

Cautiously, fearfully, the intern opened the door just enough to call out, "Hello! I'm Dr. Jampolsky. I have to come in here to help you."

Then came the brilliant insight, honestly and beautifully spoken: "Are you" Dr. Jampolsky said, quivering with fright, "are you by any chance afraid . . . like I am?"

Suddenly the patient's demeanor was transformed. He looked. He heard. He trembled. He cried. He dropped his weapon. And Dr. Jampolsky walked in. He hugged the frightened man, and healing began.

At a very deep level, fear is the taproot of anger. "Perfect love casts out fear."

"So the opposite of love is not hate. The opposite of love is fear." Face, then, the angry person with this insight and this disarming question, "What are you afraid of?"

Assume that the angry are basically decent persons and not sadistic psychopaths who find pleasure in inflicting pain. "How can I help you?" is a question that reflects respect and can be amazingly effective in turning an angry person into a friend.

This then is a *command meant* to inspire us to respect persons by giving them life free from anger that can kill so much, in so many persons, in many ways.

Withhold respect or insult someone's pride, and you run the risk of causing anger that can kill.

So Jesus issued one of His greatest warnings against anger in the sentence "Whoever says to a person, 'You fool!' will be in danger of hell fire."

What does that mean? That means you really destroy people when you insult them, demean them, strip them of their dignity, embarrass them, shame them, and leave them humiliated. A positive fulfillment of this commandment is never to go to a person and say, "You fool," but rather go to people and tell them how great they really can become if they will only let God's love flow through their lives. This is Christ's answer. It is His way of saying that the fulfillment of this commandment is the development of self-respect in people.

6

4. Restore life! Begin by practicing forgiveness. This miracle power will always work wonders!

Of all the messages I have ever delivered, no single sermon drew more positive reactions than the one with this long title: "I Never Knew How Heavy My Luggage Was Until I Stopped Carrying It." I have always been greeted at gateways at world airports by someone who would invariably reach out for my hand-carried luggage, offering, "Let me take your bags."

I always resisted the gracious offer. I'm not sure why. Then one day I surprised myself by saying, "Thanks!" And I handed the garment bag and valise over. I was suddenly free to shake hands, to respond positively to requests for a prayer, and even to reach out with a hug to a friendly stranger. Freedom!

What heavy luggage have you been carrying too long? And at what price?

> **Old sorrows?**
> It's time to bury the dead.
> **Old sins?**
> It's time to accept Christ's forgiveness.
> **Old setbacks?**
> It's time to believe in beginning again.
> **Old insults?**
> It's time to let the past be the past.
> **Old hurts? Angers?**
> It's time to accept the spirit of
> forgiveness.

Let God exercise justice: "Vengeance is mine. I will repay," says the Lord.

You'll love yourself more (and properly so) when you give and receive forgiveness.

It takes more inner strength to forgive than it does to inflict revenge. And remember, God has declared that justice is His right to exercise. Forgiveness, on the other hand, need

6

not imply compromise with wrongdoing. Only the strong, self-assured, self-confident will have the inner power and patience to become "peacemakers." Ghandhi, Dr. Martin Luther King, Jr., the proponents of nonviolence, understood that.

Discover the pride of becoming a peacemaker. Now, quite possibly, you can build a bridge of communication with the enemy. Together conflict resolutions can begin.

The killing has to stop with someone leading the way.

Ego power becomes eagle power when it lifts us above the levels of those who do damage to our dignity.

Someone must be bold enough, be big enough, and rise high enough to put an end to war. Why not you? Discover the pride of being a peacemaker!

> You shall be called the Repairer of the Breach,
> The Restorer of Streets to Dwell In.
>
> (Isa. 58:12)

Does this mean you'll have the world hurling honors and thrusting awards your way?

Possibly.

Probably not.

Peacemaking is dangerous business. But the reward—your rising, soaring self-respect—will be worth the risk.

"Blessed are the peacemakers, *for they shall be called the children of God.*"

How's that for an honor? Try topping that accolade!

5. Release life when it is imprisoned.

How many lives are oppressed by social or self-inflicted negative forces. Liberate persons to come alive with hope.

The real killer today is low self-esteem, no doubt about it. We will never effectively battle social injustice unless we begin by building self-esteem in persons.

Live! Love! And Lift—Yourself—And Others!

6

This destructive force of low self-respect happens to groups of people as well as persons. You can see the desperation generated when dignity has been violated in the red face of the revolutionary demanding freedom. Oppressed people yearning for freedom will find their repressed honor turning to righteous rage. This energy that churns in persons who are victims of injustice is the passion for liberty. And this passion for liberty is the cry and call to be treated with respect.

Every person's inalienable right to be free is justified by his humanity, a high and holy privilege to enjoy the dignity that is their divine birthright.

The "have-nots" of this world are made up of two kinds of persons, those with such low self-esteem that they cannot imagine survival short of plunder and violence and those with enough self-esteem to believe that somehow, somewhere, some way they can make it to freedom from social, political, or economic oppression.

How can we positively confront social and political injustice in the world? By building pride in persons!

You probably know who Wally Amos is through his delicious Famous Amos chocolate chip cookies. Wally was born in Tallahassee, Florida. His mother was a domestic worker. His father was a common laborer at the local gas plant. Neither parent was able to read or write. He grew up in poverty. And he was black.

When Wally was twelve, his parents divorced. He moved to New York City to live with his Aunt Della. His aunt, her husband, and their son lived in a little one-bedroom apartment. Aunt Della shared her living room with Wally as well as her love and her recipe for chocolate chip cookies.

How easy it would have been for Wally to have allowed himself to become imprisoned by negative thoughts. How easy it would have been for him to have become swallowed up by the anger that understandably raged in the inner city. But Wally was determined to make something of himself. After various pursuits, including a stint in the Air Force, Wally found himself on a corner in Hollywood on Sunset

6

Boulevard, selling his Aunt Della's chocolate chip cookies.

Wally describes the idea this way: "I had the idea of a product that was so basic and so simple that many people said, 'You can't do that.' Since no one else had done it, I figured it was time for *me* to do it! I had a tremendous faith, a very strong belief in myself, and I made a commitment. I declared, 'I'm *going to open this door* selling chocolate chip cookies.' I didn't say, 'I guess' or 'I hope' or 'I'll try.' I said, 'I *will!*'"

Five months later, Wally did it. He raised $25 thousand initially to open that first store. He formed a corporation. He shared his vision with some friends who invested in him and his dream. I asked Wally how he did it, how he got so many people to support him and his wild dream.

"I was so excited," he said, "and so enthusiastic that others said, 'Let me do this for you. Let me help you.'"

"Wally," I asked, "what do you say to all the people who don't have this vision, who don't have this enthusiasm?"

"Well, I say to them, *get it!* Life begins and ends with the individual. We're not victims. It has been an evolution for me. It has been a process for me, because growing up in Tallahassee I didn't have it. I had what we called an inferiority complex. Now we call it low self-esteem. But, I began to think and observe the aspects of my personality that I could be proud of."

Wally did it! He learned that he could be proud of himself. He was successful. He received the Horatio Algier award and the Presidential Citation for entrepreneurial excellence. And the shirt and hat he wore for the picture on his cookie package have been immortalized in the Smithsonian.

Wally has done something remarkable. He has looked at himself from a positive perspective. He didn't ask, "What's *wrong* with me?" He asked, *"What's right with me?"*

Wally serves today as a spokesman for the Literacy Volunteers for America. He is busy serving the large population of our society, the twenty-seven million adults who cannot read or write. He is sharing the gift of literacy, he is helping people to live by releasing them from their prison of illiteracy, and it all began when he released his own gifts through possibility thinking.

6

6. Revitalize life! Restore life! Revive life! by respecting people as persons!

"All that is necessary for evil to conquer is for good men to do nothing." Let's extend that thought: "All that is necessary for killings to spread is for nice people to ignore persons who are hungry for attention, recognition, and respect. All that is necessary for suicides to become epidemic is for fine folks to be too busy to look, see, hear, listen, touch, and feel!"

So what do we do when we reject people? Or neglect people? Or fail to respect people? Or miss opportunities to inspire and encourage them to dream great dreams? Or fail to affirm their value and worth as persons? What are we doing to people when we insult, embarrass, humiliate, taunt, or simply snub them? What damage do we do when we withhold respect? Do we let their life's potential die while we let them alone, uninspired to "play little games"? Do we ' leave them vulnerable to stress that will move in and kill in many ways? Yes.

Stress, the big killer, moves in and takes over when the preventative shield of life-giving enthusiasm has never been injected into the emotional system. So the silent killers today are sometimes such seemingly decent folks: teachers, preachers, doctors, parents, managers, theologians, educators, peers who fail to motivate, inspire, and enthuse.

7. Respect people and Rescue life!

The savage lurks just beneath the civilized skins of those persons who are pushed, shoved, ridiculed, taunted, demeaned, dishonored, disgraced, and dehumanized by an uncaring world. You can feel the tension at any level—high and mighty or low and outcast. You can feel it in the penthouses and in the poverty pockets.

"I am a human being! Treat me with respect!" is the tortured, sometimes wimpering or screaming cry from painfully insulted human beings.

Does society realize what it is doing when it ridicules persons, however sophisticated the style of the

6

insult may be? Do we know what we are doing to persons when we fail to show them real respect regardless of their rank or station?

Do we have any consciousness of what this is doing to those of us who are inflicting the indignities? Shame begets shame. Honor begets honor.

Where there's life, there's hope.

Where there's life, there's hope. And the opposite is also true: where hope is lost, the will to die takes over. So we fulfill this sixth commandment and reap the pleasant and proud fruit of beautiful self-esteem when we respect, protect, and revive life by being messengers and generators of hope.

8. Revive life! Spread joy! Share humor!

How dramatically this came back to me as I reread from the lengthy, private personal interchange between myself and Mother Teresa. Here is the transcript from my interview with one of Christianity's greatest living saints:

RS: I am a compulsive, joyful person because of Christ within me. And I almost feel guilty smiling when I talk to you.

Mother Teresa: Keep on smiling always! Keep on smiling because smiling is the beginning of peace.

RS: Is it true that the capacity for joy is one of the requirements you ask from your missionaries?

Mother Teresa: Yes. And I have a number of the sisters who have not been able to smile with the people and be a cause of joy to the people. They found out that this is not their vocation, and they have gone back home. The missionaries who smile and express joy do great work.

6

RS: How can you keep smiling when you've seen so much suffering, so much poverty, so much dying, and so much death?

Mother Teresa: All people need smiles! Joy is the best medicine for them. When you come to them in their sorrow and their suffering and their pain and you really make them feel happy, love brings new life in their life.

RS: Do you call this the joy of Christ alive, resurrected in us?

Mother Teresa: Yes, exactly.

RS: Through His Holy Spirit?

Mother Teresa: Sharing the joy of loving!

So positive thinking revives life. And negative thinking kills first faith, then hope, then love, then joy. So we will not begin to keep this sixth commandment until frowns, scowls, cynical sarcasm, and angry countenances give way to a positive spirit. Many a devout, orthodox, disciplined, scholarly, stern, fundamentalist, and liberal Christian must learn a terribly basic and profound lesson here, from Mother Teresa, from Jesus Christ! Failure to project joy is failure to release, revive, and restore life!

> # Failure to project joy is failure to release, revive, and restore life!

Only hours before His crucifixion, Christ prayed, "Father, I pray that the joy that is in Me may be in [the disciples]."

Science is increasingly confirming that positive emotion is a life-giving force. Negative emotion is a killer. Norman Cousins' landmark work taught us that humor can heal. "If negative emotions kill—and that is well established—and despair leads to death, then should not positive emotions do just the opposite?" Cousins reasoned. So when faced with what was seemingly an incurable illness he gave himself prolonged "laughter therapy."

And the results were remarkable. Following up on that observation, doctors have now proven that the brain is a gland that, like all glands, secretes chemicals under the stimulation of thoughts. This is understood by the person who breaks into a sweat under fear or anxiety. The chemicals released by the brain under positive thinking stimulation are called endorphins.

More than forty different endorphins have been chemically identified and labeled. So I want to shout to my colleagues who claim to be in Christian work, "Get with it!" It's not silly or shallow, but lifesaving to spread this joyous message: "Don't worry! Be happy!" The Bible taught this years ago: "A merry heart does good, like medicine" (Prov. 17:22).

Keep thinking positively, and you'll develop a personality that can restore life. This is the real secret behind the greatness that the world recognizes in Mother Teresa. Let us go back to the interview:

RS: Mother Teresa, you are viewed by so many people as a saint, so I have to ask you this question: Do you ever struggle against sin?

Mother Teresa: Of course. That's why I need confession, also.

RS: Do you ever become afraid?

Mother Teresa: Afraid? No. Because I know God's great mercy.

RS: Do you ever worry?

Mother Teresa: I don't worry because He's there to love me. He loves me.

RS: Do you ever cry?

Mother Teresa: Not lately, I don't [Laughing]. I've no reason to cry. Only I've often cried when I've seen the mother and the child suffering. That I can't accept.

RS: Do you laugh a lot?

Mother Teresa: Lots, plenty.

Live! Love! And Lift—Yourself—And Others!

6

Christ prayed, "Father, I pray that the joy that is in Me may be in [the disciples]."

RS: You have a good sense of humor.

Mother Teresa: Yes, thank God.

RS: Where will you be buried?

Mother Teresa: I don't know. Whatever happens or whenever Jesus comes to take me [Laughing].

RS: That's great! Do you have any regrets?

Mother Teresa: Nothing. If I had to begin again, I would do the same thing.

RS: You walk in the will of God—that's your purpose?

Mother Teresa: Live for Jesus!

Yes, Mother Teresa lives! She smiles. Laughs. She radiates joy. And at the age of seventy-eight walks off briskly, almost running. She is *full of life*!

9. Love—the Big Lifesaver! Savor it, and share it!

Of course! And this can be your purpose in living, too.
Enjoy the humble, holy pride of being a life giver, life rescuer, life reviver, life restorer, life releaser.
This goal raises some important questions.

1. Q: How do you bring life to people?
A: Give them love! This commandment is ultimately fulfilled with the eleventh commandment, "Love the Lord, your God, and your neighbor as yourself."

6

We can either take life away from people, or we can awaken life within people. A ministry of love! A ministry of hope! A ministry of faith! This builds up self-esteem in others and in yourself. And hope is born.

If you never terminate another life, does that mean that you'll feel good about yourself? Not until you build hope and build life.

So we look for the best in persons and believe the best about people. That is respecting people as persons created in the image of God. We believe that there is some possibility of goodness in every person. We must believe that and never underestimate the power of salvation and redemption.

2. Q: Do I have the freedom to choose to do anything I want to do with my life?

A: Not really.

My freedom must be compromised if my actions will contribute to the lowering of social self-esteem. So my freedom must be considerate of the sensitivities of the society where I live. To do less is to be disrespectful of the community.

I still am shocked recalling the time I was in the Hilton Hotel in Washington, D.C. A bellhop pointed out a room that had been totally sprayed with broken glass— everywhere. I was so depressed. Why? I wondered. It wasn't my doing. It was no expense to me. I analyzed the depression as an expression of inner shame. But why should I be ashamed when I didn't do it? Then the insight came clearly. I was ashamed because I knew this was done by one of my relatives. Yes, it was done by a human being, not by apes or dogs or animals. And every human being is a distant relative of mine. And by despicable behavior, some fellow human being had just contributed to the lowering of my self-esteem!

6

TO LOVE IS TO LIFT.

TO LIFT IS TO MAKE A GIFT—

OF LIFE!

3. Q: How do you deal with injustice, with evil, without losing your self-respect in a silence that appears to condone sin? Or at the other extreme: a destructive reaction of violence—verbal, emotional, or physical—that will leave deeper shame behind?

A: My answer to that is framed beautifully in the life and ministry of the Nobel Peace Prize winner, Mother Teresa.

I will never forget when I first visited the teaming city of Calcutta. I was there to meet that tiny little woman with an enormous heart. She walked the streets of Calcutta looking for the dying. There were many, far too many, who fit the bill. She built a home for these souls on the brink of death and called it Home for the Dying.

When I met this beautiful soul, this Mother Teresa, I took her gnarled hands in mine. Hers had gently closed the lids of hundreds, thousands, of eyes that no longer could see the light of day. She said, "Everyone has the right to die in dignity!"

Everyone has the right to die in dignity! How right she was. (That's the horrible thing about murder—it is so utterly degrading, to both the victim and the perpetrator!) So she gathered the dying from the streets, gave them beds, and *loved* them! She sang to them, touched them, let them know that someone cared.

The amazing, totally surprising thing is that when these people were loved, many of them stopped dying. The home of the dying has become the home of the living because it is a home of the loving.

The commandment "You shall not murder" has often been interpreted from the point of view that we are not to take life from people. Such an interpretation falls short of what God intended when He gave us this commandment. This commandment really means *You shall bring life!*

And you'll never be ashamed of who you are.

This is Mother Teresa's message. To complete this chapter

LIVE! LOVE! LIFT!—
YOURSELF AND OTHERS!
SHOW LOVE, AND
SHARE LIFE.

6

for this book, I went to meet Mother Teresa in Tijuana, Mexico. I asked her several questions.

RS: You probably won't remember this, but many years ago you sent me a postcard that you had written in your own hand. You wrote, "I am trying to save people dying from physical starvation. You, too, are saving people from emotional starvation. In Calcutta, people are starving physically. In America, people are starving emotionally." Does it make a difference how a person dies—if he dies from physical starvation or emotional starvation?

Mother Teresa: Oh, yes! It's terrible to die from the effects of physical starvation. But worse is the hunger to be something to somebody. When I find a person starving for food in Africa or in India, I can simply take him to my home and give him something to eat. I have removed that immediate difficulty. And if I keep him with me longer and put him on his feet, then my work is finished.

But to a person who is lonely, unwanted, and uncared for and left alone, there's a terrible bitterness that comes in and even closes the heart to anybody and anything.

I will never forget one day when I met a man in the street in London. He looked so terrible. I went to him and I took his hand and the hand I held was very warm. Then he said, "Oh, for a long, long time I craved the warmth of a human hand."

Then he sat up and he gave me such a beautiful smile! I reached out again, and then that old bitterness took hold of him again. It was so sad.

My sisters and I often go to clean a house where lonely people live. Once I saw in such a place a big lamp. I said, "Don't you light this lamp?"

He said, "For whom? For years, nobody has come."

I said, "If you'll light the lamp, we'll send a Sister." He said, "Yes."

So a Sister came, and the light was lit. Then, after two years he sent me word, "My friend, the light you have lit in my life is still burning!"

That is what people are hungry for. Love.

6

RS: If love makes people feel so good, why don't people rush to love?

Mother Teresa: Because they are preoccupied with other things. They can only love one thing at a time.

RS: Mother Teresa, the heart of my theology is dignity, self-esteem, and that's what attracted me to lots of the writings of the Holy Father and yourself. You have tried to put dignity in dying.

Mother Teresa: Yes.

RS: How do you do that? By showing love?

Mother Teresa: Yes. Nobody is taking them—like I picked a man from the drain. Then I brought him to our home full of worms, full of death, and finally he says, I've lived like an animal in the street, but I'm going to die like an angel, not dead cattle. And he died with a big smile on his face.

It took three hours to clean him, to take off all the worms. But he died with a beautiful smile because he felt love, prayer, and at peace with God. But there was no bitterness, no anger, no nothing—so happy to die.

RS: He died with great dignity! How do you put dignity in the living *to keep them alive*?

Mother Teresa: I feed my people. When I pick them up from the street, it only takes two fish. Then, when they are strong, I will hand them over to you. You can teach them how to hold their rod and catch their fish. And they never ask for another fish.

RS: [I am quiet. I am thinking, *This is how our ministries join in giving life.*] How do you build their dignity while you give them charity?

Mother Teresa: Well, charity is only the immediate need of that moment. But after that, we start giving them work and so on and so on. But many people that I have picked from the street have lived—now have a little house of their own, and they are working! They have dignity again!

If we want to discover real dignity we must learn to be

6

meek and humble of heart. And to be able to talk to God! Because God speaks in the silence of the heart and we listen! Then we speak to God from the fullness of our hearts and He listens! That's prayer!

And to be able to do that, we need a clean heart, for a clean heart can see God. And we see God in each other, especially Jesus, who came to bring us the good news that God loves us and wants us to love one another.

He made it so easy for us to love one another by saying, "'Whatever you do to the least of My brethren, you did it to Me. If you give a glass of water in My name, you did it to Me. If you receive a little child in My name, you will receive Me. I was hungry; you fed Me. I was naked; you clothed Me. I was homeless; you took Me in.'"

Hunger is not only for bread. Hunger is for love. And the clothing is not only for a piece of clothes; it is also to be clothed in a beautiful dignity. Then homelessness is not only not having a home made of bricks, but being unwanted, unloved, and uncared for. And this, today, is the greatest homelessness—to be unwanted, unloved, left alone!

That's why love and peace have been destroyed from the very heart. But I have a beautiful example in Russia.

RS: In Armenia? The earthquake? You were there?

Mother Teresa: Yes. There was a mother who was caught under the debris, trapped for eight days with a little child, maybe two or three years old. When they found this mother, they saw that she had cut her finger, and she had fed the child with her own blood, put her finger in the child's mouth. Yes! She fed the child for eight days on her own blood.

RS: [I have no words. I am profoundly impressed and deeply moved.]

Mother Teresa: And this child was in perfect health! The mother was in terrible condition. But it's wonderful to see what mother's love can do.

RS: So, this is what life's purpose is all about, isn't it? Giving our spiritual life's blood, sacrificial love. The cross. Life preservers! Life restorers! Hallelujah!

6

And so the commandment is fulfilled! How beautifully! The sixth word is a *command meant* to release life! To restore life! To revive life! It is a rule for life and living that leaves you proud to be a human being and a follower of Jesus Christ.

CHAPTER 7

LOVE OR LONELINESS— IT'S YOUR CHOICE

"THOU SHALT NOT COMMIT ADULTERY"

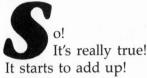

So!
It's really true!
It starts to add up!

It really makes sense!

The ten *commands* are *meant*—Not to *take* the *fun* out of life, But to *turn* the *sun* on in our life!

They are designed to put pride back into our life and keep shame out.

Which explains why even though the Ten Commandments have been violated ever since they were written, they are indestructible. They are broken often, but they are never destroyed.

The anvil wears the hammer out.

Gibraltar still stands. For all the pounding of the ages, the law outlives and outlasts the lawbreakers. Whether the rock hits the glass or the glass hits the rock, it's the glass that really gets hurt.

Yes, these Ten Commandments have earned moral immortality!

Why? Because they're one of the best things ever to hit the human mind!

How so? They contain:
- A blueprint for decision makers
- A map to guide our thought processes as we wade through the jungle of our daily choices
- Safety shields to protect us from the dangerous radiation of carnal temptations that assail every mortal.

So we've turned a new page in this book.

What's next?

The seventh commandment: "Thou shalt not commit adultery." One sizzling sentence helps us make the right choice between:

7

- Fidelity—or philandering,
- Integrity—or ambiguity,
- Trust—or deception,
- Pride—or shame,
- Pleasure—or pain,
- Love—or loneliness!

—These are the real choices!
—This is how the options really stack up in real life!

"Thou shalt not commit adultery."
Modern rendition?
And God said to His children, "I just don't want you to get hurt where the pain is the greatest—in broken hearts!"
We need wisdom to make the right decisions when we're faced with the choices that carry such lasting consequences. Some choices are so important that wrong selections leave scars that can't be covered with fresh paint. Remodeling and redecorating can cover a multitude of sins. But adultery? The very walls of the home are infected with a foreign element that will continue to seep and stain every new application of wall covering.
On my first trip to the Holy Land I purchased an antique water jug. It cost a mere quarter, but it was a priceless souvenir that contained memories and feelings of a spiritually uplifting visit to my Lord's homeland. I packed it in my flightbag along with some rocks that I had picked up along the way.
In retrospect, I can see it was folly to mix the rocks with the pottery. When the strap of my flight bag broke, the rocks crashed against the fragile pottery, breaking it into pieces. I started to throw out the broken parts when my wife protested, "Bob, I can fix that." I took it all home.
Here she painstakingly glued it back together, piece by piece. Believe it or not, she repaired the jug. Each piece was in place. But you could still see every crack, every line where the pieces had been joined. The jug was repaired, but nothing could ever cover up the damage that had been done.
That jug sat on a shelf in my office for years to come. I used it often as an illustration for couples whose marriages were torn apart by the pain of infidelity. I would take down

7

the jug and tell them that they could put their marriage back together again if they were willing to work very, very hard at it. However, the trust had been broken. After time, faith could be recovered. But the scars of infidelity would never be completely erased. The couple would have to turn those scars into stars. They would have to learn to forgive, for they would never be able to forget completely.

"Thou shalt not commit adultery."
We need this word desperately to manage the choices that suddenly confront us when the fire begins to burn in body and soul.

To a person or a society that knows no moral restriction in the exercise of sexual activity, the possibilities for pleasure are seemingly unlimited.

A smorgasbord of stimulating options is spread out before the sexually liberated people: In a morally relativistic culture, a beautiful buffet table is spread with an embarrassing assortment of enticing temptations. There's something there to satisfy any and every taste.

How easy it is to reach out to the attractive, colorful, and even dazzling displays and help ourselves. It's all so generously offered to anyone who passes by with a plate large enough to load and carry away the secret delights to a private corner where he can freely indulge his whetted appetite.

Voices tempt with offers too good to refuse, such as:
• "Take all you want."
• "Come back for more."
• "Sample it all."
• "Don't miss out on this."
• "You must try this delicacy."
• "One price covers all."
• "No charge for an extra helping."

"No extra charge?" Really?!

7

Well, so it seemed until our connoisseur stepped on the scale the next day and suddenly felt uncomfortable in clothes that mysteriously seemed to shrink overnight. Now he hated himself for his unrestrained indulgence. When he loaded his plate so full that he spilled on the front of his new garment, he caught his breath.

No extra charge?

"Don't worry," whispered the friend who shared the sinful orgy with him. "The spots will come out, and no one will ever know."

But the cleaners, unable to remove the stain, sent it back. He couldn't bear to throw it away. So he kept it for months and years in a dark and lonely corner of the closet until one day, growing older, he sadly took it out and disposed of it.

So there *was* an extra charge after all for all of the free food on the fabulous smorgasbord. A stain. A soiled garment. An ill-fitting shirt. A touch of shame.

Sadder and wiser, he realized he had been seduced that night.

He was betrayed by a beautiful buffet!

He wondered how he could have been so easily tricked by the stunning array of enticing choices. He remembered what a perfect, unspoiled picture that buffet table was before he started to load up his plate. When he first checked the festive arrangement, it presented itself as a single harmonious creation in which all of the separate colors, textures, and shapes seemed to blend together perfectly to form one coordinated creative plan—a beautiful picture indeed!

He circled the buffet and without hesitation or restraint filled his plate until no corner or hollow was left. Somehow he balanced the overflowing plate and managed to get it to the table.

As he slid into his seat, he looked at the incredible collection of clutter he had selected and noticed that his undisciplined choices turned harmony into disharmony. Creativity had turned into chaos.

Mustard meant for cold turkey had touched the edge of the chocolate chip cookie.

Somehow his indiscriminate, undisciplined, unrefined, undignified exercise of freedom had disgraced the artful

presentation. The lust of his eyes had led him sadly astray.
To his dismay, the contradictions of flavors left him with a
disagreeable aftertaste. What went wrong? Where did he
make his mistake?

"We really got our money's worth," he heard someone say.

For some reason, he wasn't sure that he agreed. He felt
strangely, sadly, dissatisfied. Embarrassed. Ashamed.

He remembered seeing another couple who walked ahead
of him at that buffet. They passed by so many tempting
portions. They chose small helpings of a refreshing green
salad and a slice of lean breast of chicken. They seemed, he
noticed from the corner of his eye, to be genuinely enjoying
the blending of these simple, complementing choices. And
later, he observed slyly, they returned to the buffet to select a
clean plate and one (only one) sweet dessert which they
apparently relished—slowly and with genuine satisfaction.

There was, it seemed to him, belatedly, a dignity to their
dining that somehow escaped him with his confused
collection.

What a sharp contrast they were to him. As he recalled his
unchecked indulgence, he had a mental image of a shallow
philanderer and playboy, who had impulsively and
disgracefully indulged every wistful whim. Now suddenly he
saw the kindness and caring heart of God expressed in the
wise advice, "You shall not commit adultery."

Indeed! The light dawns!

Dignity! Of course!

Isn't dignity always the rich reward, the natural by-product
of a discerning eye, a discriminating mind, and a disciplined
body?

Dignity! The big prize! The satisfying feeling that greets
you the morning after you dared to say no.

Dignity! Nothing saps the life out of it more surely or
swiftly than unbridled lust.
Nothing produces or preserves dignity more
sincerely or securely than committed love.

So—this is a *command meant* to lead us to a . . .

Love that lasts!

"In sickness and in health."

Love that lasts!

"For better or for worse."

Love that lasts!
   "For richer or for poorer."
Love that lasts!
   "'Til death us do part."

"Thou shalt not commit adultery."

Indeed! This is a *command meant* not to limit our love life. Just the opposite! *This is a command meant to extend and expand our love life, to eliminate loneliness, not pleasure, from our lives.*

It follows! This is a *command meant* to safeguard our dignity. So when our memory strolls back into the intimate hallways of our personal history, opening private doors, and the light is turned on in the secret closets, there is no shame to spoil or stain the sweetness of nostalgia.

But are we not told today that adultery isn't really that serious? For if we listen to the laughter or respond to the lusty stimulations that surround the scenes of illicit adultery in movies; or if we take our cues from the TV talk shows; or if we accept the opinions of self-appointed secular sex therapists as the final word on this subject—are we not left with a cavalier attitude toward infidelity?

Then why does God sandwich this commandment right between *murder* and *stealing*?!!

In the mind of Moses, adultery was no laughing matter. It was deadly serious. Why?

Because a person who breaks the seventh command breaks all ten! For all of the other nine commandments share the nest with this seventh commandment.

It's important to see the Ten Commandments not as ten separate, free-standing columns as in an ancient Roman courtyard: Knock one over and the other nine will still remain standing strong. Rather, we must see them as an ancient Roman arch of stones carefully leaning on one another, mutually supporting each other, to frame the entrance over the pathway to self-respect that leads to the inner court of human dignity! Take out one stone and risk the collapse of the entire portico blocking the pathway to noble pride, leaving you stranded alone, outside, in your shame.

You see, adultery is a breaking of relationship and commitment. Each of the first six commands, as well as the remaining three, are affected by this one act.

7

Commandment Number One:
Adultery is choosing another God, like pleasure, sex, or materialism.

Commandment Number Two:
Committing adultery will seriously flaw the reflection of God's image in your life.

Commandment Number Three:
Adultery is taking God's name in vain, for adultery betrays a relationship.

Commandment Number Four:
We make a mockery out of Sunday religion if we are unfaithful in our day-to-day love relationships. Adulterers are the real hypocrites.

Commandment Number Five:
Break commandment number seven and the family honor is violated. The family name is shamed. Cracks appear in the bridge. Society starts to crumble.

Commandment Number Six:
Yes, adultery is killing. It destroys trust, faith, and true love. A beautiful marriage is devastated in one foolish ill-fated obsession.

Commandment Number Eight:
Adultery is stealing. Betrayal is thievery. Something precious and priceless is deceptively stolen from a relationship: love, joy, peace, hope.

Commandment Number Nine:
Adultery is bearing false witness—deception, deceit, duplicity, lying. It's all here! Yes, the philanderer is a prevaricator.

Commandment Number Ten:
Adultery is coveting another person, another passion. Compulsive tension saps contentment from the human heart.

The moral collapse of the triumphal arch of personal dignity is complete! Damaged beyond repair? Possibly. Permanently scarred? Most likely.

FIDELITY: THE POSITIVE ALTERNATIVE

This commandment, remember, is not intended to take the joy out of our sex life, but to put more pride and pleasure into our sexual activity by protecting us, first of all, from shame and low self-esteem, then from alienation, bitterness, cynicism, and fear, and finally—loneliness!

If sexuality serves to inflate your unredeemed ego merely by counting or weighing your "scores" or "conquests," then

> The little fellow didn't realize what he did when he hammered a nail into the furniture. The father, of course, scolded him sternly.
> "I'm sorry, Daddy! I'll pull it out."
> The lad carefully removed the nail. Then tears filled his penitent eyes, "Daddy, the hole is still there."

your self-esteem is on a self-destruct path. But if sexuality is channeled to experience and enrich a beautiful love life, then it can, in fact, be a positive and genuinely pleasurable experience. *For perfect love is nature's food to nourish a healthy self-esteem.*

What's so great about a solid commitment made by partners in love? To answer this question, check these values: 1) secrecy; 2) right to privacy; 3) human dignity; 4) ultimate pleasure; 5) healthy intimacy; 6) the possibility of perpetuity. All of these six human values are interrelated in sexual activity:

1. *Intimacy* isn't possible if you have any reason at all to suspect that your sex secrets will be unwillingly exposed. Happy is the couple that collect exciting, safe secrets in their memories!

2. You cannot have that assurance of unbroken confidentiality unless your *right to privacy* is guaranteed.

3. If your sex life is not secured by a binding guarantee

7

Perfect love is nature's food to nourish a healthy self-esteem.

to privacy, your *human dignity* will be terribly vulnerable to embarrassing exposure. Under this threatening possibility you'll fail to experience . . .

4. *Ultimate pleasure.* The fun of sex will be diluted by fear of possible shameful revelations. Even if you are sure that you have taken careful, precautions to guard your shadowy secret from shameful detection, you will still not dare to "tell all" to your uncommitted lover. And *ultimate pleasure cannot be experienced without unrestricted intimacy.*

5. *Healthy intimacy* is where great sex really happens: When and where the lover is allowed to enter every room and any closet in the mansions of your soul! Only then, at the subconscious level, will there be true and total freedom! Only a secure subconscious allows wild abandon, which triggers stimulating spontaneity! Now you're free to fully enjoy total, unalloyed sexual joy.

6. All of the above five principles work well, of course, when there is an underlying *possibility of perpetuity.* Young lovers walk hand in hand, fingers interlocked. Positive feelings are aroused. Passions are ignited. *They want this to last forever.*

Great! Then the first wise step is to *plan to take steps to safeguard the possibility of perpetuity.* To neglect this first step before going all the way may weaken, at the outset, the incentive and resolve to make a commitment to continuity. Remove or ignore this primary principle, and principles 1-2-3-4-5 listed above become virtually impossible!

Now, adopt and apply the above six principles and let's see where the road leads!

PRIVACY—PLEASURE —PRIDE—THE KEYS TO SATISFYING SEXUALITY

How easy it is to be shamed when privacy is stripped and total exposure occurs. So in the Garden of Eden, the first emotional reaction of a fallen Adam and Eve was shame in their nakedness. Enter the proverbial fig leaf.

In virtually every culture, anthropologists find an almost universal human inclination to cover the "private parts" with leaves, gourds, skins, grass skirts, or woven fabric. Is this meant to suggest that nudity is a shameful sin? Or does it really suggest something more profound: that *every person's dignity demands the right to set limits beyond which the public cannot probe? These limits define space that must not be invaded lest the person lose his freedom to have and hold sacred secrets. Lose that liberty, and you lose your dignity.*

Yes, *privacy protects pride* and shelters from possible shame. This explains why human rights and property rights go hand in hand.

So the invasion of privacy is prohibited by law in free societies and nations. Laws protect the private closet; private articles; private property; private thoughts; private correspondence; private financial position; and finally, the ultimate privacy, personal sexual activity.

"Do not hold me up to full exposure," the soul of human dignity cries out. *"Allow me the right to secrets that will not be whispered around bars, board rooms, or bedrooms. Leave me alone with my intimate information that is secret, sensitive, and sacred."*

Intimacy loses both its pleasure and its pride when the possibility of total disclosure threatens. Passion and private performance have the right to be shielded from potentially embarrassing review, critique, and judgment.

So feel free to draw the drapes and lock the door. Now, assured that no one will ever tell tales or violate private secrets, feel free to exercise unrestrained abandon. Real freedom (and fantastic frivolity) is impossible without a guaranteed right to permanent privacy. Without the absolute assurance of secrecy subconscious restraints will restrict the ultimate pleasure potential.

The subconscious is always ahead of the conscious. If there is any assumption, any suspicion, or any remote possibility that a secret may someday be revealed unwillingly, then the subconscious mind, like a commanding general hidden from sight far behind the front line, will do its defensive job to protect its pride. Secret emotional defensive moves will be called out:

"Be careful!" "Be cautious!" "Don't show and tell too much." "You'll be shamed if this secret ever gets out."

So sound the commands of the subconscious protective commander.

Finally, the genitals get the message from the general, but too late!

Result? The fullest release of emotional joy and energy is never set off! Yes, in the absence of a trusted and total commitment, both persons will subconsciously hold something back. After all, love can only fly freely and fully if the companion in pleasure is trusted to preserve and protect—forever—the secret pleasures they choose to share together. *So "thou shalt not commit adultery" is a command meant not to limit, but rather to enhance our pleasure.*

Studies indicate that maximum pleasure in sex is only possible in a context of the trust that only comes with a true, total, trusted commitment to continuity. "'Til death us do part" is a setup for super sex. Yes, few, if any, human pleasures match the joy of sex, providing it is "safe sex," which means something more than protection from sexually transmitted disease. Almost as important—perhaps more important—is safety from any form of blackmail, extortion, or embarrassing reports that could devastate valued professional or personal relationships. No wonder the human being finds secure and safe sex in monogamy.

So what does the future hold for marital fidelity? Good news! Marriage will never go out of style. Cultural cycles may arise declaring the law against adultery old-fashioned. Liberated people will race to explore new frontiers of sexual freedom. But human nature will examine the classic pleasures guaranteed by privacy. And once again, the discipline of fidelity will be welcomed back into the culture. And a new cycle of marvelous, yes, delightful morality is resumed. For marriage—faithfulness between bonded and committed lovers—not only maximizes the joy in sex by making real love possible, but enhances self-esteem as well. This, in the final analysis, is the Big Pay-off!

Here's how it works. Real identity is discovered when you are loved by someone you trust enough to fully disclose yourself—body, mind, and soul. The lover tells you more about yourself, and the better you know yourself, the better you can love yourself.

It really is that simple. Can you love a stranger? Can you love someone you don't know? Can you love yourself without a mirror?

So the question is, can you—will you ever—really love yourself if you don't really know yourself? And can you really know yourself until you get an honest opinion and a reliable and revealing report from someone who knows you intimately?

You won't have to fear what your best friend tells you about your deepest self. Your self-esteem will be enhanced even if you discover your negative qualities, for your trusted lover will affirm, encourage, inspire and help you to improve yourself.

In an adulterous relationship, on the other hand, sexuality separated from a commitment to continuity fails at this crucial point: *total knowing.* The result? A shallow relationship that will be interlaced with hollow promises and hypocritical platitudes!

In the Bible, sexual intercourse is described as "knowing" a woman; or "knowing" a man. "She never knew a man" was a way of saying this woman was a virgin.

Intimacy is the key to love, self-esteem, and joy. Mind you, you can be totally undraped in body, but if you have kept your emotions shielded and haven't really bared your innermost feelings, you have not experienced intimacy.

You'll miss out on *totally knowing* this person and perhaps, in the deceptive, dishonest dance, miss out on knowing yourself, too. Intimacy only happens when first you feel safe enough to expose yourself completely at every level— physically, emotionally, and spiritually.

Do you dare to know the real you?

Are you afraid to find out who you really are?

Is this another reason why people fear intimacy? How

wonderful it is to have one essential friend that you can trust, one who will promise to love you, "for better or for worse," one who will promise to build you up and help you become a more beautiful person even when that friend discovers your secret shortcomings.

SELF-ESTEEM IS BOOSTED— OR BUSTED— IN AN INTIMATE RELATIONSHIP!

Uncertainty of the outcome is a primary impediment to intimacy. If all is bared and nothing held back, then you will be fully discovered. That's great if you can rest assured that you will never be embarrassed by the report. It could be devastating if someone you allow to know you fully reports back to others that you are a person or a performer who earns low marks.

Is there a way to take the risks out of intimacy and go on to enjoy the peak pleasure it promises?

Yes!

And no!

No—never in adultery.

Yes—if there's a binding, bonded agreement to fidelity.

Fidelity! It gives you the courage safely to explore and experience the possibilities awaiting you in life's intimate experiences. Faithfulness (powerful word, just the opposite of adultery) is fantastic because it leads you safely into life's hidden chambers.

SEARCH FOR INTIMACY

So intimacy is a God-created prescription to full-blown joy! The pleasure comes to full flower when you find a friend with whom you can laugh and cry; talk honestly and openly; be happy or angry; sit for hours and say nothing or scream in ecstasy or frustration.

The first reward of intimacy is a love that cures loneliness. "In the beginning God created man. And God saw that

Adam was lonely and God created a companion. Male and female, God created them, and God saw that this was good!"

There is a deep, innate hunger in mankind to ease the pain of loneliness. Few, if any, emotions are more disabling than those that come with abandonment, loneliness, isolation, obscurity, being forsaken and forgotten.

This need to find someone to whom we can commit ourselves, with whom we can enjoy total intimacy—a best friend, a trusted companion—is a God-designed impulse. It is the Creator's way to bring people together to support each other, to build up each other, to believe in each other.

> **The first reward of intimacy is a love that cures loneliness.**

We were never meant to find fulfillment alone. If we were able to achieve that, we would too easily become arrogant.

There is no doubt that every man and every woman needs intimacy. We all need that *one essential friend* to explore intimacy's great possibilities. When we find that friend, we will replace loneliness with authentic love.

What a prescription for true joy! Daring to be intimate, you will really enjoy *true love!* Your dignity is affirmed! It's possible to love yourself when you are loved by someone who will always respect and never betray your intimacies.

Yes, we all need to be affirmed, valued, and respected as unique, distinctive persons. Self-esteem is our deepest emotional need, and love sustains it. That's why we all seek desperately to be loved. When we're loved, we're filled—full. Now we have something we can give away—love. The empty cup can give nothing. The full cup has much to share. The life filled with love has a sweet something to offer to others who thirst for this life-giving nourishment. And in giving we enjoy a burst of new self-worth. *I'm important to someone after all!* I have something precious to give to somebody who has a great emptiness, hungering for fulfillment.

Remember: The deepest need is the need to be needed.

Love Or Loneliness—It's Your Choice

7

This need—in your life and in mine—is safely, perfectly satisfied in safe intimacy.

When, at what point, did my self-esteem blossom, open wide with delightful fragrance to pour its perfume over my personality? Was it when I bravely opened my life, my heart, my soul to welcome and receive the love that was tenderly tendered to me? Was it after I took and tasted of this precious gift of love? Or was that awakening of the hidden beauty within me uncovered and aroused when I *gave to others what I had taken in?* Real, satisfying, sustaining love is a cycle of satisfaction. I accept, and I give. I give, and it comes back again.

Giving never moves in a straight line—it always moves in circles!

So, self-esteem—a pearl of great price—finds its most satisfying and sustaining source at the spring of trusting love. This precious, priceless sense of self-esteem must be protected at all costs. No competing value, no alluring temptation, is worth accepting or enjoying if it risks poisoning or polluting this precious wellspring of emotional health and well-being!

- Loss of love is a price we cannot and must not pay as we check the choices offered to us on the smorgasbord of life, for

> # Daring to be intimate, you will really enjoy *true love!*

- Loneliness is too high a price to pay for any pleasure adultery offers, and
- Loss of self-respect is too high a price to pay for any temporary pleasure.

Yes, we all pay a price for everything, even when it's free.

When you are tempted to indulge in the extravagant temptations of life, ask yourself, Is it worth the price of the loss of love?

Love—I must not, I cannot, I will not risk losing it. Or polluting it. My pride cannot survive without it. I must preserve it. I must guard its refreshing purity.

I will not play the game of shame.

Love that flows free, pure, and precious is life-giving. Love is a wellspring of enthusiasm! Optimism! Creativity! The joyous spring of love must never be allowed to run dry and must never, ever become cluttered with litter or polluted with foreign elements.

God loves us enough to say, "Thou shalt not commit adultery." This commandment is God's way of saying, "I love you, and I don't want to see you get hurt."

This is a *command meant* to be a key that opens the door marked, "Sex can be beautiful." God created every human being with an appetite for food and an appetite for sex. And both are meant for great personal fulfillment and enjoyment.

> # Love is a wellspring of enthusiasm! Optimism! Creativity!

There was a soldier whose parents were members of my church until they passed away. His only sister was a charter member of the Crystal Cathedral Congregation. This soldier became something of a national celebrity during WW II when he was on an aircraft carrier in the Coral Sea. In the midst of a terrible battle he was on deck when an explosive 20-mm. shell from a strafing Japanese plane went through his chest into his stomach and lodged in his hip without exploding. They didn't know what to do with him. With the slightest movement, the bomb could have gone off and killed everyone around him.

They hung a tag around his wrist that said, "Caution—live bomb!"

He was then strapped to a cot strung on a cable and was moved from his ship to a hospital ship across stormy waves. Then he was transported to New Caledonia, and two weeks later, surgery was performed. When they safely extricated the 20-mm. shell from his body, they shot it through a piece of tissue paper. When it hit the tissue paper it exploded. For two weeks, he had indeed been a living bomb.

7

Psychiatrists, psychologists, anthropologists, and theologians all know that the potentially explosive power of the human sex urge is incredible. Its ramifications are reflected in creativity or lack of creativity, in civility or incivility, in antisocial behavior or in constructive behavior. The question is, How will you handle this living bomb that is in you and in every human being?

There are three ways, you see, to handle the sex urge. *The first is to repress it,* deny its existence. That was the overriding inclination during the extremely puritanical period in American life. Of course, this is not our problem today.

About thirty years ago there was almost a neurotic repression, and you couldn't even mention the word *sex* in mixed circles. Today the pendulum has swung to the opposite point, the strategy now is, "Don't repress it; *just release it."* But release without certain moral restraints, we are discovering, is very dangerous, even deadly. It's like saying, "Let the river flow; forget about the dikes; banks aren't necessary; give the waters natural flow."

Morality is not based on natural instinct.

How do you handle this great God-given urge? Release it? Yes, *if* it's truly Safe Sex. Yes, but make sure you understand the controls dictated by healthy morality. *Restraint*, not repression, is the best way to handle sexuality.

SEXUAL ADDICTIONS

Our ministry has, today, one of the first church-connected clinics to treat sexual problems. The clinical director, Dr. John Lybarger, has some interesting findings that are relevant here. He specializes in treating addictive and compulsive behaviors, focusing specifically on compulsive overeating, alcoholism, drug abuse, and a new area called "sexual addictions."

Hear what he has to say: "Sexual promiscuity has been

7

I'll never forget a woman who came and sat next to me on a plane. "Whew! I got good news today!" was her opening line to me.

Being neighborly I asked, "Oh? What's that?"

"My AIDS test came back negative!"

Well, of all the "good news" I could think of, I surely was not thinking of that! I was, needless to say, taken aback. But before I could recover she plunged on, "I think all this 'safe sex' stuff is boring! Life is short. I want to have fun. I have no intention of curtailing my lifestyle just because of some disease."

She was, I suspected, afflicted with a spreading social disease called promiscuity.

around almost from the beginning of time. But it has been recognized as a legitimate disease or disorder probably for twelve to fourteen years now.

"God has created us as sexual beings, and we have a continuum. For example, on the left we have sexual dysfunction where someone is unable to be sexual. In the middle is healthy sexuality. At the other extreme we have compulsive out-of-control sexual behavior. Sexual promiscuity could be defined as sexual behavior that is unmanageable in the person's life. All the while it creates an incredible amount of guilt, shame, and despair."

"Would you then classify sexual promiscuity as a sin or a disease?" I asked him.

"That's a common question," he answered, "and I think Scripture is very clear that sexual promiscuity, extramarital affairs, and premarital sex are sinful. The difficulty, though, is that there are people who are very much aware that their behavior is counterproductive to their self-esteem and not representative of the mature Christian lifestyle, yet they are unable to control their behavior. This adds to their guilt, shame, and remorse often resulting in a double life of

7

pornography, anonymous sexual contacts, or relationships outside of marriage.

"Meanwhile, in public life, they are responsible, upstanding citizens. They may be actively involved in their church, and the majority of people in their life are not aware of what is going on, literally behind closed doors."

Now listen to the therapy that is prescribed in our clinic. "We work on building self-esteem and a positive self-image. I think two of the core issues that are involved in sexual promiscuity and sexual addiction are a very low self-esteem or a negative self-image added to an incredible fear of intimacy," Dr. Lybarger says.

THE JOY OF INTIMACY—MISSED

Dr. Lybarger goes on: "The promiscuous persons have a very intense drive or craving for intimacy or closeness coupled with the fear of being rejected, abandoned, or betrayed. So they will get close to someone to achieve intimacy, and then be fearful that this person will leave them. So they cut off the relationship, and they turn to compulsive sexual behavior to anesthetize themselves or deaden the pain or the fear. This turns into a vicious cycle because, after they've acted out sexually, they not only have the original fear and the low self-esteem; they now have added guilt and shame. It keeps them locked in."

"Faith," Dr. Lybarger reports, *"is the critical issue because it requires a spiritual intervention.* We borrow the twelve steps and twelve traditions from Alcoholics Anonymous for treating all of the addictions that we treat at the New Hope Treatment Center. In the first step of the twelve-step program, the addict says, 'I've come to believe that I am powerless over my addiction and that my life has become

> # Morality does not ask, "What do I desire?" Rather it asks, "What is right?"

7

unmanageable.' The second step is that 'I've come to believe in a power gretaer than myself to restore me to sanity.'"

He concluded our interview by freely sharing the secret to his successful program. "In our Christian Treatment Center, we freely ackowledge that Jesus Christ is that higher power and that the Holy Spirit is the One that empowers us and gives us victory over the addiction. So we respectfully and sensitively lead addicted persons to turn their wills and their lives over to Jesus Christ, to receive the Holy Spirit so that they can experience day-to-day victory over their addiction."

Morality is never dictated by "normal" or "natural" desire. Morality does not ask, "What do I desire?" Rather it asks, "What is right?" Immorality, on the other hand, is doing what you want to do when you feel like doing it, as long as it makes you feel good.

Morality is not based on natural instinct.

To do what you naturally feel like doing is not morality. After all, what's the difference between colonies of civilized humans or herds of animals? An animal society is a noncivilized society. A civilization is a collective society of human beings who have agreed to restrain some of their normal drives to improve the social condition of the human family as a whole.

Morality is not a matter of doing what's natural. If you did what was natural, you'd kill people when you got mad at them. If you did what was natural, you'd steal from somebody when they had something you wanted. If you did what was natural, you would probably have promiscuous sexual relationships any time you felt the desire.

Here's the million-dollar question. *What is right?* Man has used every rationalization in answering this question. But, in reality, does every human being have an equal capacity to determine what's right and what's wrong? Who's to say what's right? Are the hosts on talk shows or performers on soap operas or fabricators of fiction—novelists, screenwriters, playwrights—are these to become the moral Bibles of our society?

Each "expert" has a personal view of what's right and

7

wrong, but few agree. Confusion abounds. Who's right? Is there some inviolable law to clear up the confusion and give us all the insight we need? The ancient Jews thought so. They were given the Ten Commandments, including "Thou shalt not commit adultery," as their shining lights in the darkness of decision making. Through these ten keys, the Bible guides to what is really right.

The Bible tells the truth. Remember, it's not true just because it's in the Bible. It's in the Bible because it's true. The Bible teaches us to redeem the sex drive. Yes, redeem it, take it, and use it positively, creatively, and constructively within the constraints that will allow you to enjoy it to its maximum potential.

I make this case: Nobody will enjoy sex more than someone who has both a fantastic marriage and a beautiful relationship with God. Sex within the bonds of marriage is beautiful, and it's undeniably the best sex.

BACK TO THE BIBLE

So we are finally drawn back to the Book of ultimate wisdom—the Bible. Here we can clear up the moral confusion that surrounds sexuality. Here we can confront the five major philosophical flaws, modern misconceptions, when it comes to this whole sexuality subject.

Misconception #1:

Marriage restricts your freedom to enjoy sex.

The truth is marriage may appear to limit your freedom, but remember, freedom is not freedom if it enslaves us to guilt, embarrassing secrets, and a lower self-respect! In fact, marriage increases your pleasure. It promises sex without shame, fear, or guilt. My wife has written a book called *The Positive Family.* She tells of the time that she was on a television talk show opposite a model from Paris. The model took the position that if you really want to enjoy sex, you should have total freedom from the "restriction" of marriage, that married sex, because it is limited to one partner, is boring and unfulfilling.

7

My wife's wise, perceptive observation to her was this: to experience sex only on the biological or social level, is to miss out on the best and most complete dimension of sexuality; to be "one" with each other is to transcend the physical and social to the intellectual, emotional, and finally the spiritual dimension. Then one experiences sex with total trust, pure pleasure, and satisfying, unalloyed euphoria. No negative emotions, no suspicions or hints of distrust spoil or pollute the sacred, safe, sexual pleasure in marriage.

Misconception #2:

You have to live together to find out if you're sexually compatible.

Nothing could be more shallow or erroneous for two obvious reasons:

1) Without a bonded commitment, there cannot and will not be present that joy-releasing power called TRUST. The six-fold process we observed earlier in this chapter cannot unfold naturally, fully, or freely. *So the experiment will be flawed and incomplete.*

2) A second fallacy with this position is that you are changing; your partner is changing; and you may actually grow apart unless and until the two of you are bonded together in a commitment to stick with each other through the good times and the bad. Outside of commitment the tendency is to draw apart. By contrast, the tendency under a beautiful, bonded, and binding commitment is to draw closer.

Outside the bonds of commitment normal adjustments will always be a downward trend. The upward movement is never an adjustment; it is always a commitment.

So unless you are committed to each other "for better or for worse, for richer or for poorer, through thick and thin," you're more likely to grow apart. Without a commitment there is no way that you can fully experience a true test of what your real sexual compatibility will be. With the slightest frustration, you'll be tempted to go your separate ways.

Even if you have a good relationship but no commitment, there is no guarantee that this "good relationship" will still be a good relationship a year from now. You say, "The same could be said about a marriage." Yes, with this difference: marriage is a commitment to *make it work!* So a commitment releases vast potential for creative positive adjustment. "When you dare to trust all things become possible," Caryl S. Avery comments in a lengthy *Psychology Today* (May 1989) article on this very subject.

Dr. Ruth Westheimer reported recently that living together before marriage isn't a guarantee of successful marriage.

Q: Do you think it is wise to spend "living" time with your future spouse before marriage? Would this help avert a divorce later on?

A: We know from divorce statistics that people who have lived together before marriage do not have a lower incidence of divorce. Living together does not ensure the future of a marriage.

When the idea of living together was, in this country and in most European countries as well, a pretty daring idea, people often discussed the idea of partners having a trial period of living together before marriage. This seemed a logical idea, and people often cited, in their wise discussions, certain peasant customs of youth and maiden not getting engaged until she was pregnant—that is, until the outcome of the marriage in terms of children seemed reasonably well assured. But much experience of premarital living together has not shown this procedure to have any advantage over keeping that close experience of each other until after the wedding.

In fact, one often hears, "It was all pretty good until we went and got married." Many things keep couples together, not always for the best. *Two strong influences for preserving marriages, more reliable than premarital living together, are a shared belief in marriage or in the beliefs or philosophy or religion that the couple share.**

*Taken from the *Honolulu Advertiser,* March 2, 1989

7

Misconception #3:

Sex between consenting adults is O.K. as long as nobody gets hurt.

The problem with this is: How do you know nobody is getting hurt? How do you know you won't get hurt? If there is no commitment, how do you know that tomorrow morning he or she won't pack up the suitcase and walk out? Of course! Somebody is going to get hurt!

A few years ago a young lady engaged to be married sought counseling from me when the engagement was broken. She said, "Dr. Schuller, he just walked away. *I told him all my secrets. I don't know if I'll ever dare to trust anybody that deeply again."*

Outside of a marriage bond, you had better be careful what secrets you tell to the person in bed with you. How do you know you're not going to get hurt? And how do you know your behavior might not be hurting a lot of other people? Including persons you'll never know who are silently looking to you as an example?

Misconception #4:

Religion somehow restricts sexual enjoyment.

That is simply not true. Studies have been made and published that scientifically established the fact that Christians get greater pleasure out of sex than non-Christians. There are several reasons for that. For one thing, we don't have to pay the price that the non-Christian frequently has to pay. What am I talking about? *For one thing we don't have to worry as much about cervical cancer.* An extraordinarily high incidence of cervical cancer is found in those who have promiscuous sexual relationships. And *we don't have to worry about sexually transmitted diseases.*

Two teenagers approached their happy and jovial grandparents as they celebrated their Golden Anniversary. What a blast. What a party. "What did you and Grandpa

7

use," they asked their Christian grandmother, "to keep from getting sexual diseases when you were young?"

"We used this," the wise old woman replied with a twinkle as she pointed to her wedding band.

Misconception #5:

A commitment will limit my individual development.

Not true. Psychologically, *when I make a commitment* "for better or worse," *I grow.* I have grown through my marriage. I have grown through my wife. And she has grown through me. If I'd not had this lasting commitment, I would not have grown in many areas of my life. It's obvious when I make commitments I:

1. set goals,
2. agree to "pay the price of self-sacrifice,"
3. resolve to solve problems,
4. learn to work through difficulties and *not run away* from them!

That is a positive prescription for emotional and mental maturity. This is an undebatable formula for "growing up" as a person.

Furthermore, a fantastic paradox comes into play here. The deeper the commitment, the deeper the trust, the deeper the freedom for both parties offer each other. So deep is the trust in a true marriage that both parties enjoy far more freedom.

> **The deeper the commitment, the deeper the trust, the deeper the freedom for both parties.**

Trust liberates. Suspicion oppresses. "Where were you?" "Why are you late?" "What were you doing all this time?" How oppressive is distrust!

My wife believes in my love. And it is this trust that keeps me on the path. "She believes in me!" is still the strongest source of moral power.

7

Without faith there is no freedom. Without freedom there is no joy. If I could give my wife gifts of jewelry, home, clothes and did not trust her, or she me, all the pleasure and happiness in the relationship would be gone.

CONCLUSION

Now, what if you are coming from a past that may be so contrary to all of the above that you may emotionally reject these truths in a defensive posture or accept the truths, only to fall into guilt or depression? You may have been thinking as you have been reading, *I wish I hadn't.* Or *I wish I had.*

Both responses are negative, counterproductive, and totally nonconstructive. A positive reaction is to accept the forgiveness that Jesus Christ offers and start a new life—here and now! Decide to live by a higher, safer, more satisfactory moral standard!

Adultery, after all, is a *forgivable* sin.

Do you remember what Jesus said to the accusers as He shielded the woman caught in adultery with His own body? He said, "Let him who is without sin cast the first stone."

To the woman He said, "Your sins are forgiven. Go and sin no more."

Accept Christ's forgiveness for the past. Then begin to improve your future and the future of society by setting higher standards than those which were set for you by a society skilled at self-deception, and rationalization.

"My father's life was hell," a young man said to me. "My father had his mistress; my mother had her affairs too. The home life was really bad. They put on a hypocritical front. Hypocrisy isn't setting a high standard and missing it through weakness. Hypocrisy (he correctly pointed out) is pretending to be something you're not. *Hypocrisy is at its worst when we start out rejecting the so-called ideal in favor of what is surely a lower level of moral expectations.*"

I applaud that! He went on to make an upward moral climb—he got married!

"Watch me, Dr. Schuller. I'm going to build the marriage and family my parents never had!" He is determined and dedicated irrevocably to sparing his children from the torn

7

and tortured home life he had to face. Good news! He's making it! He's on his way to a golden anniversary!

HERE'S MY HAPPY HISTORY

Now, agree or disagree with what I've written, but no person can debate or deny the truthfulness of my personal history. My wife and I were both raised and trained to believe that we were created in the image of God and were prohibited by God's law to engage in sexual intercourse until we were bonded together in a commitment to continuity called Marriage.

Our courtship lasted two years. We were married on June 15, 1950, and that night both of us joyously and jubilantly abandoned our virginity.

Accept Christ's forgiveness for the past.

We will never forget the first time.

What an incredible way to launch a lifetime together!

The christening of a ship!

The unopened bottle of champagne is cracked across the hull in a sparkling celebration!

The ribbon-cutting—who can forget it! The grand opening—an indelible memory! The first time—unalloyed pleasure without guilt or fear or shame!

So what a honeymoon we had! Freedom! Fun! Frivolity! And it has never stopped.

"Adultery." It has never even been a temptation or a problem in our marriage. It simply was never an option.

Now, what's so great about fidelity, faithfulness in marriage? Where does this road lead?

Here's my observation, backed up not only in my life but, believe it or not, in the laboratory of sexual research in millions and millions and millions of marriages since this seventh commandment was written nearly three thousand years ago.

- Profound emotional power is released when sex is totally guilt-free and fear-free.

Believe In The God Who Believes In You

7

- Marvelous and mysterious pleasures are tapped into when we can safely enter the room called Life's Secret Intimacies. Wild and wonderful experiments are safely enjoyed in exciting adventure together.
- Real liberty and true freedom and release from oppressive controls are experienced when unquestioned trust is the foundation to our sexual friendship.
- How beautiful and perpetual true love really is as it creates precious, passionate secrets that crystalize into diamond memories to be enjoyed more with each passing year until you grow old with a treasure chest full of jewels that puts a sweet, sexy twinkle in the eye of the jolly old gent and his silver-haired sweetheart.
- How peaceful, relaxed, and tension-free life is when you are never lonely anymore. True commitment releases total trust which gives rise to the ultimate companionship.
- How peaceful and fulfilling married life can be when faithfulness is never broken. Hand in hand the married lovers walk through life. A baby is born. (How their values change.) Another child. (The focus now changes to the children.) So a deeper commitment to their family moves lovers from selfish, greedy, shallow materialism and shallow sensuality into unselfishness. They grow to become *genuinely caring adults.*
  Generosity replaces greed. A touch of hardness turns to softness. Focusing on their family distracts them from their selfish, petty, shallow frustrations. Quite accidentally they discover joys and sorrows they never knew before.
- Now all of life becomes one unending series of celebrations: wedding anniversaries, shared birthday parties, and holidays together as a family. Thanksgiving with children. Christmas shopping together for the children and the grandchildren, graduations, weddings!

Tears? Yes. Hurts? Yes. Pain? Perhaps. But the *bonding without bondage* becomes more *binding* and beautiful with every passing year.

7

Life's a never-ending process of collecting mostly happy memories.
 • How easy is the journey . . .
 • How light is the luggage . . .
  . . . when you have no regrets to carry with you!
        Then finally—
 • How sweet the sorrow when separation finally comes. "Parting is such sweet sorrow."

Life's a never-ending process of collecting mostly happy memories.

*A*fter the funeral they were all gathered at the family's home. The children were all there. Johnny flew in from the East. His brother picked him up at the airport. "Mom's gone" were the first words that fell from their quivering lips as these two six-foot-plus men hugged, trembled, and cried quiet, happy tears. Then they broke their embrace and headed for the baggage counter. Soon they were laughing again, through their tears.

"It was a wonderful service. Thank you, Reverend Schuller." They all said it.

I answered, "Thanks, but I didn't write it. Your mother did. She wrote it with her life and with the love of her husband—your father."

SO!
That's what the seventh command is meant to deliver!

SO!
That's where the high road leads!

SO!
That's why faithfulness in marriage is so fantastic!

7

SO!

That's why sex without shame, guilt, fear,
remorse, regrets, recrimination is . . .

SO FANTASTIC!

SO FABULOUS!

SO FULFILLING!

So go for it! At this point, its no longer a debate; it's a
decision!

CHAPTER 8

THE PRIDE OF EARNERSHIP AND OWNERSHIP— EXPERIENCE AND ENJOY IT

"THOU SHALT NOT STEAL"

8

*W*ho are they, these thieves? Are they desperately poor people?

Greedy rich people? Are they workers who give a partial effort in return for full wages paid?

Managers who exploit laborers with an unequitable share of profits?

Their collars come in a variety of colors and types: white, blue, even turn-around collars.

They hitchhike and they own private jets.

They travel economy and first class.

Why do they do it?

• *Bread and milk for their babies?* I doubt it. Such thieves are few in number. They're not the ones who concern us.

• *Drugs?* Yes. This criminal is genuinely to be feared, for he carries a knife, and a gun, and he'll use them if he has to.

• *Excitement?* Most juvenile car thieves never intended to keep the wheels. They jumped in for a lark.

• *Power?* Here's where the big boys come into play. The stakes are high. No penny-ante stuff here. A dangerous demonic ego challenges this sophisticated criminal to rip off the government in false billings, cook the books, and prove to himself how clever and smart he is. What a kick—power!

• *For no reason at all?* Yes, there are the kleptomaniacs. Obsessive-compulsive behavior is the scientific description. They really don't want it. They will never eat it, wear it, sleep *in* it or *on* it. They'll never even bother to buy the batteries that didn't come with it.

• *Social Justice?* Any government can be oppressive, wasteful, or immoral in its expenditures. "I'll protest silently and the IRS will never know." "Pay me in cash and I won't have to report it."

• *Economic injustice?* "I've worked hard: I deserve to give myself a bonus. Many in my company don't work as hard as I do, and they get paid more. I'm not stealing; I worked for it!" "Somebody's got to give me a raise!"

• *Greed?* Why do they do it? In one word: *more*. Enough is never enough. "How much land do you want?" the little farmer asked the big rancher. "Just the land that touches mine," he answered.

Who are they? All kinds, colors, and classes of people.

Why do they do it? For understandable and for crazy reasons.

What do they steal? Anything, including the most precious of all possessions: another person's pride. Shakespeare said it: "Who steals my purse steals trash, twas something, tis nothing. But he that filches from me my good name robs me of that which not enriches him, And makes me poor indeed."*

Enter the gossip, the tabloid journalist, the bigot in the pulpit, the lawyer at the bar, the reckless and unrestrained reporter. If a person is innocent until proven guilty, why don't we wait to report the news until the verdict is handed down?

Do they get by with it? Or will they all be caught and brought to trial and sentenced in proportion to their crime?

Good news! No guilty soul ever "gets off" free. *That's not what I read in the magazines and newspapers,* you argue.

But final justice isn't handed out in a court or in the evening news.

How, then, can we say, "They're all caught and punished"? When and where is justice handed out? To understand, we must ask the next question.

Who are the real victims? The homeowner who finds his TV stolen? The businessperson who is "short" on inventory? The government that is robbed of its legal revenue every April 15? Yes. Yes. Yes. But don't forget the most pathetic victims: the thieves themselves.

For they rob themselves of the one value that is most precious of all. Their pride!

For starters, they deprive themselves of the pride of

(Othello, 3.3.155)

achievement. Ask the student who cheated, who in the final analysis *robbed himself of knowledge.* The cheating will come back to haunt him.

Ask the driver of the stolen car, "Where did you get the money for that?" Now he'll pay: he'll miss the pride of sharing an honest success story.

Yes. The thief robs himself of the really big prize—like a bank robber that scooped up the loose change and filled his bag with bundles of one-dollar bills and rushed off to escape. "He overlooked the bundles of hundred-dollar bills in the next drawer," the bank teller reported to the police.

The really big prizes every thief robs himself of are:

The Pride of Workmanship:
And with it the pride of serious, sincere, and unselfish effort.

The Pride of Earnership:
"I did it! Wow! I did it! I earned it; I really did!"

The Pride of Ownership:
It's not his property just because he took it, and deep down in his heart he knows it.

The Pride of Stewardship:
He misses the greatest treasure of all, the joy of giving. After all, you cannot give what you do not own.

Yes, *The Pride of Workmanship.* A skill, a trade, a profession, an art, a service—all can become such ennobling, honorable, joyous sources of human dignity.

The dedicated craftsman, the patient artist, the conscientious laborer—all are driven by a compulsion to excellence. They win the big prize that no lottery can ever offer.

The really big winners are those honest workers who "did their best." Perfection? Probably not. When you simply and sincerely do your best, you strive toward excellence without being caught in the trap of perfectionism. And that's called: *Pride of Effort.*

The pursuit of excellence is, of course, a spiritual endeavor.

8

If I believe in the God who believes in me, I'll believe that He will give to me—and to every person—some idea, some dream, some desire to achieve or acquire. My duty is to see this as a divine opportunity entrusted to the care and keeping of my imagination, my ingenuity, and my industry. I must seize the moment, develop the possibility, and return my accomplishment as a gift to God, worthy to be an offering of thanksgiving to the God who entrusted the treasured opportunity to me.

So why did God give this command? Mind you these ten laws were given to the Hebrews just as they were released from years of slavery. For generations the Hebrews had been slaves in Egypt, deprived of property and more seriously, deprived of freedom to discover, develop, and excel in life's opportunities. Now they were set free! Free to experiment and explore! Free to succeed or fail. Free to work and win! Free to risk, to adventure, and to taste the dignity that comes with every act of courageous effort. In the end they would be free to enjoy the pride of workmanship, the pride of ownership, and the pride of stewardship.

So how should a society solve the problem of thievery?

By simply removing the challenge to hunt? Or fish? Or make tents? "The hardest job in the world," a philanthropist once said, "is how to give money away without doing more harm than good."

• "I didn't feel much pride when I went to the mailbox to get my welfare check," someone once told me. "Then you, Dr. Schuller, you made

> **If I believe in the God who believes in me, I'll believe that He will give to me—and to every person— some idea, some dream, some desire to achieve or acquire.**

me believe I could do better on my own. I went back to night school and today I *hire* people!"

• "They're some of the best workers I have," Carl Karcher told me. He was referring to the physically disadvantaged young people he hires in his fast-food outlets. "And they're the first ones to donate to the United Charities fund," he added.

Pride of workmanship, pride of earnership, pride of ownership, pride of stewardship—this is the really great reward.

And there is more. They now enjoy the *Pride of Friendship*, the joy of knowing they have earned the respect of their fellow workers. Friendships flow to them to give them a dignity that is really rich.

So how can a society fight theft?

Pass tougher laws to send the crooks away *for good?* Probably, if that's necessary to impress upon would-be criminals that the risk isn't worth the effort. But being tough on criminals alone will never do the job.

Develop an economic philosophy backed by *laws that will guarantee* enough income to *every person* so that incentives to crime will be eliminated? But what if this solution would also eventually and unavoidably remove incentives to creativity, productivity, and ultimately *Pride of Achievement?*

How can we distribute the financial resources to maximize the individual's self-respect? In this process how can we avoid penalizing the productive worker while we reward the lazy person?

Could a nationalistic state, like an autocratic megacorporation, fall into the trap of stealing from its best workers through unfair taxation? Where, then, would this road lead? To increased productivity and prosperity and an expanded tax base that all of society could benefit from? Or will the selfish state, like a greedy corporation, see economic growth diminish as human motivation is stifled? And in the process deprive persons of their potential human dignity? How can we fulfill the potential productivity, prosperity, and pride that this eighth *command* is *meant* to release? How can we maximize the possibilities for all persons to be free to

8

discover the pride of workmanship, earnership, ownership, and stewardship?

Freedom! This is the key word. "Let my people go," was the rallying cry Moses shouted to the Egyptian slave masters. No person must be a slave. Let every person be free to discover and develop his God-given talents.

Education for all! That's the first positive step—freedom from ignorance.

Equal opportunity for all to enter and compete in the marketplace! That's the second positive step. Social customs, cultures, or laws that would bar people from the freedom to learn, then to earn, save, invest, and give back, must not be tolerated. Equal opportunity laws to give persons unprejudicial freedom regardless of race or religion will be a welcomed, necessary positive step.

But will this be enough to open the door of opportunity for all to strive for success until they enjoy the big prize? Pride of workmanship, pride of earnership, pride of ownership, and pride of stewardship?

Not quite.

Freedom isn't enough—not without faith. Freedom without faith will drive people back to slavery. In their fear they'll choose the security of a promise of food and shelter in exchange for the risks of

> **Freedom without faith will only lead to new forms of oppression.**

freedom. Freedom calls for courage. Freedom can't survive without it. Liberty won't make it without self-reliance. And self-reliance runs into trouble without a faith that can carry it through tough times.

Freedom without faith will fail.

So the final solution to theft is this positive prescription: *possibility thinking.*

What's that? It's a philosophy designed to give people hope. To *inspire every person to believe in himself!* Any effort to

8

motivate persons without first laying down a solid foundation of strong self-esteem will be doomed to disappointing results. *The "I am" will determine the "I can."*

- "I may be poor and financially deprived, but *I am free* to set goals and try!"
- "I may be living in a deprived neighborhood—but *I am free* to pack up, migrate, and, in some cases, emigrate!"
- "I may be academically or professionally handicapped, but *I am free* to choose my own destiny, and slowly but surely take steps to acquire the knowledge, learn the skills, and pursue my dreams until I will have the pride of improvement, the pride of achievement, and then the pride of contributing something meaningful to my family, my community, my country, my church, and my world!"

So that's where this road called possibility thinking leads! The pride of workmanship leads to the pride of earnership, which leads to the pride of ownership, which leads to the pride of stewardship!

"I'll take the starving person and give him a fish to keep him alive today," Mother Teresa told me. She continued, "Then I'll turn him over to you, and you can give him possibility thinking so he'll learn to fish."

The process of possibility thinking then releases *the creative power of healthy pride.* Here's how it works.

Every human being—without exception—is inspired to become an opportunity thinker—to see, size up, and seize the possibilities.

See how this process unfolds. A positive self-confidence will inspire persons to believe in themselves until they affirm:

1. "I am free" to set my private goals. This is step number one. I'm proud of my freedom to dream. Yes, my dignity demands the freedom to dream. *No person is ever poor if he is free to dream great dreams.*

2. "I need not be afraid of failure" is the second inspiring affirmation we must instill in every person. Honest failure is no call for embarrassment. But not to dream, not to discipline myself, and not to deny myself the passing pleasures in favor of pursuing long-range goals, in short not

8

really to try and in trying give my opportunities my best effort—that is a basis for personal disgrace. "I'd be more proud if I'd tried and failed than I'd be if I never made a serious effort and accomplished little or nothing."

The famed Washington attorney Edward Bennett Williams once hired Vince Lombardi to coach the Redskins. Before his death Williams shared lessons learned in sports: "Let me tell you about Lombardi and learning to lose. I was in Miami in the mid-'60s at a National Football League meeting right after Coach Lombardi had taken the Green Bay Packers into the NFL championship game against the Philadelphia Eagles.

"Vince lost that match and was terribly depressed.

"I said to him, 'You know, Vince, you and I think we always have to win. But the truth is nobody wins all the time. I don't care how great you are; you've got to lose once in a while. In fact, the more you go into battle, the more you'll lose. What we have to do is learn how to deal with a failure now and then.'

"I then shared the secret of how to deal with losing: You just have to get ready for the contest. You burn your body, burn your spirit, tax your psyche. I prepare for everything. In court, I never ask a question to which I don't know the answer. So you tax yourself to the ultimate for a contest, whether in sports, politics, or court.

"If you leave nothing undone, if you are 100 percent prepared and there is nothing further that you could possibly do to prepare for battle, you will leave the contest with an inner victory. *You won't be ashamed of losing if you can be proud of the effort you put out. You will leave fulfilled and satisfied.* You will say, 'I have won because there is nothing further that I could have done.' Now, the chances are great that the inner victory will be reflected on the scoreboard. But not necessarily. In any case, win or lose, you will build insulation against despair and against exterior defeat."

That's possibility thinking. That's the foundation of human freedom. That's the solid rock upon which human dignity is built. The process continues:

3. *"I'm going to make the most of the opportunities I'm free to pursue."* This is the third step in the process of creative economics. This is the exciting moment of great awakening.

8

Congratulations! You've begun the transition from negative thinking to positive thinking. Now you have been set free from the ultimate oppression: impossibility thinking. Bravo for you! You have revolted against your most dangerous oppressor—yourself. You are beginning to experience real liberation from your own oppressive negative thinking.

Choose to be a positive thinker, and you'll be free at last!

One of my dear friends is W. Clement Stone. For years he was reputed to be one of America's wealthiest men. That may or may not have been true. But his wealth was legendary in his time. Today, W. Clement Stone is remembered as a great philanthropist. He has contributed tens of millions of dollars to mental health, prison reform, medical care, religion, and positive thinking. I think I can honestly say that the most respected people I know respect W. Clement Stone. Born into total poverty, he started selling newspapers as a six-year-old boy. Along the way he read the book of Napoleon Hill, *Think and Grow Rich*. He also read Horatio Alger stories of people who had nothing, caught a dream of becoming wealthy, and went out to become very rich. Bitten by the beautiful bug of ambition, he began selling life insurance. Then he discovered OPM: Other People's Money. And he learned that you can borrow money to buy a business. He learned that you can take a small business and make it bigger and better if you are serving people's needs more effectively and economically. He learned that if you do this sincerely, you can become wealthy in the process. So he purchased a little insurance company. He offered job opportunities for people who were poor and wanted to work. He created generous employment opportunities. He opened the doorway to dignity for thousands of poor people. Now he was on his way toward what would amount to great wealth. He has since inspired untold thousands to follow in his tracks. "Just because you are poor doesn't mean that God wants you to be poor. . . . Just because you don't have wealth doesn't mean that you can't get it—honestly and honorably," he preached. He is today a motivator of men and women. "Anything the human mind can believe, it can achieve," is a line Clem Stone repeats often. I was captivated by his teaching on the power of a positive mental attitude.

PMA, he calls it. I learned from him that every person is free to *choose* to have a negative mental attitude or a positive mental attitude. I learned that a positive mental attitude will produce positive results and a negative mental attitude will produce negative results.

"I have the freedom to choose my mental attitude. What am I doing with this freedom God has given me?" I asked when all I had was five hundred dollars. I was now on my way to real economic liberation! So long as I have sanity, why shouldn't I therefore choose a positive attitude?" I asked. So I did. So with only five hundred dollars in total assets, I decided to build one of the greatest churches in the world—for the glory of humanity and for the greater glory of God. I still have to remind myself every moment I'm always free to choose PMA or NMA. And every time I make the positive choice, it turns my life instantly in the direction of light, joy, hope, and optimism. And that spells *health*!

When I invited Clem Stone to speak in my church, I asked him, "What does it feel like to be wealthy?" He answered in one word. *Power*! "Power is a wonderful feeling if you use it right," he told me. *"Wealth is power. Power to do good!"* And do good he has! So his pride of workmanship led to the pride of earnership, which led to pride of ownership, *which led to the pride of stewardship.* His money has helped build hospitals, universities, and the Crystal Cathedral. It all started when he chose to live with PMA.

> **You are moving out with exciting freedom as you become an opportunity thinker, believing in the God who believes in you!**

8

*F*ree at last! Thank God you're free at last. You
are moving out with exciting freedom as you
*become an opportunity thinker, believing in the God who
believes in you! Only when a force is set loose in society
that turns persons into opportunity thinkers, then and
only then have we fulfilled the positive challenge of this
commandment: "You shall not steal!"*

"We shall overcome! We shall overcome! We shall
overcome some day!" Listen to the song of these marching
opportunity thinkers.

These possibility thinkers are coming out of their ghettos
and barrios.

They are the opportunity thinkers of the world.

Look at them.

Listen to them.

Step up and join them.

They are bringing pride back into the human race.

Become an opportunity thinker and you too can experience
success.

What did I hear you say?

*I shall stop focusing on my adversities and disabilities and start
focusing on the possibilities and opportunities.*

Congratulations! With this positive mental attitude your life
will begin its dignifed turnaround.

So get set. Learn how to be an opportunity thinker in *nine*
steps.

**Find a need and
fill it. Find a hurt
and heal it. Find a
problem and
solve it.**

1. EXPECT opportunities.

Be on the alert. Opportunities
often appear without advance
alert: a knock on the door; a
telephone call; a newspaper
story; unsolicited mail; an idea
out of the blue. Keep the
"opportunity antennae" up, or
the ideas will pass in and out
of your mind and you'll never
notice.

God often sends His
creative ideas subtly.

8

So sharpen your imagination. Tune into your intuition. Heighten your expectations.

Try praying this morning prayer: "Good morning, Lord, what do You have in mind for me today? I'm awake. I'm alive. I'm alert. I'm ready to be active! Let's go!"

Expect opportunities, no matter how disadvantaged a position you are in. God has a plan for your life. It is a plan for good and not evil. It is a plan to give you a future with hope (see Jer. 29:11).

2. PROSPECT for opportunities. If you expect them, you'll start looking for them. *Bloom where you are planted.* The odds are they're very close to you, even in your own backyard. More often than not, they're disguised as problems—yours or somebody else's. When you're frustrated enough to swear it's time to invent something or start a new business. Check the new course offerings in adult study groups. Look for the changes in the workplace. Find a need and fill it. Find a hurt and heal it. Find a problem and solve it.

"Where's David? I haven't seen him around all week?" I asked. David was the head bellman at the hotel where I stayed on my visits to Hawaii.

"Oh, he's not here anymore. He started his own business. You know those T-shirts with pictures on them? He's doing so well he is shipping them to all the islands and around the world."

Prospect for opportunities—close at hand and far away. "I've just started a business in Iraq," a friend told me as I wrote this chapter.

"Iraq!?" I answered, shocked.

"Yes," he explained. "I saw this brass and bronze foundry in Indianapolis, Indiana going into bankruptcy. 'What a shame' I thought. I was able to take it over without any cost to speak of. I then was able to renegotiate contracts, salvage a lot of jobs, and fly to Iraq to get an option on all their used brass and bronze." "But why Iraq?" I asked. "You know the Bible says 'turn your spears into pruning hooks and swords into plough shares'? I thought of all the spent shells lying in the desert sands, left as waste from the horrible war. No one else was even thinking about that" he explained. "You have to look where no one else is thinking of looking."

3. RESPECT opportunities. Treat these ideas reverently when they come to you. Just because they're impossible doesn't give you the right to laugh them off, rudely discard them, or cynically reject them. They may, after all, have come from the God who believes in you. Take them seriously. Check them out. Pray about them. Almost every person who ever succeeded turned an impossibility into a possibility. "If you have faith as a mustard seed, you will say to this mountain, 'Move' . . . and nothing will be impossible for you," Jesus said in Matthew 17:20.

Respect for opportunities is an early first step to earning self-respect. Self-respect starts when you start respecting your own ideas.

Is your dream unreachable? Unattainable? Impossible? That's good. It's one indication that the idea may be a gift from God Himself. For He always calls us to be more than we are. His plan is always bigger than our perceived abilities. This is His strategy for stretching our thinking until we leave the calm, snug safety of our comfort zone and break loose, move out, step ahead, and become more than we have ever been before.

> **Self-respect starts when you start respecting your own ideas.**

4. INSPECT opportunities. No, you won't plunge in with a major investment of time, money, energy, or effort without asking safe, sensible questions. Does this fit in with my value system? That's the first inspection every opportunity must pass.

Faith, focus, and follow-through are wise words to guide the opportunity thinker. (1) Do I have the *faith* to catch the vision? (2) Shall I *focus* on this opportunity? Should I *focus* on this opportunity *now*? Does it complement or supplement my main line of business? Or would it scatter my attention, divert me from my first and primary calling? Don't let any and every new opportunity distract you from focusing on what you do best. (3) Now if you decide to go for it, there is

8

a final inspection: Ask yourself if you're prepared to *follow through* and pay the price.

Remember this before you begin: *Failure follows those who fail to follow through.* Faith, Focus, Follow-through—these are the three inspectors who must approve your opportunity. Are you still with me? Then move on and make the decision to do it.

5. SELECT the opportunity. Grab the moment. Take action. DIN: Do it now. This great opportunity may never come again. Be decisive. Make the decision. Dare to try.

I know of a teenage girl who chose never to learn to snow ski. She stayed in the mountain cabin all alone while the rest of her family went to take skiing lessons. Why? Because she was afraid she would be embarrassed in front of her family or she might look clumsy in front of the teenage boys that might be there.

What a loss! Everyone came home from the skiing expedition laughing and exhilarated. They had had such fun. "Dad kept falling, and did he look funny!" They teased. Yes, there had been some embarrassing moments for the father who had the courage to try, but he also had the reward of the fun memories. Not so, the girl who stayed at home, protecting herself from embarrassment. Or did she? *Later she would admit she was embarrassed because she lacked the courage to risk being embarrassed.*

You can choose not to run for the election; you can choose not to become romantically involved; you can choose not to audition for the part. You can choose safe withdrawal rather than risky involvement, but be sure of this: You'll rob yourself of the pride of accomplishment.

Jim Abbott was born with one arm and one hand. Growing up, he fell in love with baseball. He desperately wanted to play, not just sandlot baseball, but major league baseball. He harbored the dream deep in his heart. If he had dared to voice the dream, people surely would have responded, "You need two hands to play baseball in America."

Nevertheless, he dared to dream, and he dreamed of ways that he could play as well as anybody—even with only one hand. He asked himself, "Is there any position that a one-handed player can play?" The amazing answer turned out to be yes. He could be a pitcher; a pitcher only

8

God always calls us to be more than we are.

needs one good arm to throw.

So he dreamed of becoming a great pitcher. He became so good, in fact, that he earned the right to be the pitcher for the United States team at the 1988 Summer Olympics in Seoul. He pitched to a gold medal and was drafted soon after as a starting pitcher for the California Angels. April 24, 1989, at the age of twenty-one, he won his first major-league game.

He dared to be what he wanted to be. He dared to think beyond the limits that others naturally would have set for him. He dared to try, and in the final analysis, that is the most important step any person can take in feeling good about himself. *Where you end up is not as important as what you learn along the way.* Dare to give it a try.

6. PROTECT the opportunity. Yes, get a net around it. Take out an option on the opportunity. Put yourself in a control position to explore and research the development. Don't let it escape.

Strike while the iron is hot. Timing is everything. Call a meeting. Form a company.

Protect the opportunity from procrastination and from predators. Copyright the idea. Get a patent on the possibility.

In the process protect yourself as well. Measure with eyes wide open the risk that's in every opportunity. Weigh the risks carefully. Develop a risk management plan. Can you bail out? Be smart. Put on a parachute before you leap. What's the worst that can happen? Could you live with that? What are the odds of the worst happening? Can you largely protect yourself in advance? Do you need another safety clause in the contract?

Protect your opportunity from negative thinking—your own and everybody else's negative thoughts.

Now, give that opportunity all you've got. Most opportunities that passed inspection and failed to lead to

8

success stumbled and fell apart in the hands of halfhearted trustees. Yes, most failing opportunity thinkers fail not because they lacked opportunity or talent or training or resources but because they didn't give their opportunity their wholehearted effort. So they quit too quickly. Possibility thinkers really get started when they hear a "no!" How do they do this? Why, they . . .

7. INJECT opportunities full of enthusiasm. *En* and *Theos,* the Greek for in-God, is the origin of the word as well as the real definition of enthusiasm. Enthusiasm is a spiritual power designed by the Creator God to fuel human beings to be *the creative creators of creative offspring.* Enthusiasm is a mysterious, marvelous, miracle-working, mountain-moving power. Simply keep on believing in the God who believes in you, and never, never give up.

I'm constantly amazed at how many people choose to fail. How? By failing to inject this God-power into their human spirit. So they miss the drive, the ambition, the determination, the motivation to make the most of the opportunities that are made freely available to them. Without this power of enthusiasm, problems, difficulties, obstacles, and frustrations become excuses for not trying or for giving up.

Disappointments—and they're inevitable—turn into discouragement without constantly reinjecting enthusiasm into the human spirit. Remember this:

Disappointments are realities. Discouragements are reactions. I may not be able to control my life and manage to avoid all disappointments, but I can choose never to let the disappointments discourage me.

Consider this true story of a girl who really had nothing going for her—except freedom and faith.

> **Enthusiasm is a mysterious, marvelous, miracle-working, mountain-moving power.**

8

Her father was Dutch and lived in Indonesia. He married an Asiatic, which meant Joyce was mixed blood. So when World War II broke out and the Japanese invaded the country, they placed Joyce and her Indonesian mother in an internment camp. When she was only two years old, her father died. So far, a tough start to say the least. With the war over her widowed mother got a job as a secretary.

Poor? They lived in a Quonset hut with no electricity or running water. For a bathtub they used an old oil drum. For a toilet they used an open-air ditch. There had to be an opportunity to improve their lot. It came with a chance to emigrate to the Netherlands.

Joyce was fourteen when she arrived in Europe and saw a telephone for the first time in her life. Now she could go to school. But her toughest time was still ahead of her. Two years later at the age of sixteen she contracted an infection that required the amputation of a leg. Pain. Handicap. Tough times.

When she was twenty-one her mother chose to make still another move, this time to America. Joyce settled down to work as a secretary. She saved her pennies. So did her mother. And six years later she suffered her biggest loss. Her mother died, leaving her alone, but with a total inheritance of only five thousand dollars.

"I'll go back to school again! This is the land of opportunity," she thought.

So at twenty-seven she enrolled in college and graduated four years later with a 4.0 average. She didn't stop there. She went back to U.S.C. and graduated now with her degree in law—once more winning a 4.0 average. And as I write this chapter, she has just been appointed a supreme court justice in the state of California—Justice Joyce Kinnard.

Wait a minute! Don't withhold the honor she deserves by suggesting she was naturally bright and brilliant. Again and again the top students are on top because they simply never believed that high scores were impossible. "I got straight As," Walter Anderson, now editor of *Parade* magazine, confesses, "simply because I got a scholarship and all the time I was working under the false impression that I'd lose my scholarship if I didn't get straight As!"

8

8. CORRECT the opportunity. Yes, be prepared to shape as well as seize your opportunity. If there's one quality that stands out in the operational style of opportunity thinkers, it's their ability to compromise, adapt, adjust, and make midflight corrections in their flight plans. Skillful and successful entrepreneurs will maintain management flexibility.

For opportunities have a way of suddenly expanding—or with equal surprise—shrinking. Rather than being disappointed when progress is slower than expected, opportunity thinkers make adjustments downward. So the student may take fewer semester hours of study when a really tough course is required. So the businessman lays off employees during slack times. So this author, Robert Schuller, shelves some of his projects during the pressure time when a book, like this one, demands completion. Tough times are encountered by almost anyone who is seriously pursuing any goal. When problems or pressures mount, you simply retreat, regroup, reorganize, and reprioritize your resources, but you don't get discouraged and quit. Cycles come and go, but your eye never loses sight of your ultimate goal.

The rocket is launched. The computer locks it into the track to its predetermined target. And midflight corrections are made rather than abort the launch.

That's how I have succeeded. I was five years old when I set my goal to become a minister. That meant four years in high school, four years in college, and three years in postgraduate theological school. And eventually I made it! In 1955 I committed myself to begin a church with five hundred dollars. I carved out a forty-year plan. Thirty-five years have passed as this book is published. Today we are more successful than I ever imagined. Through depressions, runaway inflation, and unpredictable challenging times I have had to revise and reschedule my goals again and again. Sometimes I would suddenly have to move faster to "grab the moment" and buy real estate quickly when it became available. Be prepared to move fast to collect and cash in on the opportunity before the divine offer expires.

And when problems challenged my well-laid plans, I would, in wisdom, slow down, be patient, revise my

8

calendar, wait for the base to grow stronger, perhaps putting aside, temporarily or permanently, lower priority opportunities to secure, to salvage and strengthen, our primary purpose that was passing through unexpected storms. But I never, never, never lost sight of my primary objective. Yes, opportunity thinkers simply cannot lose sight of their God-given dreams. And eventually they will collect on their opportunities.

9. COLLECT on your opportunity?! Yes, if you will keep the faith, keep the focus, and keep following through, then *partial success is inevitable, and total failure is impossible.*

This I can guarantee to any and every dedicated, disciplined opportunity thinker: At the end of the road there will be a worthy prize. *Pride of effort is the reward given to everybody who enters the race.* Now collect the big prize, and pick up the trophy that really has value. Enjoy the pride of earning the highest honor: *recognition* as one who was faithful to his God-given dream.

Yes, be proud of the self-discipline you have demonstrated in the whole process of living as an opportunity thinker. Simply say yes to the beautiful, possibility and saying no to attractive, distracting temptations. Now take note: You've changed! Do you realize that? You're not the same person you were when you started. You have now built self-respect into your moral character. So pick up your award. You earned it! Be proud of your dedicated, determined, disciplined effort!

> **Pride of effort is the reward given to everybody who enters the race.**

Be proud of the courage you demonstrated when you made a noble commitment to a grand opportunity.

Truly, all opportunity thinkers always win something in the pride category. No opportunity thinker ever loses completely. Everyone at least wins self-respect in the *daring.* Courage is still the one human trait that is both a source and strength to

8

every person's self-worth. The person who attempts the impossible in the face of possible failure exercises courage, which—without delay or denial—brings immediate and authentic pride. Win or lose, succeed or fail, you now look into the mirror and, with either the smile of success or the disappointment of a setback, your head remains high, with the pride of knowing you were not defeated by fear. You had the courage to step into the arena and face your competition. *Whoever dares to try can never be a total failure.* Yes, at least you succeeded in overcoming timidity and cowardice. That happened the moment you made the commitment, stepped out of the circle of safe security, and exposed yourself as an adventurer who dared at least to give God a chance to do something wonderful.

Few people have inspired me more than Dan and Dennis Hayden. These twin gymnasts were certain to be on the U.S. Olympic team in Seoul, Korea, in 1988. They had dreamed of competing in the Olympics for seventeen years. They had started gymnastics when they were only six, and together they worked and dreamed and dared to be the best they could be. They dared to compete; they dared to face the possibilities of injury and losing.

They did well. They did better. They became the best in America. Dan, especially, began to shine in the national competitions. He won several of the biggest events and won *four national championship titles.* So the eyes of America were on Dan as the Olympic trials began. After all, he was our national champion. He was now our brightest and best male gymnast. But Dan suddenly became ill during the tryouts. He managed to get through the routines and still pull high scores. But during the eleventh routine he dislocated his shoulder. A muscle ripped. Pain shot through his body. In one awful, horrific, shattering moment, his seventeen years of effort were wiped out. He could not go to Korea. His dream was over. Dead. Finished.

Two days later, he and I had dinner together. Dan and Dennis were very quiet. Dan was hurting so badly that he could hardly lift the knife to butter his roll. He said to me, "I have worked seventeen years for this, and now it's all over. I'll never be able to go to the Olympics."

For seventeen years he worked. For seventeen years he

8

dreamed. For seventeen years he denied himself pleasures and fun. And in one split moment, his dream was shattered. I said, "Dan, I don't see anger in your eyes. I don't sense self-pity in you. How can you take this? How can you give everything for seventeen years and lose it in one split second and not be bitterly consumed by a devastating disappointment?"

Whoever dares to try can never be a total failure.

"I draw upon my faith in God," he answered, misty-eyed. "When I knew that it was all over for me, I prayed a prayer that went something like this: *Father, please give me the courage and the strength to get through this. For we know that it is Your will that counts.* Then two Scriptures came to me: One Scripture is, Do all things to 'the Lord, knowing that your labor is not in vain' (1 Cor. 15:58). And the other Scripture is 2 Corinthians 12:9 and 10. 'My grace is sufficient for you, for My strength is made perfect in weakness. . . . Therefore I take pleasure in infirmities . . . for Christ's sake. For when I am weak, then I am strong.'"

Dennis added, "Even though I did not make the Olympic team, I felt an inner purity in my spirit. After the Olympic trials were over, I chose to put my faith in the Lord. And I'm believing that the Lord has a better plan for my brother and me."

That's believing in the God who believes in you!

Neither of the twins ended up where they hoped they would. Neither one of them has an Olympic gold medal. But they both have a beautiful faith in God that has crowned their lives with honor. *That's called keeping a disappointment from becoming a discouragement.*

Losing can be tough, but you won't fail to win the biggest prize, pride of personal integrity. You were faithful to your God-given opportunity.

Yes, those who succeed as well as those who fail must find their real reward in the personal pride of heartfelt integrity. For you can be sure—and you had better beware—that you will not be

8

universally honored, applauded, appreciated, or respected if you succeed. Champions, achievers, yes, rich people too, are often hated. Successful people are, after all, a judgment upon many of those who, for whatever reason, noble or ignoble, never rose above the level of mediocrity. The play-it-safe persons, who choose to live safely on the shallow slopes, never striking out to scale the peaks or take risks or climb mountains, will probably watch your climb up the side of the cliffs attempting the impossible.

Some will applaud. But there will be others who will be jealous. You should expect this. They may even mock you for what they may call a waste of human effort. They may downplay your achievements. They may fault your efforts, however noteworthy and honorable. They may even accuse you of cheating when they are the real cheaters. They have stolen from themselves the possibilities and opportunities to succeed. For sure, those who stand on the summit will be noticed and complimented and sometimes criticized.

If you become number one in your class, you will be in an extremely vulnerable position. Do not expect everyone to honor or respect or compliment you. In fact, belittling and demeaning criticism will often be a normal and natural reaction. So your inner pride of achievement must be your real reward. That sense of integrity will more than compensate for implied insults and critical reviews. This is the truth: When you have received a divine dream, grasped it in fervent faith, and pressed it with passion to the peak, your inner fulfillment will so inspire you with surges of humble pride that you can stand before God and be proud of who you are, what you have done, and how you get there! That is the great reward. This is the challenge in these blunt words: "You shall not steal."

So

- **Earn All You Can!**

- **Save All You Can!**

- **Give All You Can!**

The Pride Of Earnership And Ownership—Experience And Enjoy It

8

THE PRIDE OF STEWARDSHIP

Here then is an exciting philosophy of creative economics that can build a global society in which human beings can have the hope of peace, prosperity, and pride.

"A gentleman," George Bernard Shaw wrote, "puts more into life than he takes out of it."

Yes, the pride of earnership and the pride of ownership without the pride of stewardship will finally become a hollow, shallow, empty pride.

So this is where this positive eighth commandment points us: out of greed and into generosity.

> "Bring all the tithes into the storehouse,
> That there may be food in My house,
> And prove Me now in this,"
> Says the LORD of hosts,
> "If I will not open for you the windows of heaven
> And pour out for you such blessing
> That there will not be room enough to receive it."
> (Mal. 3:10)

If you really come to believe in the God who believes in you, you can become a tithe generator—a giver who returns one-tenth of his hoped-for earnings to God.

Then will you be absolutely assured of financial prosperity? Well, prosperity is a relative word. I can promise you this: You'll never, ever suffer from the indignity of poverty. I promise you that you'll never feel poor and you will feel rich.

You will never feel poor if you are rich enough to give away 10 percent of whatever you earn. No matter how slight or slim your income, you'll never feel the embarrassment or shame of poverty as long as your mind and mood are stirred to philanthropy.

My childhood family may, in fact, have been poor. We did wear hand-me-down clothes. A tornado completely wiped out everything my father owned. But a small ($5,000) insurance check came. And one-tenth of that went straight into the church offering: "A gift of thanks to God for sparing our lives." You'll never feel poor if you'll go to church every Sunday and drop a tenth of your weekly income in the offering. Somehow you *manage to live on the balance.* The result? *The pride that comes when you are preserved from the poverty complex. So I never felt poor—I always had something to give.*

Well, after the tornado we went on to salvage broken planks, bent nails, and cracked bricks to rebuild with our bare hands a new house to live in. Yes, my father prospered. Tough times, we learned, never last, but tough people do. And my dad came to the end of his life satisfied and fulfilled, having tasted to his joyful end the pride of earnership, the pride of ownership, and the pride of stewardship.

Good news: *You can never lose what you choose to give away.* But you can never be sure you won't lose what you choose to keep for yourself.

So stewardship is the secret of financial peace of mind.

John duPont, who is a member of my board of directors and a good friend, was born into the legendary wealth of the duPont family. He could have done what some wealthy children have done—become a playboy and squandered the wealth. Instead he looked upon his wealth as an inheritance of responsibility. Interestingly—and very importantly—he was true to his own unique personhood. Early on he was interested in birds. As a boy, he was fascinated by these beautiful creatures. When he went to school, he found that his part of the country didn't have a good museum of natural history. He took an interest in ornithology and proceeded to study until he had earned his doctorate, whereupon he decided to personally build such a museum. Now boys and girls growing up could see samples of the different kinds of birds in the world. He went on to use his wealth to travel to all of the far corners of planet earth acquiring and collecting birds, carefully making sure they were properly prepared by taxidermists. Today his museum houses a fabulous bird collection. He himself discovered in the Philippine Islands a species of bird that had long been considered extinct. He heard the natives talk about "strange little mice." And on close investigation he checked out the creatures to find they were not mice—they were actually a rare and wonderful

8

species of fowl long considered extinct. He went on to discover and name species of birds that have never been recognized or recorded before. Not only did he build and equip the museum but he has endowed it. Now something beautiful remains to be enjoyed by thousands and thousands of schoolchildren and adults today and for years to come.

Some years later in 1987 the stock market crashed. "I lost fifty million dollars in one day," John told me, adding, "but what I gave away I never lost. I know where it is."

America is a most unique country in this regard. There have been the very wealthy who not only acquired great riches but embraced the values of the Christian faith: love, compassion, tolerance, generosity. And they found their greatest joy not in gaining or acquiring their wealth—by achievement or inheritance—but in giving this money to wonderful causes. The greatest universities in America, for instance, are not the state universities funded by taxpayers but institutions that were privately founded and privately funded: Harvard, Yale, Columbia, Stanford, Princeton, and Duke, to name only a few. Likewise some of the greatest breakthroughs in medical research have been made with funds from individuals who earned it, owned it, then shared it generously.

Armand Hammer is a man I profoundly respect. He was educated to be a doctor like his father. Both graduated from the College of Physicians and Surgeons at Columbia University. Armand's forebears were Russian Jews who feared persecution under the Czars. His grandfather came to America the first time in 1875 and became a U.S. citizen. Later he returned to Russia to engage in business there and later, once more, returned to the United States with his family, including young Julius Hammer, Armand's father. Then came the Russian revolution. Lenin established a communist state. "Anybody who destroyed the Czars had to be a good guy," so Armand Hammer's father reasoned. He saw the revolution as freedom from oppression and became a founding member of the Communist party in the United States of America. However, Armand would never share his father's viewpoint but would become quickly and faithfully a great capitalist—in the finest sense of the word.

"Armand, I want you to take over the tiny drug business I

8

started," his ailing father said to his son, then attending college. "Will you do this?"

Armand took over the business. He decided he could mix, then sell, his father's prescriptions cheaper than the cost of advertised brand drugs and thereby bring needed medicines to people who otherwise couldn't afford them. With that simple, compassionate attitude, the young capitalist went to work, managing the drug business even while he was attending medical school. In a few years he would graduate from medical school at the top of his class. In the meanwhile, through Armand's astute business sense and marketing talent, the drug business expanded into a flourishing pharmaceutical establishment. With a medical degree in his pocket and financial success in his hand, he looked at the life ahead of him and wondered what he would do.

The first thing he did was to sell the now hugely successful drug manufacturing business to his workers. They bought it by purchasing shares. Now they had the Pride of Ownership as well as the Pride of Earnership. So Armand Hammer found himself, at the age of twenty-three, free of the business and with well over $1 million in cash! With this base he began his career upward and onward.

When Armand learned of a great typhus epidemic in Russia, he decided to help by purchasing an ambulatory hospital and taking it to the Soviet Union. Because of his father's communist commitment, he was trusted enough to be admitted to the Soviet Union for a visit. There he saw people dying from starvation and realized they needed food more than medical help. "I'll make a deal with you," he told the Russians. "I'll buy wheat in the United States and have it shipped to you. It's deplorable that men, women, and children die of hunger when we have an excess of wheat in America! I've got a millon dollars to buy the wheat which sells at $1 a bushel. But I need something in trade in return for my entire investment." It was decided he would receive furs, hides, and other goods. Thus, the deal was consummated and Armand's wheat saved the Urals from starvation!

Armand's humanitarian efforts brought him to the attention of Lenin, who invited him for a meeting. Lenin offered him an asbestos mining concession—the first made to

8

*H*ow and where do you begin—*if you have nothing?*Maybe you have to go back to Chapter 1. Or perhaps close this book and meditate on the title, *Believe in the God Who Believes in You!*

"Many of the poorest of the poor," Mother Teresa told me, "have gone on to learn how to earn, then save until they own their own home today." It's amazing how people can be motivated and inspired to achieve after they have learned to believe in the God who believes in them.

a foreigner. This was the beginning of Armand Hammer's business dealings with the Soviet Union.

He went on to save the lives of many people through his business transactions. His compassion and his belief in capitalism made it possible for him to be generous toward worthy causes. He would go on in his life to acquire immense wealth, giving 90 percent of his income away every year! At the age of twenty-three, he was a millionaire. Today, at the age of ninety-one, he's leading a campaign to raise $1 billion to help "find a cure for cancer" before the end of this century!

One of the men in the world I count as a personal friend is Woo Choong Kim in Seoul, Korea.

As a young man Woo Choong Kim was among the poorest of the poor. He had survived the unspeakable horrors of the Korean War. His country was decimated, denuded of all trees and shrubs. They had all been eaten by the starving people. Now the war was over. He had nothing. He could steal? No. For his Christian mother had taught him that stealing is a sin. *Believe in God and you can succeed.* How? Where? He prayed. He believed. Into his mind came an impossible dream "to earn and save until he could reach his goal of having $15,000." How do you earn when there are no jobs? Well, you can always become a scavenger, collect litter and sell it and even collect cigarette butts from the gutters around the American military base. He cut off the filter and burned ends, tore open the paper, collected the used tobacco

8

and sold it. Imagination. Ingenuity. Integrity. Enthusiasm. He was motivated.

Beginning is half done. Today he heads one of the world's great corporations, Daewoo.

"Dr. Schuller, my sales last year were over $12 billion dollars. But I find my greatest joy in lifting my countrymen from shame to pride by giving them opportunities to escape from oppressive poverty to liberating prosperity. I create job opportunities. Yes, and I build churches too, like you do, Dr. Schuller. Whenever I get an overseas contract to build a major construction project, the first thing I do is build houses for my workers to live in and then a church where they can know God."

If Joyce Kinnard could do it,
    so can you!
If Woo Choong Kim could do it,
    so can you!

Become an opportunity thinker now! Become an actual participant in this exciting global system of creative economics. Don't call it capitalism or socialism; call it "creationism." Believe in the God who believes in you: this is real "liberation theology."

You are somebody! You can do something! Tap into the creative power of healthy pride!

HOW DO YOU BEGIN
IF YOU'VE LOST EVERYTHING?

First, *you have not lost everything.* You still have life left.
So *look at what you have left. Never look at what you have lost.*

Honestly, you haven't lost everything. You have not lost your faith. For faith is not something you can lose. You can decide to abandon it. But you can't lose it. You cannot lose what you can always choose.

It's not lost if you know where you can find it. And you know where to find it, by going to the God who believes in you even if you don't believe in Him.

In Washington, D.C., the stunning National Air and Space Museum stands connected with the Smithsonian Institute and houses a great collection of aircraft, airplanes, rockets,

8

and space capsules. The dramatic entry features a spectacular nine-story-high painting of the sky. Billowing clouds rise layer upon layer, gray over white against a blue sky. And then you see it—painted by the artist is one solitary jet airplane flying nearly one hundred feet above you. The sleek, silent silver streak of a jet trail forms a long white path against the azure sky.

The artist—a friend of mine, now gone—was the famed Eric Sloan. I met him when the Hammer Galleries in New York City exhibited his work. I was admiring the exquisite, elegant sketches of sky and clouds at sunrise and sunset, after the storm, over mountains, and above the deserts.

He started life a very rich young man when his father died and left him with $1 million cash in the bank. It was his inheritance; he never earned it. And that may be why he didn't appreciate the value. He simply "enjoyed it," or so he thought.

"Dr. Schuller, what you teach and preach—self-esteem and possibility thinking, is so, so true!" His eighty-year-old eyes twinkled. "You know I took my inheritance and traveled the country. I spent it, wasted it, on 'riotous living' like the prodigal son. I had no religious faith or scruples. One day in a western city, I went to the bank to request cash to be transferred from my fortune back East. To my everlasting shock and horror the banker gave me the unbelievable news, 'I'm sorry Mr. Sloan, it is all gone. There is nothing left.'

"When the awful reality hit me, it left me with total despair and depression. I wandered down the lonely street. Lost. Confused. Broke. In the pit of the darkest discouragement, I found myself two days later in one place I had never been before—a church! It was Sunday! The minister started to talk. He announced his message, and the title hit me like a thunderbolt: 'God's Providence—Your Inheritance!'

"The minister said, 'God loves you! He has a plan for your life! He has given you talents. Develop them. He has given you some gift. Discover it! He is giving you opportunities. Seize them. God's waiting to provide you with all you need! This is your inheritance. No man can take that from you!'

"I went out of that church alive for the first time in my life! I had done some dabbling with paint and brushes. I now went home and wrote beneath my easel these words: 'God's Providence is my inheritance!' Yes, Dr. Schuller, today I am eighty years old and, some would say, a wealthy man. Carved into the wooden mantel in my Santa Fe, New Mexico, home are those words: 'God's Providence is my inheritance.'

"And, Dr. Schuller, when I die, they can write these words on my tombstone: 'God knows—I tried.'"

We shook hands and said our fond and affectionate good-byes. Three days later he was leaving the gallery walking tall, proud, and natty in his double-breasted, navy topcoat when, as someone reported seeing it, he stopped for a moment to lean with dignity against a New York

> **Beginning is half done.**

City lamppost. Slowly, quietly, he slumped down and was gone. Did Eric Sloan find success? You bet! I'm so happy that my last words to him only seventy-two hours before he died were, "God loves you, and so do I!"

You can always start—or start over again—if you'll only believe in the God who believes in you.

CHAPTER 9

HOW TO GET OTHERS TO HOLD YOU IN HIGH SELF-ESTEEM

"THOU SHALT NOT BEAR FALSE WITNESS"

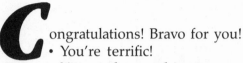

9

Congratulations! Bravo for you!
- You're terrific!
- You are honored in your community!
- You are respected by the most respectable people in your neighborhood. People really are impressed with you!
- Few, if any, persons are held in higher esteem than you.
- You are one person who is never the subject of negative gossip.
- You have your faults, too, but they're never noticed or at least not mentioned.
- How did you manage to become such an admired, respected, and highly esteemed person?

Surely it's not the result of your financial standing in the community? For others you know in the same class do not enjoy the respect you enjoy.

And it's not your educational credentials. Many names come to mind with equal and higher levels of academic accomplishments than you can claim, and they're not given the honors you receive.

And it's not because of your home. It's nice . . . but . . .

Nor your wardrobe. It's in good taste, true . . . but . . .

Nor even the block you live on. It's pleasant, agreed . . . but . . . (There's that recurring *but.*) How do you explain it when there are so many others that have matching status symbols but they're just not as well liked?

It can't be your physical appearance. For there are others more attractive in body and face than you, and they're really not that well liked. And, oh yes! There are others definitely not as beautiful as you, and they're respected as much as you are.

No, it's not your club or church connections. There are other members of clubs and churches that are as well respected as you are.

9

What is the secret? Yours and all of the others who are accorded great dignity by most of the fine people in your community?

You don't know? Come on. You're kidding. Your modesty is too much. O.K. Think of the people you really admire, respect, and esteem. Now, why do they command your sincere admiration? Remember, it takes one to know one.

They're always so positive! you say.

Oh! "What do you mean by that?" I ask.

I can't remember that I've ever heard them gossip, criticize, or run others down.

Interesting, Revealing. Anything else?

Yes, they're always so encouraging. They're so affirming of other people whether they are rich or poor.

They're so quick to compliment people. Not flattery, mind you, but they can always find something truly good to say about others.

So that's why this ninth commandment is so important. In the final analysis (and we're almost there—after all, this is the second to the last commandment), *if you want to respect yourself, it helps if you feel that you are genuinely respected by respectable people in your community.*

> **If you want to respect yourself, you have to feel that you are genuinely respected by respectable people in your community.**

It is so obvious, isn't it? You may have all of the material things that high culture would dictate as important to social standing and still miss getting the one acquisition that's most important: respect. And without that, suddenly the car, house, club membership, and designer labels lose their luster. *Being really respected by the most respectable people becomes terribly important.* Of course.

9

Here, then, we have this ninth word: "You shall not bear false witness against your neighbor." Yes, this *command* is *meant* to turn you into such a positive person that you'll be protected from the shame of negative gossip and shielded from hypocritical smiles. In fact, quite the opposite, you'll enjoy the self-esteem that comes with sincere and well-earned compliments.

So, this is a *command meant* to turn people into really beautiful human beings, respectable and respected.

How does this happen? It happens when a person is recognized as a positively honest human being.

What words can we choose to describe them?

Honest?

Yes, they have integrity. They speak up, but always with respect, even when they're not in full agreement.

Constructive?

Yes, yes. Even their criticism, which seems to be rare, is always constructive. They never seem to attack; they just seem to come up with better ideas.

Motivational?

Right! They are always inspiring to family and friends. "Of course you can do it." I hear them say that a lot!

Thoughtful?

Very true. They seem so slow to join in swift, negative, impertinent, impulsive, insulting judgment, as if they're reserving their opinion until they are better informed.

Tolerant?

Yes. That's it! While others get so upset when contrary views are voiced, they always seem to be saying, "Well, on the other hand," or "But they do have a point, you know."

Sincere?

Oh, definitely. When they genuinely dislike something, they're often quiet and say nothing. And when they do offer compliments, you know it's not hollow flattery—they really mean it.

9

Loyal?

For sure. They are never two-faced. Never. I mean never!
And you can count on them to come to your defense if you
are unfairly criticized.

Neighborly?

Yes, they're *wonderful* neighbors. They really are outstanding
and upstanding, and they stand up for the other neighbors
and the neighborhood.

Dependable?

Yes, and reliable too. Their word is as good as gold. Their
handshakes are better than any legal contract any lawyer can
draw up.

There are no loopholes in their handshakes.

So that's where this ninth command leads. And these are
the kinds of people that are turned out by God, who drew
up these ten *commands meant* to design and develop
wonderful character.

Real respect has to be earned. There are some accolades
you can attract honestly to yourself, but respect, that one
noble quality without which you cannot happily live, is not
handed out in a cavalier manner.

*No, it has to be earned. You may inherit wealth. But you cannot
inherit respect and you cannot buy it.*

A study of reputable families makes the point quickly and
clearly. If anything, children who are born into famous
families have to work harder to earn the respect of their
world in their time. Those who are born less privileged are
inclined, if they are negative thinkers, to be jealous and to
resent young people born to rich and famous families. How
the children themselves handle this position into which they
are born is itself a fascinating study.

Now, you're ready to meet some of the friends I've come
to meet, love, and respect in my life:

Meet Jane Owen. She is one of the most remarkable
women I've met. Recently Mrs. Schuller and I spent another
evening with her. She was one of three sisters known in the

highest social circles as the Blaffer sisters. Jane lives with her husband in Houston, Texas, and New Harmony, Illinois. The other two sisters married into the highest social and royal ranks of Europe and make their residences abroad. Jane's father was one of the founders of the Humble Oil Company. Jane said, "When I was a young girl, my family thought my friends should be the friends of the other wealthy families. I resented that. I did not appreciate the fact that I couldn't have as friends, just plain girls, maybe even from poor families."

It would be interesting to know whether this was, in fact, the intent of her parents or whether this was Jane's childhood impression and possibly an inaccurate interpretation of her family viewpoint. Our perceptions are frequently clouded, confused, and distorted at any age, and childhood perceptions have their own peculiar challenges. Nevertheless, Jane was born into a family highly respected in the higher social circles of her day.

I hold her today as a woman that I respect as much as any woman I've ever met. Not for the family into which she was born but for *what she did with what she was given.* This is what impresses me.

After Jane married Mr. Owen, she became fascinated and intrigued by his family roots. She understood her own family roots and wanted to understand his as well. This study would lead her down a path that would eventually consume her life with a passion, putting increasing demands upon her inherited wealth.

And so it was that she found herself visiting a quaint and quiet little town called New Harmony, Indiana. She discovered that it was a settlement established in the nineteenth century by a devout and spiritual people who believed in generously sharing themselves and their substance with their neighbors in the community. The selfish and greedy aspects of capitalism at its worst were not only frowned upon but were looked upon as major evil forces in society. So the social structure of New Harmony was one of mutually agreed-upon cooperation. The pursuit of material things was notably absent. The people found their self-respect, and they in turn projected this respect upon their neighbors and colleagues as they accepted and exercised human values like industry. They were indeed industrious. Nothing was to be wasted.

On her first visit to New Harmony, Indiana, Jane found no hotel and spent the night in a simple little house. The next morning she heard stirring on the lawn outside and saw the neighbor lady lowering a pail into a well and pulling the rope to lift a bucket of water out of the well. The neighbor turned to see Jane looking at her with an amazed stare. After all, Jane had never seen anyone draw water out of a well before.

"Oh! May I give you some water?" the neighbor lady offered generously, naturally, and honestly.

It was Jane's baptism into the simple lifestyle in which old-fashioned values dominated the behavior of people.

"You should make jelly out of those berries that are ripening on your bush," one of the plain and simple women said to Jane one day.

"But I don't know how to make jelly," Jane answered.

"Oh, I'll give you my recipe." the gentle friend offered. The next day she could smell the berries as they were simmering in the pan on the stove. The fragrance wafted through the clean and clear country air. Soon other neighborhood women were attracted to her house.

"You're making jelly?"

"Yes," Jane answered.

"Whose recipe are you using?" someone asked.

And immediately upon Jane's answer there was a chatter of pleasant disagreement among the ladies. Each had her own favorite recipe. Each found something unacceptable about the other person's recipes. So Jane was to observe that love is not to be confused with agreement.

Now Jane discovered a few of the original settler log houses still standing.

"They must be preserved," she said. So today, many years and millions of Jane Owens' dollars later, this pleasant and plain town is an internationally recognized center for the study of such human values as peace, love, prayer, and faith in God. So Jane Owens, with a remarkable inheritance, preserved and plucked from extinction the soul of a unique American town.

I was invited to go to this wonderful village place and

9

conduct a service of worship in what is called the "roofless church" designed by famed architect Philip Johnson. I shall never forget the spirituality that hung in the open air of this remarkable church.

What did Jane Owen really do? She fulfilled this ninth command—that's what! "You shall not bear false witness." She *bore a true witness* to the good people of this small town.

• You have a noble history—respect it.
• You are good people—believe that.
• You are the salt of the earth.
• You are the light of the world.
• Your inheritance of faith is precious—understand it! Value it! Treasure it! Enjoy it!

That's how Jane Owens helped that little settlement find its soul. That's what happens when we affirm and encourage our neighbors to believe in themselves and in the God who never lost faith in His children. We fulfill the positive challenge of this commandment.

Respect? No, it cannot be bought. It cannot be inherited. It has to be earned.

You don't, of course, need to be rich and famous to be respected. Anyone can earn respect by becoming a truly beautiful human being.

To begin with this means that a person must become a positive person. I recall a visit to my hometown in Iowa. While there I went to make a call on an aunt who was dying of cancer in the hospital.

"Oh, there's another friend of mine in an adjoining room," my brother and my driver said. "She would love to meet you. Would you mind stopping in to see her?"

I could tell by my brother's intensity and tone that he would be very pleased if I went along with his suggestion and so I rather reluctantly agreed. He briefed me as we walked down the corridor to her room.

"Mrs. Cambier is ninety-three years old. She has been here now since her husband died. She isn't able to get out anymore. So she spends most of her time in her chair and will spend the rest of her life here. She is a wonderful, beautiful person."

9

When I stepped inside the door I saw her sitting in a large chair with her shoulders and head bent forward in a stoop brought on by age and illness. She was unable to turn her head to face the persons coming into her room. But her eyes moved full orbit so she could see. Her eyes met mine even though her face did not turn. I was instantly, immediately, moved by her personality. An excitement was coming from those eyes and from the smile on her face. There was an energy of joy in that face! It was as real as the fragrance of flowers hanging in the air. She was really attractive, appealing, and exciting!

Instantly she began to talk about my uncle Henry.

"He was my first date!" She went on to brief me on history that I found fascinating! Her mind was so keen. Her memory was so sharp. Her attitude was so positive. Her enthusiasm was so contagious!

"Do sign my book," she said. And she handed me a book that recorded the names of all who came to visit her. It was nearly three-hundred pages thick, and it was nearly full. On every page there was a different name of someone who had paid her a visit.

"That's my second book!" she said with zest and zeal. "I've already filled another one."

What an unbelievable array of callers and visitors she had in her months of confinement in this nursing home. I was impressed.

I recall her even now and salute her, honor her, respect her as a truly great and beautiful human being. I admired her instantly. I esteemed her most highly.

She won my respect swiftly and sincerely. How? By being so positive in her mind and in her spirit.

"I came to call on her last week. I call on her once a week," my brother said.

"How are you feeling today?" I asked.

"Fine," she said. Somehow I felt she was forcing it a bit.

"Oh, I could complain," she added, "but I never grumble or complain—or I wouldn't get any company!" She twinkled and laughed.

"This is my prayer book," she said as she fondly took back her book after I had signed it. "You see, Dr. Schuller, I spend

9

Instead of putting people down, pray them up!

many hours alone here in my room. I never get discouraged or lonely. I just pick up this book and read it, praying for the people who have been here. I ask the good Lord to bless them.

" 'Yes, Lord. There's Dr. Schuller. He's doing Your work, bless him. Yes, Lord. There's Mary. She's a wonderful wife and mother, and she's having problems. She's such a good woman, Lord. Bless her.' "

Now that's bearing good witness in favor of your neighbors! This is really fulfilling the positive possibilities for this commandment.

"You know, Robert," my brother said, "everybody knows that when they call on her, they can't come bearing idle tales or suspicious gossip!"

So here is her key to winning friends, influencing people, and earning the precious and powerful wealth of respect.

Be positive! Be optimistic! Be careful! *Instead of putting people down, pray them up!*

It's really true. You, I, anyone and everyone can earn respect from respectable people.

Yes, anybody can win the respect of most important people. And the most important person whose respect you want to win is a person called *YOU!* You'll be proud of the person you are when you know you are a person of your word. A handshake! Anybody can become that kind of a person.

Let me introduce you to another person, a friend of mine, who is no longer living and for whom I had profound respect. His name is J.C. Agajanian. J.C. was born to a rather poor family. His father collected garbage to feed to his hogs. As it turned out, he became very wealthy. And that's because he was willing to take on a job that few people were willing to take on. So he turned a dirty job into a high-paying job—collecting garbage and feeding it to hogs. Obviously, the major cost of producing a hog for sale is food. If you can get the food free, you're on your way, especially if people will pay you to take their garbage away. He saw great possibilities and made a great success of his business.

So J.C. tried to get his wealthy father to agree to buy him a racing car and let him become a professional race driver.

"Never will I let you drive a racing car, J.C." his father said sternly.

"I'll never finance you on that venture. I will loan you money so you can buy race cars and have the fun of watching them race. I don't mind buying you a racing car as long as *you don't drive the car!*"

J.C. respected his father, and that's how he got into what would turn out to be a lifetime career. He became one of the world's great auto racing promoters. The Indianapolis 500 speedway in Indianapolis, Indiana, saw J.C. Agajanian wearing his classic white cowboy hat at every event. He was loved. He was admired. He was respected. He even established his own racing track in Southern California and promoted races. It became a very successful enterprise.

Now comes a remarkable story that needs to be told. One evening at dinner I noticed that J.C. had a gold chain running from his trouser pocket to his belt. Attached to the gold chain was an accessory that looked like a miniature bird cage about an inch and a half high and about an inch in diameter. And inside this gold bird cage was what looked like a solid gold nugget. Attached under the bottom of the bird cage was a round gold disc that hung like a flat coin hanging, like the clapper of a bell.

"What's that disc on your watch chain?" I asked J.C.

His eyes twinkled, "Oh, before I show it to you, I'll tell you the story.

"Many years ago a young man walked into my office and demanded to see me.

"My secretary stepped in and said, 'There's someone here to see you and he is very insistent.' So I let him come in.

He strode confidently into my office and declared, " 'Mr. Agajanian, you don't know me but I have a dream. I ride motorcycles. I do stunts with these motorcycles. I have an act that I have perfected, and I'd like to perform that stunt before your races some Saturday night.' "

9

"'I don't need you, thank you, and I'm really not in the stunt business,'" I answered abruptly.

"The man leaned forward, looked me in the eye, and said, 'Mr. Agajanian, let me tell you something. *Just let me do it!* All I'll ask you to pay me is one dollar for every person above the highest attendance you've ever had on a Saturday night. Let me advertise myself and it won't cost you a thing. You can't lose, so give me a chance.'"

Something about the man's intensity struck J.C.'s fancy. He stood up and shook hands.

"'O.K., it's a deal. I'll pay you a dollar for every person over my average attendance."

This young man then had pictures taken of himself on a motorcycle that appeared to be flying through the air.

"See the world's most daring stunt driver on a motorcycle!" shouted the billboards that were plastered around the race track and in local stores around the town.

The event was held. He did, in fact, draw a larger crowd. The next day the man came to the office to collect his check. Before he arrived, J.C. ordered his secretary to write out a check for 500 dollars.

"'But Mr. Agajanian,' my secretary protested, 'he only pulled three hundred more and you only owe him 300 dollars. Wasn't the deal a dollar for every person?'

"'Yes I answered, 'but he was good and I'm very grateful for what he has done for us. Just make it 500 dollars. After all, I made a lot more than 500 dollars extra from the three hundred tickets we sold!'" Laughingly, he admitted, "I'm still coming out on top of this deal."

The secretary stepped out, closed the door and when the stunt man arrived she handed him the check. He looked at it, stared, looked up at the secretary and said, "I've got to see your boss."

"I'm sorry. He is busy," she said.

He pounded on the desk, "I insist on seeing him. He's made a big mistake! A big mistake! We had a deal."

Now the secretary stepped up, walked into J.C.'s office, closed the door, and reported, "I gave him the check, but he seems angry. He said you made a deal, and you made a mistake."

9

"Send him in. I'll take care of him," J.C. answered. Now it was J.C.'s turn to be upset. He had been overly generous and the fellow apparently wasn't satisfied.

Now they were eye to eye.

"What's the matter with you? What's wrong with that check? What mistake did I make?" J.C. demanded.

"Listen, Mr. Agajanian, the check is a mistake. It is for 500 dollars. I only drew three hundred persons, not five hundred!"

J.C. was really taken aback. How did he know?

"Well, how did you know how many were at the race last night?"

"I had friends of mine doublechecking and counting the people as they came in. Mr. Agajanian, you owe me three hundred dollars, not five hundred."

"Well, I have a right to give you a tip, don't I?" J.C. laughed. "I think you were great, and I think you are terrific! Moreover, I feel you earned more than a dollar a person. Call it a bonus."

The men shook hands, and they became fast friends forever. And now with that story J.C. reached down to his gold chain and handed me the gold birdcage.

"This is a gift from the grateful performer."

"Yes," he added, "that *is* a solid gold nugget in that birdcage." And underneath I could now read on one side of the flat coin these words, "To J.C. Agajanian from Evil Knievel." And on the opposite side of the coin, "Your word is as good as gold."

"Thou shalt not bear false witness against thy neighbor."

Just think! What a beautiful, wonderful world it would be if the spirit of this ninth commandment were in charge of the minds, moods, and manners and mouths of people in the world today.

The first persons who must hear this message today are the preachers, the press, professors, professional colleagues, parents, and all other important people—like you and me.

9

PREACHERS

Preachers: Yes, my profession has often broken this commandment: by *omission* in failing to point out the truth and goodness in other preachers and by *commission* in false judgment and criticism of others.

False witnessing by religious authorities set the stage for the crucifixion of Jesus. Ironically it was Pontius Pilate who came closest to earning respect for critical judgment when he asked sincerely, "What is truth?"

The world of religion can be so beautiful when preachers, evangelists, authors, and theologians look for areas of agreement with other faiths.

Surely where understandable, sincere, and irreconcilable differences remain, *we must at least be respectful, dignified, and courteous in our comments and critique.*

Cheap shots, cute insults, faulty criticism, and cynical sarcasm clearly violate this ninth command. At least we must be humble and consider: "I'm not sure I am being completely fair if I articulate my opinions as they are being formed now."

We will begin to keep this commandment when we become humble and *fearful of one thing:*

Be afraid of damaging a good person by unfair criticism. (Pinning labels on people can really be dangerous.)

Do you really want to become a respected and respectable communicator? Then interrogate—don't pontificate. Ask questions—don't level accusations. Inquire—don't attack.

Can you imagine negative, critical articles and even books about living persons being put into unforgivable print before the author has verified the facts or his opinions? Of course, it happens all the time. Who's hurt? Everyone, of course. Not least of all the irresponsible author. He will end up losing his own self-respect if and when the unclouded truth reveals his judgment to be biased and faulted.

One pious church leader spread vicious rumors about a priest. When confronted with the truth, she realized she had made an awful mistake and was sincerely penitent.

9

"Then take this feather pillow to Nob Hill," the priest ordered, "and let the feathers fly like untrue rumors."

She did as she was told. Nob Hill was the highest point in the town. Here the winds always blew. Alone on the top of the hill she opened the pillow and emptied the feathers to the wind. They were carried like little birds and tiny butterflies until all were gone. She returned to her priest with an empty pillowcase. She put it dutifully on his desk and, with tears in her eyes, said, "I have done as you ordered. I have come to claim my pardon."

He looked down at the empty pillowcase, picked it up carefully, and handed it back to her. She hesitated. He said, "Take it. I say take it." She did. "Now go back and pick up every feather and bring them all back to me."

THE PRESS

The Press: Like preachers who enter their pulpits inadequately prepared, the press have often been leaders in bearing false witness against their neighbors. When the pressure of daily deadlines, added to the pressure to be the first to break the news, joins with the pressure to increase circulation, then the conditions are right for a dangerous, destructive societal thunderstorm. Under our wonderful freedom of the press, reckless, ambitious, unethical reporters literally can and do get by with murder, all under the virtual blanket of immunity granted by our Constitution.

One of the most respected spiritual leaders with an impeccable reputation came dangerously close to being gravely damaged by the press. At the height of the television ministry scandals in the late '80s, a woman entered a courtroom (with reporters trailing at her side) to present to the judge a request for a legal order demanding that "Reverend So and So" be restrained from sexually harassing her. The entire episode was a fabrication. When she could submit no evidence for her accusation, the judge dismissed her.

"If you can come up with some basis for your complaint, then come back tomorrow."

9

"All right, your Honor, I'll be back tomorrow." The lawyer of that falsely accused minister went directly to the daily newspaper and barely convinced and persuaded the editor (minutes before the presses started to roll!) not to go with the story. Had that desperate, urgent, passionate appeal not been made this story would have appeared on the wire services worldwide: "Local Preacher Accused of Sexual Harassment." The next day the plaintiff again approached the court, again with reporters. Before she entered the courtroom, she approached the attorney for the minister and whispered, "Don't you have something to offer to me?" When no money was offered, she left.

How do the innocent people handle irresponsible, peremptory strikes leveled against their reputations and ruthless reporters? How do these victims of false witness deal with it when the press does not need to "swear to tell the truth, so help me God"? If you are tried in the press by the press, which enjoys immunity from perjury laws and more often than not lacks the time to check and double check the details (the presses are rolling!), how do you handle that? Fight back?

Well, there is great wisdom to the painfully true advice, "Don't get caught in a war with those who buy ink by the barrel."

Sue for libel damages? Maybe. My friend Carol Burnett did and won. But check the odds: To succeed in a libel suit you must prove that the press *intended* to do damage. Unless damaging memos outlining a campaign or a conspiracy to do damage exist, how can you prove a reporter intended to damage someone's reputation?

Think positively? Is this the strategy for survival under unfair attacks? Now you're on the right track. But that's easier for some persons and some professions than others.

A friend of mine, the late U.S. Congressman Clyde Doyle, learned how to practice positive thinking when he was viciously attacked in the press, most unfairly and irresponsibly. "How do you handle this?" I asked him. "Doesn't it lower your dignity?"

"Well, I am in the business of getting elected to office to

serve the people. When the people come to the polling place, they will vote for the name that is most familiar. That's been proven time and time again. So I can absorb the negative stories in the press—AS LONG AS THEY SPELL MY NAME RIGHT."

Yes, be challenged by the false accuser!

Jesus was. He remained silent. He lived and died with such divine dignity that He brought honor to Himself and disgrace to His critics.

So live that when you die you'll have proven your enemies to be liars.

THE PROFESSORS

Professors: Yes, the preachers and the press are not the only people who need to hear and heed this commandment. Even academic professors bear false witness. For instance, conclusions are often taught as scientific truth and later proven to be incorrect. The development of jet-propelled aircraft was blocked for years by professors heading the study of aeronautical engineering. The late Walter Burke, past president of the McDonnell Aircraft Company told me, "We were taught in schools of aeronautical engineering that flying faster than the speed of sound is scientifically impossible, that if a material object goes through a sound barrier, its molecular structure breaks down."

"Then how did we ever achieve the breakthrough?" I asked him.

"Oh, World War II came along, and they drafted farm boys who became war heroes and got promoted to top brass positions. They didn't know it couldn't be done, so they innocently ordered research and development to find and invent a way to build jet aircraft."

Elitism of course is part of the problem.

We cannot forget the scornful slights that leave scars on our self-esteem through aristocratic elitism. There are the intellectual elite who consider themselves the mental Lords of society. Academic arrogance can look down with disrespect upon the men and women whose educational backgrounds fall far short of the lofty achievements of those in the academic aristocracy. There is also the cultural

9

aristocracy that produces its own circles of the sophisticated elite. They will be the pacesetters and in their own way demean those who are trapped, more often than not, by economics and who must wear last year's clothes.

THE PHYSICIANS

Physicians: What? Doctors? They aren't really in the communication business are they? Well, not mass communication, not generally.

Case Number 1: Dr. Bernie Siegel in his book *Love, Medicine, and Miracles* writes:

"Ten years ago a woman with diffuse histiocytic lymphoma and widespread metastases came to see me. Her doctor in North Carolina had told her to go home and die. 'Why go three hundred miles to the nearest medical center only to be made sick with chemotherapy?' was his comment."

You could call that bearing false witness against your neighbor. The oncologist that Dr. Siegel sent her to was not at all encouraging.

"'As you know,' he wrote me, 'this is a rapidly progressive illness; survival for more than fifteen months is unusual, the average being six months.' He told me he really didn't think he had much to offer her.

"After she met me at the hospital, however, she told her friend. 'I knew I'd get well when he held my hand.'"

The letters from her oncologist tell the story: • July 1979 (just after starting treatment)—"continues to be weak"; • August 1979—"Marked response, weight gain, total regression of lymphadenopathy, and slight regression of lung nodule"; • October 1979—"Continues to do well . . . an objective decrease in all disease"; • December 1979—"In complete remission." Letters covering the next three years report, "Continues to do very well" or "extremely well" or "amazingly well;" • July 1983, "She came in today looking the best she has in two years. Her physician at home thought the family had switched people (she looked so well)."

One day in the corridor of the hospital the oncologist said to me with a twinkle in his eye, "Isn't chemotherapy wonderful?"

9

"When she first came to me, I was concerned," Dr. Siegel writes, "about the high hopes she obviously had for her treatment, because I knew her chances were not good.

"I began by feeling upset that her hopes were so high, and ended by having learned something—about the value of hope.

"Anything that offers hope," Dr. Siegel believes, "has the potential to heal, including thoughts, suggestions, symbols, and placebos."

Dr. Siegel concluded with this powerful insight: "I am sometimes accused of creating false hope. The only truly false hope is false NO HOPE.

Case Number 2: In the *Journal of the American Medical Association* (JAMA), Jane A. McAdams wrote about how a message of hope affected her mother at a time when doctors were expecting her to live only a few weeks more. Her mother had grown up during the Depression and as a consequence was very frugal and opposed to waste of any kind. She wrote:

> I resolved to lift her spirits by buying her the handsomest and most expensive matching nightgown and robe I could find. If I could not hope to cure her disease, at least I could make her feel like the prettiest woman in the entire hospital.
>
> For a long time after she unwrapped her present . . . my mother said nothing. Finally she spoke. "Would you mind," she said, pointing to the wrapping and gown spread across the bed, "returning it to the store? I don't really want it." Then she picked up the newspaper and turned it to the last page. "This is what I really want, if you could get that," she said. What she pointed to was a display advertisement of expensive designer summer purses.
>
> My reaction was one of disbelief. Why would my mother, so careful about extravagances, want an expensive summer purse in January, one that she could not possibly use until June? She would not even live until spring, let alone summer. Almost immediately, I was ashamed and appalled at my

9

clumsiness, ignorance, insensitivity, call it what you will. With a shock, I realized she was finally asking me how long she would live. She was, in fact, asking me if I thought she would live even six months. And she was telling me that if I showed I believed she would live until then, then she would do it. She would not let that expensive purse go unused. That day, I returned the gown and robe and bought the summer purse.

That was many years ago. The purse is worn out and long gone, as are at least half a dozen others. And next week my mother flies to California to celebrate her eighty-third birthday. My gift to her? The most expensive designer purse I could find. She'll use it well.

Case Number 3: "I'm afraid we physicians have sentenced millions to die," a prominent medical doctor told me. "We do this by failing to give patients hope. We are afraid of hope, Dr. Schuller. For if the hopes don't materialize, we'll be accused of failure. Perhaps even sued—unfairly, of course— for malpractice. So if we paint the darkest picture and the predictions prove correct, we'll be viewed as bright and good doctors. Our prognosis was right on target. If our negative prophecy doesn't come to pass, we win as well—we prolonged his life!

"God only knows how many patients would have benefited from the health-producing power of *HOPE!*" this doctor concluded.

PROFESSIONAL COLLEAGUES

Professional Colleagues: Professional jealousy too has caused many professionals to bear false witness. One of the great architects of the twentieth century was Richard Neutra. His published works are studied by most architectural students in the world. He was the architect I chose to design my first church building in California. We became close friends. I knew him well.

Strangely enough, he was a pained and unhappy person.

9

Why? Because he never felt he received his just honors, and recognition from his peers. Insults may be as slight as simply being ignored. Deserved recognition withheld is still another way to bear false witness. It was so with Richard Neutra. Powerful architects in the sophisticated parts of the United States tended to look down on California architects. This cultural bias led to Richard Neutra's being virtually ignored and never being taken seriously by the establishment of his day. Yet Richard Neutra was responsible for bringing the best classical architectural principles to modern architecture. Regrettably it was not until he had been dead for seven years that the American Institute of Architecture dared to recognize him with a gold medal award.

We discussed the oversight while he was alive. He admitted that it hurt him. He was not alone. Many of the truly creative pioneers have been overlooked when the promotions or awards were handed out. We are not always judged fairly. Frequently we are victims of jealousy. People who are threatened by our abilities are quick to criticize. Consequently, oversights, snubs, and criticisms are common.

All of us have been hurt at one time or another, and if the truth be told, we probably didn't deserve it. We all deserve to be treated with respect and with dignity, but unfortunately that doesn't always happen.

In the often-fierce competition for rewards and recognitions, the professions are always faced with the temptation of jealousy. I entered the ministry and was horrified to see this green-eyed monster at work among my colleagues while I was still in theological school. The most talented and gifted preacher was criticized behind his back by his classmates. The ninth commandment was being broken all around me.

It's almost impossible for jealousy to be honest. Jealousy is a faulted, flawed attempt to rescue self-respect from the positive challenge that comes from competitive centers or circles. Do I build myself up

Running others down is no way to build oneself up.

9

by tearing others down? In my own mind, perhaps. But this is at best a counterfeit pride. It will simply prove to be counterproductive. For jealousy is a hollow way to try to win the admiration and esteem of my professional colleagues. Only concrete, creative, constructive achievement can do that. So running others down is no way to build oneself up.

PARENTS AND OTHER POWERFUL PEOPLE

Parents and other powerful persons: These people bear false witness too.

I was standing at the cash register in the men's department.

In front of me stood a young mother with a young man. She looked young enough to be his sister. He was, in fact, her son.

"Well, you picked up some sun today," she spoke to her son in what I felt was a sarcastic tone. Her son said nothing.

Looking at me, a total stranger, she said, "He skipped school today."

"College?" I asked.

"No, he's only a junior in high school."

Then came the zinger. Looking alternately at me and at the clerk at the cash register she said, "Yes, he has the body of a man and the brain of a baby."

The insulted son simply turned away, left the scene, and headed for the exit. She turned to watch him leave, then flipped her head and shoulders with the what's-a-mother-to-do? gesture.

"Please," I offered to her as she turned her back, "don't ever again put your son down like that in public!" She stopped, and turned briefly to see who was offering her unsolicited advice. Her face was flushed with well-earned embarrassment.

Impossibility thinkers I call them, these people who by omission or commission put people down or fail to encourage them.

Then how can we harness the positive possibilities of this ninth commandment? By becoming possibility thinkers, that's

9

how! By becoming beautiful encouragers of our neighbors.

Look how the positive people—parents, teachers, trainers, coaches, managers, supervisors—respond to the challenges of this *command meant* to motivate people, to bring the best out of others.

"You can do it!"

"I'll help you! I won't let you fail!"

"You have the possibility if you're willing to pay the price."

"You can go for the gold! I really believe in you!"

"Someday, sooner or later, you'll get your reward!"

That's bearing and bringing positive (instead of negative) witness to your neighbor.

And it promises great rewards.

The student will come to the old teacher with these precious words: "Thank you."

The child will come to his positive parents and praise them.

The patient will bring a gift of love to the doctor who gave him hope.

The parishioner will simply say, "Pastor, you saved my life."

J.H. Jowett tells the true story of John Morel, mayor of Darlington, who was passing through the town and met a fellow citizen who had just been released from jail where he had served three years for embezzlement.

"Hello!" said the Mayor, in his usual cheery tone. "I'm glad to see you. How are you?"

Little else was said, for the man seemed embarrassed and ill at ease. Years afterward, this ex-convict met John Morel in another town and profusely thanked him.

"I want to thank you for what you did for me when I came out of prison."

"What did I do?" was the puzzled response of the Mayor.

"You spoke a kind word, and it changed my life!"

Let's start an inspiring revolution of the human spirit on the planet earth! Let us make a decision to allow ourselves to become channels of God's encouragement to our fellow human beings. We will go around boosting the spirits and elevating the self-images of people who have been bruised by

9

the failures, frustrations, and fracturing experiences of life.

You'll be surprised how good you will feel living with yourself. You'll discover that simply by being a great encourager you've found a healthy prescription for positive, personal pride.

Finally, how should the victims of false witness handle the abuse that a negative, cynical world hurls their way?

How have I, how have you, how will we *react* when false witness is leveled against us?

1. *Check your expectation level.* Discouragement is the result of a confusion of expectations—more often than not, the result of unrealistic thinking. Did you expect everyone to be honest and truthful? Did you really see the world as free from all human jealousy, sin, and evil? Did you really think anyone is always respected by everyone?

> # Determine today that you are going to be a positive person even if everyone doesn't believe you.

Does everyone respect any person who has accomplished something? Hardly! Bad people do not respect the work of good people. Negative people do not respect positive people.

Determine today that you are going to be a positive person even if everyone doesn't believe you.

Decide to be a kind, honest, and generous person. Yes, you may lose the support of some negative persons. Let them go. Pay the price. After all, they probably aren't the people that you respect the most.

Start living out the ninth commandment. Become a positive-thinking person. And when good people see you coming, they'll announce joyfully, "Here comes good news!"

2. *Don't take life's insults too seriously.* The first danger is to exaggerate the problem.

9

The great New England pastor Philip Brooks was sitting in his study one morning with one of the most admired men in his congregation. The parishioner was distraught and on the verge of panic.

"Reverend, I am ruined!"

Brooks, who hadn't the faintest idea what was going on, inquired and listened.

"Didn't you see the morning paper, Reverend? There is a ghastly story about me, and it's not true! What am I going to do?" He began to sob. Philip Brooks was a huge man, weighing over three hundred pounds. He walked over to the trembling body of a broken but a very good man.

"Now wait a minute," he said. "You have gotten this all out of proportion.

"Yes, I can understand that this could prove to be very embarrassing to you, even shameful. But now let me tell you something. First of all, I never saw the story. I never read the morning paper. Half of the people in this town don't take the morning paper. They won't read it. And by the time the evening paper comes out, another news story will have replaced the story about you!

"Of the people who read the morning paper, most of them only read the front page and the sports page. They never get to the page where your story is. Now the people who do read that page of the morning paper aren't interested in you at all, so they won't bother to read it—unless they are your enemies—or your friends! If they are your enemies, you haven't lost any ground. They are responsible for the story in the first place, I take it. And if your friends read it, they won't believe it. They'll probably become very angry and, in the process, they'll become stronger friends than they've ever been before. So cheer up, good brother, all will be well. My main concern now is that you learn how to react to what's happening to you. Think positively, and you will not be damaged by this. Unless you lash back, and that could embarrass your friends. For sure it'll keep the story alive and spread it to a lot of folks who otherwise wouldn't have heard of it.

"Your reputation? Dented? Yes. But not as damaged as you suspect!"

A friend of mine named Mitzie inherited a fortune from

9

her father, who was the founder of a great hotel chain. When her marriage ended in a terrible divorce, she made a statement that impressed me: "Whatever doesn't kill me, makes me stronger."

3. *Be on guard about being too defensive.* You could do your cause more harm than good. You surely do not want to come across guilty of the same offense others may have committed against you.

Early in my ministry, I had a problem with an elder. He was untruthful. He was unkind. And he was an obstructionist.

Finally, he said some terrible things about me, and I said to my wife, "I must stand up to him. I must confront him in the next board meeting. I can't let this go on. He has gone too far!"

My twenty-four-year-old wife looked at me with the wisdom of an aged sage and saint and said something that was to shape the rest of my life: "Honey, don't do anything. There are others in this oganization who feel like you feel. They are your friends. They will defend you. And when they defend you, it will be far more effective than when you defend yourself.

"If you were to retaliate," she went on, "even your friends would see anger coming from your face. And you aren't very attractive when you're angry. You are very attractive when you are quiet, patient, and kind! Don't reduce your effectiveness by becoming a fighter. Trust your friends. They are equipped to do the job far better than you are."

I followed her advice. I held my tongue. I remained quiet. Others put the elder in his proper place, and the problem went away. I came through it a wiser and better person.

Several years later when I was the victim of an intended insult, my respectable pride was offended. I allowed it to get to me to the point where I spent a rather wretched day, grumbling and complaining. Worst of all, I found myself snapping at my wife, who was innocent. Once again, this warm and wonderful heart reached out to me. She put her soft, gentle hands on my shoulders, brought her sweet face close to mine, quietly locked my eyes to her sweet, kind eyes, and spoke softly: "Honey, I've noticed that as men get

9

older, they either collect hurts or absorb them. So they either become crotchety and crabby or gentle and mellow." Then twitching my soft cheek with a seductive touch of her fingers, she said, "I want you to become a sweet old fellow." She winked! I caught the message. That piece of precious advice has served to forge a positive attitude that has really shaped my personality for the better.

4. *So choose to react positively, not negatively.*

Realize that when the blows come, justly or unjustly, you can determine whether this ill wind will make you into a worse person or a better person.

Trouble never leaves us where it found us. We are all affected and changed profoundly.

This is one of those times when we must remember that there is one gift God never removes from us: *our freedom to choose our reaction to what happens to us.*

We can choose to react negatively, lash back, and become defensive, only to do ourselves more harm than good.

Or we can choose to react positively: "I will prove to them how good I am." Then anger can be channeled into a dynamic energy to cause us to become better persons. We can demonstrate real self-improvement.

Always there is the possibility of a positive response, even to a horrifically self-disgracing experience.

I am reminded of a wonderful story in the Bible. Joseph was one of twelve children. He was favored by his father, which made his brothers jealous. So they did a terrible thing. They sold their brother into slavery and concocted for their father a story that he had been killed

> **There is one gift God never removes from us: our freedom to choose our reaction to what happens to us.**

by wild beasts. Down in Egypt, Joseph was eventually blessed with good fortune. As a result he was noticed and rose to become one of the most powerful men in the land. Many, many years later, his brothers, who assumed that he was dead, made a trip to Egypt to buy grain, as their land was ravaged by famine.

Imagine their shock when the man the brothers were directed to negotiate with was none other than their own brother, whom they had sold into slavery years before. Seeing his brothers, Joseph uttered a classic sentence, famous to readers of biblical literature:

"You meant it for evil, but God meant it for good."

God will have the last word, and it will be good!

This is my faith. This faith principle has worked wonders for me.

Problems arise, problems are dealt with as possibilities in disguise, and the problems will disappear or turn into positive experiences.

So long as we don't respond and react to our critics and competitors negatively, we shall win out with our pride intact. Yes, we must be challenged so to live that when we die, we will have proven our false critics wrong.

So false witnesses cause me to draw closer to Jesus Christ. Then I know I am surrounded by the peace and the presence of the eternal One. That friendly force, whom Jesus called "My Father, in Heaven," whom we call "God"—I sense He is with me, within me, and around me, and I am at peace.

"This too shall pass," He whispers to me as I face unfair attacks.

5. Don't strengthen and support the forces that are humiliating you. *Why! why! why! do so many people believe in the people who don't believe in them?* Why do we listen to the voices that don't love us or trust us? Whatever you do, don't believe the worst about yourself. Reject every inclination to berate and condemn yourself, fault yourself, and sentence yourself to deeper despair.

To have pressures and powers and persons put you down is one thing. But you don't have to join forces with them.

Don't listen for those demonic little whispers that may come into your mind to contribute to the destruction of your

9

self-respect: "I'm no good. I'm stupid. I'm a fool." Rather, replace these with positive affirmations: "I'm really O.K. I've made mistakes, but I'm still a good person. I'm a member of the human race, and nobody is perfect."

6. *Now then—let's accept all the compliments we can get.* Be a careful collector of compliments.

The shy, timid, inferiority-plagued person tends to be embarrassed by compliments.

For starters, understand that we need all the compliments that we can get, so be thankful when one is offered and simply say, "Thank you!" Smile! Someone is giving you a wonderful gift, wants to make you happy and is offering you a princely treasure. Don't insult them by spurning the accolade. Don't worry about losing your humility. By now you have learned that the easiest thing in the world for God to do is to keep a person humble. God's biggest problem is to keep us believing minute by minute how beautiful we really are. After all, we are His happy and helpful children.

So accept the honors that are honestly offered to you and enjoy them.

7. *Keep on keeping on practicing positive thinking.* Decide to look upon the credits rather than focus on the criticism that you are getting. When the company went bankrupt, I said to the founder (who was ready to commit suicide), "How long were you in business?"

"Twenty-eight years," he sobbed.

"How many people did you hire during that time?" I asked, continuing, "Stop and think how much money you paid out in salaries to employees. Stop and think about all the products and service you delivered through these many years. Now some of your creditors are stuck with your unpaid bills. That's too bad. Perhaps you can still pay them off—someday. But for how long did you give your business to these suppliers? Is it possible that the profits made on all of your previous orders are far greater than the losses they will suffer by the time you finally finish settling with them?"

8. Finally remember that *the best way to get anything back is to give it away.* That's how and why this ninth

9

commandment works wonders when you turn it into a positive force in your life. "Except a grain of wheat falls on the ground and dies, it bears no fruit," Jesus said. There is the universal principle I call the *law of proportionate return.* Jesus Christ taught, "With what measure you give, it will be given to you again."

So if your self-respect needs a boost, start looking for persons who deserve honors, recognition, and compliments. Become the president of your own complimenters club.

Look for persons who are doing an outstanding job.

Observe people who have endured hardship nobly and with dignity.

Turn every day into Appreciation Day.

Drop them a note; give them a call. Express your appreciation.

Come out of your shell.

Move out of the cave of low self-esteem into the sunlight of bright self-respect!

Get on the move. Make it a habit to turn every day into Appreciation Day. You will be surprised at how good you feel simply because you will be knowingly or unknowingly become an instrument of the God of love who wants to encourage His children who are doing well. You will be living in what the Bible calls the kingdom of God.

Now be generous with your compliments to others, and enjoy seeing their faces brighten up with delight.

How do you start? *Just choose to become somebody's best friend.*

A best friend is someone who believes in me before I've had a chance to prove that I deserve this trust.

A best friend is one who still loves me after seeing me at my worst.

9

A best friend is someone who believes the best about me when he may have reason not to.

A best friend is somebody who applauds me when no one else bothers to compliment me.

A best friend is somebody who encourages me to dream the impossible dream.

A best friend is somebody who keeps telling me, "You can do it! You're great!"

A best friend is someone who is quick to forgive me and affirm me after I have stumbled, erred, missed the mark, and sinned.

A best friend is someone who is honest enough to tell me the truth when others would yield to false flattery.

A best friend is someone I can trust with my deepest secrets.

Yes—I've got such a best Friend. His name is Jesus Christ!

And I'm going to share Him by introducing Him to others. I'll do this by letting Him live His affirming life and love through me.

Yes, Jesus Christ never broke this ninth commandment. He fulfilled and is still in the business of fulfilling it. Every time I come into His presence in prayer, I hear Him whisper to me, "You are the light of the world! You are the salt of the earth!" And he whispers one wonderful, encouraging sentence:

God believes in you! So do I!

CHAPTER 10

SELF-RESPECT: YOUR POWER AND YOUR GLORY!

"THOU SHALT NOT COVET"

10

I know how to be humiliated, how to be honored, how to be a
"have" and a "have not" person. "I have learned in whatever
state I am, to be content" (Phil. 4:11).

Contentment?

Is it really possible?

With all of the gaps in my life?

. . . gaps between what I have and what I want?

. . . gaps between where I am and where I think I should be.

It's tough making ends meet without gaps showing up . . .

. . . between bills and cash on hand.

. . . between buttons and buttonholes.

. . . between what I see and want and what I can really afford.

*Sometimes the distance between my eyes and my fingers is so
long and so far.*

"Satisfied?" Sounds wonderful! But is it possible?

*Just when I have something I've always wanted, I see something
I'd like with it or instead of it or more of it or less of it.*

*Just as I was beginning to enjoy it, I seemed to lose interest or
gain weight or discover the newest fashions. Or we decided to move.
Now what would we do with it?*

Call Goodwill?

Can we take a tax deduction if we give it to the church?

*These gaps in life between expectations and satisfactions, between
what I have and what the Joneses have.*

*I thought we were doing great until we had our high school class
reunion. I found out that some of my classmates who had lower test
scores are driving better cars, living in larger homes, wearing
fancier clothes, buying second—even third—apartments for
sunning, skiing, snorkeling, or just shopping.*

*On the way home, our conversation was something else! "Did
you see the size of her ring?" "Maybe I should get you a larger
diamond. I mean, I couldn't afford a bigger one when we got
engaged, dear. How about for Christmas? Or our anniversary?"
Silence.*

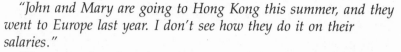

10

"John and Mary are going to Hong Kong this summer, and they went to Europe last year. I don't see how they do it on their salaries."

"But remember, they don't have any kids. They never wanted any, remember?"

"She said it is a lot easier without kids if your marriage breaks up."

A satisfying life?

Is it possible? With all of the gaps?

And then the breaks?

Somebody's always breaking up, or something's always breaking down. The car or an appliance; the watch; or my shoe. Anyway, I can't wear it today.

There's always something broken in our place. It's either a piece of furniture or a fixture on the wall, on the shelf, or in the drawer. It's either cracked, stained, torn, chipped, faded, or coming apart, scratched, mildewed . . . or the battery is dead.

Contented with life?

With all of the gaps, breaks, and sags?

How can I be satisfied when something is always sagging?

Springs, in the sofa or in my step?

It's the sags that get me down, sags in . . .

My income: I took a cut in salary;

My house: The window is jammed;

My furniture: The springs are gone in the sofa;

My clothes: The shape's gone. Something stretched; cotton, silk, wool—they all seem to suffer; or

My body: The sags are showing under my eyebrows, beneath the eyelids, at both ends of my mouth, under my chin, under my shirt, and below my belt.

What can I do? Is there any answer to my discontent? Cosmetic surgery? More cash? Fewer calories?

Contentment?

Don't tell me! Not with all of the gaps, breaks, sags, to say nothing of the bulges.

That's the problem with my life. The bulges are in the wrong places.

I'm well endowed. Trouble is, the prosperity shows more in my paunch than in my purse. What's thick should be thin and what's thin should be thick.

Somehow they got mixed up.

10

If I had more fat in the bank and less at the belt, I'd be in better shape all around.

Or would I?

Have I fallen into the trap of things—things that rust, wear out, wither, wrinkle, get weak, grow old, go out of tune or out of style?

Am I a slave to the tyranny of things?

"Purchase me!" "Possess me." "Parade me." "Preserve me—on a shelf, in the closet, or in a bigger place you build for me."

"Paint me." "Patch me." "Plaster me."

"Mend me." "Mind me." "Move me."

"Repair me." "Redecorate me." "Remodel me." "Restyle me." "Reupholster me." "Rearrange me."

"Don't throw me away. Remember how much I cost?" "Put me in the closet, drawer, or storage but don't discard me yet."

Why don't all of my things satisfy me?

Accessories! Yes! That's it! That's what's missing.

What's a sofa without the throw pillow? What's a bookshelf without the collectibles? What's a coffee table without something to fill in the empty space? Now I understand what the salesman meant when he urged me to "take this companion piece to go with it." I'll go back. "What?" "It's gone?" "Can you order one?" "They don't make it anymore?" I'm depressed.

Color coordination. Of course! Why didn't I think of it? That's what's wrong. Throw away the pillows. Sorry, but they're the wrong color now. Likewise, the pictures. Too bad, but that thing on the coffee table won't work in the new color scheme.

Wait a minute! Don't touch that. I don't care what color or shape or style it is. That's the last picture of my daughter with both of her legs—in her girl's softball uniform taken the summer before the accident. They had to amputate her left leg.

Hey! Slow down. I know that thing is cheap, but we picked that up on our honeymoon. It's special. It stays.

Contentment!

Sounds wonderful.

Is there a secret I've never learned?

Could it be in this tenth commandment? God's last word?

"You shalt not covet your neighbor's house, nor his ox, nor his ass, nor his wife, nor any*thing* that is your neighbor's."

Are we being warned here against the empty promises and false claims of materialism?

Materialism? What's that?

10

It's the temptation to relate more to things than to persons. It's finding emotional fulfillment more in things than in people.

Want fulfillment? Buy something new.

Bored? Go shopping. Spend money. Do drugs.

Guilty? Buy a gift—roses, candy—spend money. But buy some *thing*.

Fearful? Get a gun. Move to a gated community.

Insecure? Build a bigger savings account.

Feel inferior? Wear designer labels.

Need to impress people? Cars, clubs, cocktails just might do it.

Lonely? Go to a movie, a bar, or a motel.

To a materialist even people are treated like things:
- Toys to play with when you want to party;
- Tools to use and put aside when they've served their purpose;
- Trinkets for amusement, but only if and when it suits the mood;
- Treasures to buy and own and jealously possess;
- Trash to throw away and forget, easily replaced by someone young and pretty

So people become "things" made out of bones, flesh, hair, and fingernails.

It's enough to make you want to scream, "I'm a human being! I have hopes and dreams! I have a heart with pain and passion. I have a soul with hunger that needs to be fed. Help! Please help!"

Aha! *So that's what makes narcissism so pitiful! It's not simply that a person is self-centered; it's that his self-image is so materialistic.*

No, it's not the self-centeredness that makes a person truly narcissistic. After all, I had better be interested in myself. I ought to be concerned about becoming a more beautiful person, indeed! Think for a moment. Narcissus was a legendary person who preened and primped, then looked in the mirror and saw the shape of the nose, face, body. "I'm beautiful," he said, and he went out expecting everyone to admire his gorgeous body. Suddenly, subtly, he saw himself as a pretty thing more than as a beautiful soul.

Mind you, things are not in and of themselves wrong.

Self-Respect: Your Power And Your Glory!

Let's not become negative reactionaries against the materialistic culture.

Nice clothes, great architecture, beautiful interior design, lovely houses are not necessarily materialistic or self-centered objects.

So let's ask ourselves some questions.

- Do things save me or enslave me? Do I exist for my things, or do my things exist for me?
- Are my things weights? Or wings? Do they help me identify with my roots? Do they release memories? Do these memories provide a healthy moral and ethical direction to my life?
- Do these things release thoughts or positive feelings of self-worth?
- Are my things phony props for a low self-esteem? Does my ego need these things as materialistic stage sets to compensate for a deep-seated lack of self-worth?
- Or do these things inspire me to raise my estimation of the human family? Do I see some creative artist at work in this work of art? (What pride this workman must have felt in his pursuit of creative excellence!)
- Do my pretty "things" raise my level of appreciation for fine art? For great art is a ministry of hope and healing if it brings dignity to humanity.

Great art raises the collective level of human pride in a country, a culture, a race, or a religion when it inspires, entertains, educates, enlightens, uplifts, or reminds us who we are and where we have come from.

Then the monument becomes an instrument.

This tenth word is a *command meant* not to take out of our life the pride, protection, and pleasure that pretty and practical things can deliver.

"You shall not covet" is a *command meant* to put contentment, satisfaction, and fulfillment into your life.

This final warning points us in the right direction as we graduate from God's university of wisdom. This commencement address is delivered in God's hall of honor.

"Look within, don't look without. For contentment search your soul; don't envy your neighbor's material possessions."

Put your focus here: *Build self-respect; cultivate self-esteem;*

10

court a proper, positive pride in being a human being worthy of the label CHILD OF GOD.

So go out, and seek the glory and honor that only God can bestow: The God of Beauty. The God of Hope. The God of Peace. The God of Love. The God of Creativity. The God of Possibilities. The God who believes in you.

"You shall not covet. . . ."

So we have come to this!

By now we see through the glass clearly.

What we really want in life is spiritual, not material.

Beautiful thoughts are of greater value than pretty things.

Now we see why those things that we treasure most are the ones that bring us good thoughts.

I remember what a friend told me after she lost everything in a fire:

"If there's a fire, grab the family pictures. That's all you'll *really miss* if you lose everything!"

How silly then to covet my neighbor's things, after all . . .

He doesn't own my family photo album.

He doesn't possess the collection of souvenirs that remind me of happy travels and times with my family and my friends.

So things that harbor and hold positive thoughts to inspire and encourage us are truly gifts from God.

But expensive things that release no positive thoughts are empty of meaning.

I had an interior decorator fix up an empty office. When she finished, it was pretty. It looked right. But the collection of pretty things did nothing but fill the empty space. And they were, themselves, empty, elegant intrusions. Nice things that never release inspiring ideas are like great cathedrals without a congregation, like a beautiful house without family or friends. They are structures without spirit, bodies without souls, dead things. But fill the house and the cathedral with people, and the material becomes spiritual.

I like things that remind me of who I am, where I came from, and who was with me on the journey. Somehow they contribute to an awareness of my self-worth.

Those things that are of real value to me I already have. They're the objects that feed my dignity in a healthy

10

wholesome way. They release within me the kind of pride that is precious, positive, and powerful.

They wrap my important ego in a warm blanket of real humility.

I look. I listen. I touch my pretty things, and I feel something sweetly spiritual. Memories sweep over me and leave me with:

- **The pride of family;**
- **The pride of overcoming struggles and suffering;**
- **The pride of achievement;**
- **The pride of being a creative, constructive, courteous soul;**
- **The pride of being a beautiful person—yes;**
- **The pride of belonging to the family of God who believes in the positive possibilities in the human family.**

So here's to your self-respect!

I propose a toast to your self-esteem.

Do let me give you a gift box of positive ideas for your journey. When my children left the house from their wedding parties, a box of snacks to enjoy went with them— pieces of the wedding cake, sandwiches from the buffet table, napkins, and an unopened bottle of the beverage of their choice. They all remarked how much they enjoyed the food and, of course, the memories of the party that went with it.

So here's a packet of thoughts you can enjoy on your trip, ideas you can use to enjoy the pride God puts in you. Here are some ideas to nourish your important feelings of self-esteem.

Here's my first suggestion:

1. *Self-respect is a necessity, not a luxury.*

Make no cavalier jokes about it. Take this subject seriously. There's no room for frivolity on this issue of human dignity.

10

Understand, remember, and never forget that healthy self-respect isn't a luxurious emotion like some delicious dessert. It is the bread of life.

It is rice.

It is flour.

It is milk.

It is meat.

That was proven to me some years ago when I first published what has been called a theology of self-esteem.

I commissioned the Gallup organization in Princeton, New Jersey, to conduct a full-blown study of the effect of self-esteem on human behavior.

As I expected, the poll conclusively demonstrated that people with a strong sense of self-esteem demonstrate the following qualities:

- They have high moral and ethical sensitivity.
- They have a strong sense of family.
- They are far more successful in interpersonal relationships.
- They view success in terms of interpersonal relationships, not in crassly materialistic terms.
- They're far more productive on the job.
- They are far lower in incidence of chemical addiction. (In view of the fact that current research studies show that 80 percent of all suicides are related to alcohol and drug addiction, this becomes terribly significant.)
- They are more likely to get involved in social and political activities in their community.
- They are far more generous to charitable institutions and give far more generously to relief causes.

Guess what? *That's coming close to contentment.*

In summary, people with positive self-esteem demonstrate the qualities of personal character that any church would point to with pride in their members.

Twenty years have passed since I first named self-love or self-esteem or human dignity as the seminal force that helps interpret behavior both good and bad. Now these findings from the Gallup Poll have been confirmed in another study nearly two decades later.

The State of California, with taxpayer's money, funded a

10

special task force to study self-esteem and its impact on our society. The official title is California Task Force to Promote Self-Esteem and Personal and Social Responsibility.

Here, in summary, is the report:

To begin with, this is their definition of self-esteem. I like it.

Self-esteem is *"Appreciating my own worth and importance and having the character to be accountable for myself and to act responsibly toward others."*

Listen to these comments from the California task force:

"APPRECIATING MY OWN WORTH AND IMPORTANCE"

To appreciate my own worth and importance means to be aware of and to recognize the significance of my inherent worth, of my value to myself and to others, of my place in the world.

Every person has unique significance, simply because the precious and mysterious gift of life as a human being has been given. This is an inherent value which no adversary or adversity can take away.

This sense of innate worth is reinforced when each individual's unique abilities are recognized, developed, and used to enrich our society.

The more our abilities are developed for the benefit of ourselves and others, the fuller our lives and the richer the world.

The report goes on:

Appreciating is more than simple recognition. Appreciating means to cherish, to treasure, to respect and enjoy my innate and developed worth.

This is the kind of pride which arises from healthy self-regard, based on a realistic grasp of my own strengths and weaknesses. It is not the same as "false pride" or "pseudo self-esteem," an all too common condition in which vanity and arrogance overshadow a person's true self and identity, masking shame at myself.

10

The definition is further developed as follows:

"... AND HAVING THE CHARACTER TO BE ACCOUNTABLE FOR MYSELF"

Appreciating my own worth and importance is futile if it fails to foster responsible character and integrity in my actions. Character is evidenced in actions. Honesty, compassion, discipline, industriousness, reverence, perseverance, devotion, forgiveness, kindness, courage, gratitude, and grace are among the qualities which integrity of character produces.

Character is nurtured in the family which loves and accepts the child, thus affirming his or her worth and importance. Persons so nurtured are freed from the impossible burden of trying to "prove" their worth and value. They are released to be who they really are, loved and loving human beings.

Every child needs to be treated with respect, consistently, and from the earliest moments of life.

There is no fully adequate substitute for a loving family as the environment in which people learn to appreciate their own worth. There are, however, other important nurturing communities (such as schools, churches, the workplace) which can provide support to help build integrity of character and self-esteem.

"... TO BE ACCOUNTABLE FOR MYSELF"

"Being accountable means accepting responsibility for my own actions, for the consequences of my own behavior." (Good stuff, eh? Here's more!)

Too often responsibility is harsh when imposed from the outside, but when personal accountability arises from a personal, inner choice we are freed from confusion and self-deception.

Persons who are accountable for themselves value their own worth as capable, choice-making persons. They do not look to others to create their happiness,

10

and they do not blame others for their sorrows. They accept responsibility for their own lives, not accusing others of preventing their fulfillment; and insofar as it is possible, they take care of themselves.

Wow! Read on!

Persons who are accountable for themselves do not live thoughtless, haphazard lives. They make deliberate choices of the values and standards by which they live. They learn from failures, finding opportunity to learn and grow.

". . . AND TO ACT RESPONSIBLY TOWARD OTHERS"

The more we appreciate our own worth and importance, the more we are able to recognize and appreciate the worth and importance of others as well. As we grow as unique persons, we learn to respect the uniqueness of others.

We are all human beings, yet we express ourselves differently. We recognize people's rights to choose for themselves and to be accountable for their own behavior.

Yet simple awareness is not enough. A true appreciation of the worth of others will lead us to action, to deeds through which we treat others with dignity and respect.

The primary way in which we show respect to others is to step out of the state of anxious self-concern long enough to give others our attention—to listen, to understand, to care.

Responsible action is also corporate. We all belong to groups and institutions which interact with other groups and institutions. As members of families, churches, schools, businesses, social groups, a state, a nation, we must be vigilant and committed to insist that all these groups act in responsible ways as well. Our society is becoming increasingly diverse and multicultured. One dimension of acting responsibly means learning to value this diversity, to work for a peaceful and productive unity in the midst of racial, ethnic, cultural and religious differences.

10

Responsible caring for others knows when to say NO! As well as when to reach out. To act responsibly is to respect others as we respect ourselves.

In learning to appreciate our own gifts, we learn to appreciate and encourage the individual personhood and gifts of other persons.

And we become creative parts of a richer and healthier world.

This entire secular report could almost be summed up in those words of Jesus often called the eleventh commandment: "You shall love the LORD your God . . . and your neighbor as yourself" (Luke 10:27).

Yes, long before the California report came out, René Dubos, widely recognized as one of the twentieth century's great sociobiologists, made a perceptive observation in his widely acclaimed book entitled *Celebrations of Life*. The scientist began with these two provocative sentences: "The most distressing aspect of the modern world is not the gravity of its problems: There have been worse problems in the past. The greatest problem facing modern man is the dampening of the human spirit that causes many people, especially in the countries of Western civilization, *to lose their pride in being human and to doubt that we will be able to cope* with our problems and those of the future."

If that is true, **then self-esteem, or pride in being a human being, is the single greatest need facing the human race today. Our very survival as a species depends on hope. And without hope we will lose the faith that we can cope.**

If we have not faith, if we have no hope, if we cannot cope—how can we expect to be content? **Is it any wonder that we covet and long for something better?**

> As we grow as unique persons, we learn to respect the uniqueness of others.

10

Why have we lost our pride in being human? I submit that on the deepest level this condition of lost pride is the presence of an all-pervasive sin and shame—which leads me to my second suggestion.

2. *The need for self-esteem has a spiritual taproot.*

The presence and the power of a normal and natural ego drive is there. Most professionals in sociology, psychology, and theology agree that there is a strong, powerful ego. The questions we must grapple with are, Why does the human being have this ego drive? Where does it come from?

WHY ARE WE INNATELY PRIDEFUL?

Surely the ego is not the product of natural selection. Evolution may explain the genetic and organic development of the bones, hair, body, and brain, but evolution does not and cannot come up with conclusive answers to this question: Why is the human being proud by nature?

The Bible gives a clue. It says that we are created by the creative One to be His children. We human beings are meant to be the family of God on planet earth. We were designed to be creators, redeemers, producers, and encouragers and happily proud of it.

O.K. But doesn't the Bible call pride one of the seven deadly sins? Yes, it does. But the sinful pride the Bible refers to is a dangerous and pathetic attempt by shame-filled humans to recover their divine dignity.

This instinctual craving for a glory lost in humanity's primeval age lingers to lead lost human souls in a desperate, wild, wicked pursuit after that noble pride we incurably sense is our royal birthright.

For want of the honorable pride that only their Creator can supply, they established false gods, fabricated false pride, and even rejected offers of help from the Creator. It drove them to kill and steal, compounding their shame.

No wonder God, in an early rescue attempt, gave us ten commands meant *to take counterfeit pride out of life and put creative pride back into the human heart.*

Don't worry about becoming egotistical. When your pride

10

is rooted in healthy relationships, your humility is well insured. It's easy for God, friends, and family to take the wind out of your sails—if need be.

REMEMBER:

The superiority complex is conceived in the womb of an inferiority complex.

Healthy pride is the real self-esteem.

The arrogance of the conceited person is a counterfeit self-respect.

Vain narcissism; haughty egotism; destructive pride—all are distortions of God's divine design for dignity. These are dangerous emotions masquerading as the real thing. They are deviations which will ultimately prove to be self-destructive to a healthy self-esteem.

The pathetic tragedy of any phony substitute is that it deceives you into thinking you've got the real thing.

As narcotics dull the body's craving for nutritional food, so the temporarily satisfying deception blocks the natural, spiritual hunger for healthy nourishment. Eventually the alcoholic suffers from malnutrition, and becomes emaciated, and dies.

Likewise, arrogance, vanity, conceit, egotism become synthetic, counterfeit stimulants, pathetic substitutes for the real thing, opiates that dull the heart's hunger for humble pride, self-esteem, even for the God who built that hunger for noble glory in every human being.

Like a narcotics addict the egotistical soul, surviving on cheap substitutes, can never get enough to satisfy his craving. Drunk with dangerous egotism, he remains pathetically blind to his own self-destructive lifestyle.

Denial is his defense system.

He is, of course, headed for a fall. Humpty Dumpty sat on a wall.

Finally age creeps up. The foundations of his false and defective internal security system begin to crumble.

Those reassuring voices he's been listening to all his life grow weaker, are interrupted by static, and somehow no longer seem convincing in the face of his oncoming

10

transitions and death. *Too late he discovers that the egotistical "high" he'd been on all his life wasn't self-respect after all. He'd been "had."*

He went to a premium auction and paid the highest price ever for what he thought was a masterpiece only to discover that he bought a fake.

Contentment? He really missed it!

In the end his unredeemed, reckless ego produced behavior that leaves him with shame and humiliation, alienated.

On the other hand, a redeemed ego will become the powerful, creative, and positive force of God Himself within you. God can and will use this Christ-controlled ego to deliver ideas, thoughts, and feelings into the life of humanity, releasing drive, passion, and creative energy. "It is God who works in you both to will and to do for His good pleasure" (Phil. 2:13).

So enjoy those fantastic feelings of positive self-worth that positive religion offers. This is the real thing. "He that drinks from the fountain of the water of life I give shall never thirst," Jesus promised.

WHERE DOES PRIDE COME FROM?

Where do those strange ego drives come from? They are the call of your royal ancestry.

You are not a glorified ape, not a glorified animal.

You are the descendant of the first man called Adam, the first woman called Eve. You are a human being created in the image of God.

The story is told of Helen, Queen of Troy, who was carried into captivity as a slave. Here on a distant shore, in a foreign country, she was treated shabbily, until the pain and the shame brought on the added affliction of amnesia.

Meanwhile a noble warrior and prince of Troy, hoping she would still be alive, determined that he would find her.

One day in that strange and alien land, he came upon a prostitute in the harbor, seductively soliciting her loathsome trade. The warrior prince was startled to recognize an expression that reminded him of Helen. He approached her.

She propositioned him. He looked closely at her face and spotted the unmistakable scar that was an identification mark of the lost Helen of Troy. He gripped both of her shoulders, looked with passionate intensity into her eyes, and called her by name: "Helen! Helen!"

A foggy glaze in her dull eyes bespoke her complete unawareness of what he was saying. She could not comprehend her name or her true identity.

"Helen!" he called again and again. "You are Helen of Troy! You were meant to be a queen, not a harlot! Come home with me."

Suddenly a spark flared in her glazed eyes. From the depth of her memories, the powers of recall and recollection awoke her true identity within her. She remembered that she was, in fact, Helen of Troy!

Her shoulders went back, her head went high. Her lost pride was recovered; her shame was wiped away. The surge of the royal blood of the kings and the queens flowed with a new surging power through her veins. She was restored to honor! Redeemed! Saved!

3. *A positive religion can build, bolster, and boost your self-respect more than any* thing.

"Do unto others as you would have them do unto you," Jesus taught.

It's true! A positive religion that causes you to respect yourself will turn you into a person who respects others.

You have set in motion a two-way avenue of respect. As you now treat others beautifully, you will begin to respect yourself even more. You look at everyone in a new light. You find yourself admiring humbly, esteeming highly, and respecting sincerely the worth and the value of other human beings. Even the negative, destructive, and evil person is not viewed as hopeless trash, but as an individual with hurts and problems and difficulties, waiting to be redeemed, renewed, and regenerated into a born-again person. This is what a healthy faith can inspire you to be and become.

4. *Treat every person with profound respect.*

Respect others regardless of rank, economic position, social class, or intellectual attainment.

10

This is what continues to attract the world to Jesus. He treated everyone the same. Even a dying thief who was being crucified next to Him on a cross received a blessing from the Lord: "This day you will be with me in paradise."

Christ was able to see positive possibilities in the most unlikely persons.

You want to be really proud of who you are? Then look for the good in everyone:

1. *See* something positive in every person;
2. *Say* something positive to everyone you meet every day;
3. *Show* a positive face to everyone you meet.

Contentment? You're on the right road.

One of the great experiences of my life was to be invited as the guest of Commander Walter Davis, then the Commander of the *USS Ranger,* an American aircraft carrier. I was suited up and briefed on how I would experience an enormous jerk of immense proportions, once we hit the deck and came to a sudden halt. It was an experience that I hope can be repeated, a takeoff and landing on the deck of an aircraft carrier. At dinner, Commander Davis shared a beautiful experience that had happened only a few days before: "You know, Dr. Schuller, over five thousand persons make up the crew of this single aircraft carrier. We are a small, self-contained town at sea. When someone is alleged to have violated a law, I become both judge and jury. Just the other day one of our military police brought before me a young man accused of a major offense. The officer introduced him to me with the disgraceful and demeaning description: 'Captain, this man is nothing

When you discover the beauty in yourself, you will begin to discover the beauty in others.

10

but a dirt ball.' Hearing that definition applied to a human being, however faulty and felonious he might be, nauseated me.

"I stood up, confronted the officer, and rebuked him forthrightly: 'I don't ever again want to hear you call any human being a dirt ball. He may or he may not be guilty of criminal activity; he may, in fact, be found guilty of despicable behavior; but however degrading and vile his conduct may prove to be, he still is a human being. He is not a dirt ball. It is our job to build men, reconstruct broken lives, repair persons, and turn wayward boys toward honor. And we don't accomplish that by calling anybody a dirt ball. You shame yourself when you shame another person. We are here to build self-respect.'"

When you discover the beauty in yourself, you will begin to discover the beauty in others. And conversely, when you are able to discover the beauty in others, you will begin to discover the beauty in yourself.

The whole cycle of respect begins when you discover that God is God—the God who believes in you—and you are His and He is your best Friend.

5. *Let the teaching of Jesus redeem a dangerous ego.*

To succeed in the noble ideal of treating all human beings with respect, make sure your ego has been born again. It will then emerge as a healthy, humble self-respect.

Enter Jesus Christ! He specializes in the redemptive process of turning wrong egos into strong egos. A blind battering-ram ego is transformed into a humble, healthy self-esteem.

This is redemption!
This is creative conversion!
This is salvation from shame to glory.
Contentment? Can't you feel it coming on?

Jesus showed us how to redeem our egos into satisfying self-esteem when he probed deep into the meaning of the Ten Commandments. He delved more deeply than any previous prophet or rabbi when He gave the new commandment, sometimes called the eleventh commandment: "A new commandment I give to you, that you love one another even as I have loved you."

Now use the teaching of Jesus to turn a dangerous ego

10

into a safe, sensible, and satisfying self-esteem. He gives us such a reformation exercise in the Beatitudes. (It's interesting that He lays these sentences down just before He gives His interpretation of the Ten Commandments in Matthew, chapters 5, 6, and 7.) I call them the "Be-Happy Attitudes." The eight Beatitudes literally turn a dangerous ego into a sweet and satisfying self-esteem.

★

Be-Happy Attitude #1
"I need help. I can't do it alone!"
"Blessed are the poor in spirit, for theirs is the kingdom of heaven."

★

Be-Happy Attitude #2
"I'm really hurting, but I'm going to bounce back!"
"Blessed are those who mourn, for they shall be comforted."

★

Be-Happy Attitude #3
"I'm going to remain cool, calm, and collected."
"Blessed are the meek, for they shall inherit the earth."

★

Be-Happy Attitude #4
"I really want to do the right thing."
"Blessed are those who hunger and thirst for righteousness, for they shall be filled."

★

Be-Happy Attitude #5
"I'm going to treat others the way I want others to treat me."
"Blessed are the merciful, for they shall obtain mercy."

★

Be-Happy Attitude #6
"I've got to let the faith flow freely through me."
"Blessed are the pure in heart, for they shall see God."

★

Be-Happy Attitude #7
"I'm going to be a bridge builder."
"Blessed are the peacemakers, for they shall be called the sons of God."

10

★
Be-Happy Attitude #8
"I can choose to be happy—anyway!"
"Blessed are those who are persecuted for righteousness'
sake, for theirs is the kingdom of heaven."

The result? False pride gives way to humility.

Now, with self-confidence, you'll be free from coveting by
discovering the secret of spiritual contentment. It is not God's
intention for you to wander about, lost, without direction, to
come to the end of your life empty and dissatisfied, thinking,
This was it? This mess I have lived is all I have to show for my life?
God made you. He believes in you. And He wants you to
believe in yourself. He has a divine heritage and destiny for
you.

**6. *Yes, now it's possible to live with the positive power of
a living God in your life***

Can we really discover a living God? A God who really
believes in us?

If God is invisible, intangible, immaterial, spiritually
transcendent above the level of sticks and stones, water and
flesh, and hair and bone—then how, where, can we ever
hope to discover Him?

It was predicted for centuries
that God would one day, in
the long history of human
beings, actually come in the
form of a human being on
planet earth. If you really
think about it, it makes sense.
God would be most despicable
were He to allow the human
race to continue ignorantly,
blindly groping and grasping
for the truth about Himself.

Common sense tells us that
if there is an eternal God who
is invisible, then He is morally
obligated by His own
goodness to make Himself

> If we don't believe
> in ourselves, we
> may find it very
> difficult to believe
> in a God who
> believes in us.

visible and let the human race know of His existence, His character, and His expectations, if any, from us, His children.

Hence, the birth of Jesus Christ, who claimed to be God visiting earth, is referred to as the incarnation of God. An idea takes material form. And God literally visits earth in a human life.

No wonder the angel announced at the birth of the baby in Bethlehem, "His name shall be called Jesus, for He shall save His people from their sins." No wonder we sing carols at Christmas: "Joy to the world! The Lord is come!"

In Jesus we make the discovery of who God is and what He expects from us. And Jesus calls us to a delightful and totally satisfying pathway to holy pride and sacred self-respect. Jesus teaches that the central goal of human behavior is to be loved. "Love the LORD your God with all your soul and all your mind, and your neighbor as yourself."

So the focus of life changes from *coveting things* to *loving people!*

Here the Christian faith is born! A call to a trinity of affections is put before us: 1) Love yourself; 2) Love your neighbor; 3) Love God.

We must love God first. Let this be the starting point. How can we love Him? By recognizing that He created us with intelligence and creative possibilities and gave to us as human beings the greatest gift any creature on earth possesses, the capacity to have faith. *Of all creatures, human beings alone have the capacity to comprehend the possibility of God. What a wonderful gift! Reason enough for us to love the eternal One.*

Next we are called to love our neighbors.

Finally, we must love ourselves.

This is the last word. In fact, it could be said that there is no first word without a last word.

Will we be able to love God without loving ourselves? Probably not. There is a psychological defense mechanism that is called projection, which means we give out what we have within us. If we are guilty, we see other people as guilty. If we are good, we think other people are good. And if we are dishonest, we suspect other people of being dishonest. If we are generous, we expect other people to be

10

generous. If we love ourselves with a nonjudgmental love, we can love others with a nonjudgmental love.

And we can say with a perfect balance of healthy pride and honest humility, "When I'm good—I'm good. And when I'm not—I'm human. P.S. Love me anyway!" If we love ourselves and others, we will begin to love God too.

However, if we don't believe in ourselves, we may find it very difficult to believe in a God who believes in us.

In that case . . .

. . . what's a doubting person to do?

Take a long, deep, sincere look at Jesus Christ—that's what! Take a close look at the life and teachings of this Person who claimed to be the incarnation of the eternal God.

Study the behavior patterns and the lifestyle of this human being called Jesus. You will be struck by His grace, charm, and respect for all persons. His belief in others is astounding, exemplary, and encouraging.

He came to the outcast, and instead of offering them the insults they had earned by their illicit or unethical conduct, he promised them the possibility of pardon—forgiveness, nonjudgmental love!

Enter Jesus Christ. He didn't say, "I'll love you *when* . . . ," "I'll love you *after* . . . ;" He said, "I love you . . . period!" This was humanity's first encounter with nonjudgmental love incarnate.

So Jesus came to the harlots and saw great possibilities for redemption. And He pardoned them and restored their beauty.

He honored those who were dishonored by giving them the greatest gift any person can give to another, the belief that

- I can change!
- I can begin a new life!
- I can change my thinking!
- I can embrace new concepts!
- I can become a believer!
- I can be set free from destructive addictions to cynical thoughts or chemical additives!
- I can be liberated!
- I can be born again!

10

And so those who have looked to Jesus, listened to Him, and allowed Him to come into their minds, and into their emotional lives through positive thoughts truly describe themselves as being born again.

Do you want the most positive pathway to positive pride possible? Try making the discovery that God comes alive in your mind and life when you start to focus your faith on Jesus Christ.

Guess what? You suddenly realize you've joined a faith group. You have become a Christian.

- You have accepted the invitation to join the highest and most honored family on earth.
- You now are a personal friend of the most esteemed human who ever lived—Jesus!
- You can drop a name that will have impressive integrity!
- Infused within you now will be a precious, powerful, positive pride. What a sweet spirit of satisfying self-respect!

Contentment!

Now with His credentials stamped upon your reputation, you can begin to believe that you are somebody. You can therefore do something. You can cope. You can say, with the early writer in the New Testament, "I can do all things through Christ who strengthens me" (Phil. 4:13).

Disrespect, dishonor, and disgrace are replaced by respect, kindness, and honor. The ultimate shame of guilt and sin is gone. You are controlled within by a Spirit that is good! In fact, it is a Holy and Divine Spirit. Those feelings that surge within you are the presence and the power of the Holy Spirit of Jesus Himself, affecting your thinking and your behavior.

Such a Spirit within you changes your reactions and responses in daily life situations.

Now you have joy instead of sorrow.

Hope instead of despair.

Love instead of fear.

Inner peace instead of tension and turmoil.

Contentment!

After all, you know that God respects you.

For the first time in your life, you feel, honestly, that you are a wonderful person who treats people beautifully. You have discovered the priceless, precious emotional state described by Paul: "the fruit of the Spirit is love, joy, peace, longsuffering, kindness, goodness, faithfulness, gentleness, self-control" (Gal. 5:22-23).

Yes, you have found the positive path to powerful and perfect pride.

Contentment: the positive alternative to coveting.

My final word?

. . . *think! think! Think!*

Just think. It might be possible that there is a God after all.

Just think. It just might be true that there is a God, who did come in a human form called Jesus Christ, which could explain why that human being was so totally distinctive and different from all other persons.

Just think. This Jesus was crucified until He was dead. . . .

Just think. It just might be possible that He rose from the dead after all.

The fact is: Roman guards were set to watch over the tomb to prevent anyone from stealing Him. Any Roman guard who abandoned his post committed a capital offense and would be summarily executed.

The fact is: A Roman seal sealed the tomb of Jesus. Any person who broke a Roman seal would be guilty of a capital offense, and when caught . . . would be immediately executed!

The fact is: The followers of Jesus believed that He had died. They had no hope, they had no further expectations except their terrible fear. They stayed in hiding, fearful that they themselves might be caught and killed.

The fact is: Something happened on the Sunday we call Easter after His death on Friday. The Roman seal was broken. The stone was rolled away. Who did it—when the Roman soldiers were on guard all the while?

The fact is: The tomb was empty, and the body was gone. In a culture where the body and bones of the dead were treated with profound respect, no trace of Him was found. Not a bone, not a tooth, not a hair, not a fingernail. Nothing.

10

The fact is: These scattered, totally disillusioned disciples suddenly encountered a person they recognized to be the very Jesus who had been crucified. They walked and talked with Jesus three days after He had been crucified, dead, and buried. They believed that this was their Lord who had come back to life again. They believed it so much they went out into the streets, telling the world that in fact this really was the Son of God. And the grave could not hold Him! He was alive again!

The fact is: This faith spread and is more alive today than ever!

The fact is: Those who accept this faith in prayer can become transformed persons. I invite you, my reader, to offer this prayer: *"Jesus, come into my mind, into my heart. I am willing. I am not afraid, I am open to the possibility of Your coming into my life. I want to become like You, Jesus."*

The facts are: If you do this, you will experience a self-esteem that soars.

Sincerely.

Successfully.

Sweetly.

BE ALL AND ONLY FOR JESUS

"May I give you a blessing, Mother Teresa?" I offered. She smiled and nodded.

"Yes, please."

"Years ago," I explained, "when we were building the Crystal Cathedral, I wrote a prayer. Mother Teresa, your life is a fulfillment of this prayer!

Lord, make my life
a window
for Your light to shine through
and
a mirror

10

to reflect Your love to all I meet.
Amen.

Her eyes twinkled. "Wonderful. Wonderful. Will you write that down for me please." I did.

She bowed her head reverently as she folded the paper with her calloused hands. The skin was wrinkled like old leather, as if she were wearing gloves two sizes too big. With the broken fingernail of her right thumb, she pressed hard on the folded paper, folded it once more, and folded it still again. Then looking up fondly, she said, "Thank you, Dr. Schuller," as she tucked the little prayer under the folds of her tunic. She found there a mysterious pocket lodged just above her heart.

"Now let me give you a blessing," she said.

Dr. Schuller:
Be all
and only
for Jesus
without His
having to consult you first.

"Will you write it down, please," I asked, hoping she'd sign it.

I found a piece of paper. She wrote it. She signed it. I framed it. And I meditated for days on it.

What did it mean?

Intuitively I sensed it was profound, life-changing, personal. But I couldn't be sure how I should interpret and respond to it. I simply, secretly, sincerely prayed that God's intention in the blessing would come through.

It did—in the form of a prayer that flowed from my pen a week later:

Oh Lord,
I see a leaf on the wave.

Oh Lord,
I see a feather in the wind.

10

**Oh Lord,
I see a little white cloud on the breeze.**

**Oh Lord, You be the wave,
I'll be the leaf.
Oh Lord, You be the wind,
I'll be the feather.
Oh Lord, You be the breeze,
I'll be the little white cloud.**
Amen.

FAITH!
DON'T **LIVE** LIFE—
OR **LEAVE** LIFE—
WITHOUT IT!

A CLOSING WORD

Now—Keep your eye on the North Star!

Of all the stars in the sky, there is only one North Star. Many an ancient mariner took his bearings there—and sailed safely.

As a boy I used to look into the clear sky to spot the cluster of stars we call the Big Dipper. From the first star at the end of the handle all the way to the last star on the lip of the cup, my eye moved and was pointed flawlessly to the North Star!

So these *Ten Commandments* are *meant* to be guiding stars, all pointing to the North Star of human values. We have called that star by many names: Self-esteem! Self-respect! Dignity! Positive Pride!

Pride—so it's not a sin after all.

Pride—I'd better never lose it, or I'm in big trouble!

Be sure God wants you to be proud of the person you're becoming. Like Adam and Eve in the Garden of Eden, God wants you to walk at His side with your head held happily and humbly high.

LET PRIDE BECOME PRAISE!

This then is my closing word to you. Choose to live a life you can be proud of. Let your personality radiate with the self-esteem that is the presence of Christ within you, and your pride will become the praise of thanksgiving offered to God.

And if you should ever suffer an ego blowout at high speed in heavy traffic (bankruptcy, divorce, unemployment, the death of your best friend), then what?

If you are sincerely living by these Ten Commandments then resist the shame that seeks unwarranted entrance into your life.

Believe In The God Who Believes In You

If you are honestly humiliated because of sin, human error, or weakness—then repent, confess, and start again! Join the human race!

In any case, you can and must recover and renew your pride as a human being.

MENTAL EXERCISES TO RENEW AND REFRESH WOUNDED PRIDE

Then exercise the mental muscles of your self-respect, replace the disgraceful, dishonorable, embarrassing, or shameful thoughts with pride-building prayers of praise! Let this exercise be your way of saying, "Thank You, Lord, for believing in me!"

Practice the ABCs of a healthy, humble pride.

You'll be a more grateful, generous, and gracious person as a result of this act of humble worship.

A word of caution: As you read through this alphabet for self-renewal, don't expect to bat a thousand. Some—a few, probably many—of these affirmations I've listed won't fit you very well.

That's O.K.! If you're batting 400 of a possible 1,000, you're a heavy hitter. When you miss, focus on building strength.

Remember the keys to success:

Now practice these positive affirmations to give your healthy pride a hefty boost.

A
"I'm proud of my ACHIEVEMENTS!"
I've had them through the years. Chances are that I have forgotten some, so I'll take a moment to recall a few.

B
"I'm proud that I BELONG!"
The pride of belonging! Isn't it great? No person is an island. I have family, friends, associates, and institutions.

C
"I'm proud of my COMMITMENTS."
Think of all the promises I made—and kept. I thank God for the goals I had—and have. Decisions—I've made them. I dared to take a stand. I can be proud of that.

A Closing Word

D
"I'm proud of my DEDICATION."

I am imposing disciplines for self-improvement. I've grooved out some good habits, broken some bad ones, made some new resolutions, and started over again when I stumbled and fell.

E
"I'm proud of my commitment to EXCELLENCE!"

I gave it my best effort. I repulsed the easy, tempting call to mediocrity. No halfhearted attitude on my part. I did my best. Good enough is no acceptable substitute for excellence in my book of self-improvement.

F
"I'm proud that I've been FAITHFUL."

Yes, even when I didn't always live up to my own standards. I'm as proud of some of my failures as I am of some of my successes. Fidelity. You can pin that word on my character. I'm proud of that!

G
"I'm proud of my GENEROSITY."

I'm not ashamed of the gifts I gave. I'm proud of the time I gave—the money I spent, the sacrifices, the self-denial. I have not been a scrooge. I know the joy of generosity.

H
"I'm proud of my HOME."

I have made it beautiful. It's clean. See the little plant that's growing! Look at the pictures of my wife, my family. There are larger homes—true—but I'm keeping my place very nice! I'm proud of that.

I
"I'm proud that I have INTEGRITY."

My word is as good as gold. You can rely on me. I'll not lift you up just to let you down. My life's an open book. I'm an honest person. Ask the people who know me.

J
"I'm proud that I JOINED . . ."

I'm proud of my church. It's not a museum of saints by any stretch of the imagination. It's a hospital for hypocrites. We need it desperately. And I'm proud that I joined the community volunteers and that I joined a worthy cause. Yes, I'm vulnerable, but proud of my decision.

K
KNOWLEDGE—"I'm proud of my education."

"I'm proud that I didn't drop out or that I went back and picked up where I left off. I can read! I can write! I'm proud of that! So I'll help bring this pride of literacy and fight illiteracy!

Skills? I'm sharpening them.

Training? I'm not neglecting it.

L
"I'm proud of my LANGUAGE."

Language I use—and don't use! Obscenities are all around me, but they have no place in my vocabulary. Sarcastic adverbs, rude adjectives, demeaning nouns, disgraceful verbs have been replaced by a language that uplifts, ennobles, and elevates the level of social grace and human dignity.

M
"I'm proud that I'm a MOUNTAIN MOVER!"

"If you have faith the size of a mustard seed, you can say to your mountain, 'Move' and nothing will be impossible to you."

Jesus said it. I have done it. I did not quit. When frustrations, obstacles, setbacks, tough times, challenges hit me hard, I did not run away from them. I'm proud of that! Thank You, Lord!

N
"I'm proud of my NATIONAL origin."

Others may make put-down jokes on ethnic origins. But I'm proud of my Dutch blood. There are some good stock and some good genes in every blood line. I see it. I'm grateful for it. Yes, and I'm proud to be an American citizen. My nation? Yes! I'm patriotic and proud of it.

O
"I'm an OVERCOMER! And proud of it!"

Yes, I'm an undergoer who became an overcomer. I'm proud of that. Praise be to God who never stopped believing in me. He stepped in when others stepped out!

The therapy was rough, but I got through it.

The scrutiny was scorching, but I came out clean.

The setbacks were painful, but I bounced back.

The negative moods and thoughts were unmerciful, but I climbed above them! Hallelujah!

P
"I'm a PATIENT person—and proud of it!"

Yes, I'm tolerant. Some say too much so. But how can I be positive all of my answers are completely right all of the time?

Yes, I'm able to compromise. I'm thankful I'm not rigid, inflexible, stubborn—on all points, always.

"You have to kneel to be knighted," they whispered to the candidate as he approached the king. I understand that. I've learned to be patient with people and with progress.

I'm proud of the progress. The Lord isn't finished with me yet.

Q
"I know how to be QUIET. I'm proud of that."

I'm proud of the way I kept still. Just listened. I didn't lash back. God must have been in charge of the reactionary department of my mind. I'm proud of the fact that I have learned quietly to absorb insults from rude people. I actually have become a good listener. That's been a real development along with my rising self-esteem.

Believe In The God Who Believes In You

R
"I'm proud of my RELIGION and my RACE!"

"I'm not ashamed of the gospel. It is the power of God to salvation." Paul said it. I agree. I'm a Christian and proud of it. So I'm not embarrassed to be a witness to my God. I'll speak up for my faith.

My race—I'm proud of that too! I'll be a beautiful example. Help me, Lord, to do my people proud!

S
"I'm SUCCESSFUL—and proud of it."

I will not be intimidated into being embarrassed by my success. I'll use it—never abuse it. I worked hard for it. I earned it. And I helped a lot of people climb up the ladder with me.

Bankrupt businesses create few job opportunities. I made many self-denying sacrifices. I'm not ashamed to admit it.

T
"I'm TALENTED—and proud of it!"

Does it ever go to my head? How can it when it's a gift of God? I received it as a good steward. I've polished it. God is pleased—and praised at the same time! If I were embarrassed about my talent, I'd hide my light under a bushel. Who warned me against that? Oh, yes! Jesus!

U
"I'm proud of what I've UNDERTAKEN in life."

Yes—I've lost sometimes. Won sometimes.
Yes—I've had my successes. And my failures.
But—thank God I didn't back away from big ideas.
After all—I really undertook a tremendous challenge.
Whatever the outcome—God knows I tried. I'm proud of that!

V
"I'm proud of the VISION I displayed!"

That's being a leader, right? I saw problems before they were born and sold ideas to prevent them from ever hitting us. I can be proud of that.

"I have not been disobedient to the heavenly vision." Paul said that. Was he bragging a bit? Perhaps. That's O.K. He was, after all, "boasting in the Lord."

Yes—I saw possibilities, and I unveiled them! Drew the picture. That is good. And it makes me feel good.

W
"I'm proud of my WORK, my WALK, and my WITNESS— all three!"

My work? I always finish what I start. People can always depend on me.

My walk? I'm in the path, following Jesus. People know that.

My witness? I'm a living, breathing billboard, advertising the name of Jesus Christ.

X
"I'm proud of the 'XTRA' effort I put forth."

I go beyond the call of duty. I'm known for that.

I give 110 percent—people have come to expect that from me.

I go the 'xtra' mile. I have forgiven—again and again. And it pays off sometimes. But if I'm going to sin, let it be on the side of trying too hard rather than on the side of trying too little.

Y

"I'm proud that I YIELDED—and didn't insist on having my own way."

"Yield yourself to God," the Bible says. I did and I'm proud that I did. I don't want to have my own way. I just don't want to make mistakes.

People who never change their minds are either perfect or stubborn. I'm not perfect, and I don't want to be stubborn. So I can reverse myself and not be ashamed or embarrassed to do so!

I've learned how, when, and what to yield. Credit and honor included. After all, God can do tremendous things through the person who doesn't insist on getting all of the credit.

Z

"I'm ZEALOUS! Yes! And proud of it!"

"The zeal of the Lord will perform it," the Bible says
I understand that:
I cry in a heartwarming movie.
I scream at a baseball game.
I wave my arms when I'm preaching.
I hug my family and friends when I see them.
I get excited about my faith.
I'm enthusiastic about my dreams and goals.
I'm active!
I'm alert!
I'm aware!
I'm alive!

Oh, God! It feels great to be fully alive!
And to be loved by the One who believes in me!